ᴱ WEEK
7006.

Advertising Cultures

Edited by
**Timothy deWaal Malefyt and
Brian Moeran**

Oxford • New York

First published in 2003 by
Berg
Editorial offices:
1st Floor, Angel Court, 81 St Clements Street, Oxford, OX4 1AW, UK
838 Broadway, Third Floor, New York, NY 10003-4812, USA

© Timothy deWaal Malefyt and Brian Moeran 2003

Paperback edition reprinted 2006

Berg is an imprint of Oxford International Publishers Ltd.

Library of Congress Cataloging-in-Publication Data
Advertising cultures / edited by Timothy deWaal Malefyt and Brian
Moeran.– 1st ed.
    p. cm.
Includes index.
    ISBN 1-85973-673-4 – ISBN 1-85973-678-5 (pbk.)
    1. Advertising. 2. Advertising agencies. I. Malefyt, Timothy Dwight
deWaal. II. Moeran, Brian.

HF5823.A1685 2003
659.1–dc21

                                                    2003004506

British Library Cataloguing-in-Publication Data
A catalogue record for this book is available from the British Library.

ISBN 1 85973 673 4 (Cloth)
      1 85973 678 5 (Paper)

Typeset by JS Typesetting Ltd, Porthcawl, Mid Glamorgan.
Printed in the United Kingdom by Biddles Ltd, King's Lynn, Norfolk
www.bergpublishers.com

symbolic mushrooms and globes, and inscribed: 'Professor Sherry, Thank you for changing our worldview.' Later that week, a prominent colleague in another department expressed a wistful desire to take that same course, as the readings looked to him to be so 'really interesting.' Altering consciousness, motivating inquisitiveness, providing practical tools for accomplishing change, and having fun in the bargain are what anthropology is all about. Anthropologists have always been in the meaning management business. Our authors show what an intriguing playground advertising is for our practice. I commend the reader to their care.

Contents

Contents

Preface

The idea for this volume was conceived during a conversation with Kathryn Earle, editorial director at Berg Publishers, after a session at the 2000 American Anthropological Association annual meeting titled, 'In-And-Of Advertising: The Role of Anthropology.' We agreed that while interest in advertising and marketing has risen in recent years no single volume contains works that offer case studies on the subject from an anthropological perspective. The present volume intends to fill that gap. After the conference all the participants agreed to revise their papers, but in some cases could not find the time to be included here. Thus other contributors subsequently prepared papers for inclusion in the present volume.

Acknowledgements

Timothy Malefyt would like to thank Elizabeth Briody, Stuart Grau, Steve Barnett, Maryann McCabe and Monica Pons for their direction and encouragement in advertising. He also thanks his Brown University committee (David Kertzer, Shepard Krech III, and William O. Beeman) for getting him started in anthropology, and Kevin Yelvington and the Society for the Anthropology of Work for supporting the efforts of the AAA session. Brian Moeran would like to thank the Danish Research Agency for making the writing of his contributions to this book possible, and his colleagues at the Copenhagen Business School for their continued collegiality and support. This volume is dedicated to the memory of Louise Lohr Malefyt, a brilliant source of inspiration.

Foreword: A Word from our Sponsor – Anthropology
John F. Sherry, Jr.

Engine of economic growth. Underwriter of programming. Magico-religious ideology. Font of popular culture. Template of desire. Mercantile art. Distorted mirror. Inescapable leitmotif of the built environment. The most fun you can have with your clothes on. Advertising has been described in these ways, and in many others, but always with an undertone of ambivalence. Advertising is provocative and annoying, exhilarating and enervating, informative and misleading. It can exalt or debase, stimulate or lull, seduce or bludgeon. It insinuates itself into the background of consciousness, and offers itself up for public commentary. We argue with it, laugh at it, criticize it, resonate with it, deny its influence upon us, abhor its power over others and elevate it to a fetish focus on the cultural cynosure we designate Super Sunday (where the commercials are more highly touted and anticipated than the bowl game itself). We award it Clios for aesthetic merit and Effies for its impact on sales. We find increasingly ingenious ways to mismeasure its effectiveness. It has provided anthropological analysts something of a ritual annuity, becoming a scapegoat for the shortfalls of their home cultures, a surrogate, conveniently, if unreflectively, blamed for the excesses of market capitalism. Rarely has advertising been tracked to its lairs, infiltrated by ethnographers in the agencies and households where it flourishes, and described, dissected, deconstructed, improved or subverted by the anthropological habit of mind. The present volume marks a move away from our tradition of armchair theorizing and unreflective critique.

For over two decades now, I have plied my trade as an anthropologist within the precincts of a business school, teaching executives and MBA students how to comprehend the lived experience of consumers in order to market more effectively, how to anticipate and mitigate the consequences of managerial decisions for consumers and their cultures as an integral component of strategy, and how to respect the awesome power with which their growing facility with meaning management endows them, not just as custodians of brands, but as social architects. I have consulted extensively with firms across a number of industries and cultures, helping them solve problems and discover opportunities. I have researched consumer behavior around the globe, studying the creativity with which people accommodate and resist the lure of marketing and the resilience with which cultures individuate in the face of globalization.

To each of these enterprises I have brought the anthropologist's competitive edge, fascination with local detail, emphasis on grounded theory, prolonged field immersion, and a penchant for comparison to bear upon my understanding and the communication of that insight to clients. Given that my audiences have firmly entrenched folk theories that often preclude even imagining consumer behavior as it actually unfolds on the ground, I am constantly challenged to make the familiar strange in ways that resonate with decision-makers and gatekeepers. This is especially exacting with my managers-in-training, who are so exquisitely attuned to practical application that they fail to cultivate systematic introspection and intraceptive intuition, laboring instead within a kind of NIMBY syndrome of blocked access to their lives as consumers. Bumping them from the autopilot of participant observation to the hands-on engagement of observant participation in the service of deep understanding of consumer experience is at once my greatest challenge and proudest accomplishment.

The authors of this volume illustrate the heroic effort this bumping project requires, and the benefits which may either elude or accrue to managers possessed of an anthropological perspective. Whether as account planners, copywriters, or research providers, anthropologists are increasingly influencing the shape of contemporary advertising. Of all the clients to whom I act as a consultant, advertising agencies are among my favorites, as they are the most alive to the animate, numinous dimension of goods, the role of the consumer as a co-creator of the marketer's offering, and the need for ever more nuanced insight into consumer behavior. Having said that, I also believe that it is a miracle that advertising ever gets made at all, given all the stakeholders that are involved in its genesis and all the hurdles that are faced in its refashioning prior to release. Our authors convey the elation and frustration attendant upon their efforts to ethnologize clients and agencies, and demonstrate the promise anthropology holds for serving and protecting consumers.

Anthropology has lately become something of a methodological darling in marketing research circles, after its discontinuous and episodic history of virtual neglect. Advertising is in the vanguard of ethnographic practice, even if it has been slower to incorporate cultural frameworks of sense-making. I believe this recent ascendancy has much to do with an empowering of the natives, a brokering of our disciplinary lenses to our informants, and a collapse of the subject–object distinction in our research. As anthropologists collaborate with practitioners, we all gain new insight into our everyday lives. We inhabit a more interesting world as a result, and create a more interesting one in turn.

A brief personal anecdote is suggestive in this regard. At the end of a recent quarter of teaching, my MBA students presented me with a cake, decorated with

Introduction: Advertising Cultures – Advertising, Ethnography and Anthropology

Timothy D. Malefyt and *Brian Moeran*

There is, in fact, some reason to believe that fieldworkers are the leading edge of a movement to reorient and redirect theoretical, methodological, and empirical aims and practices in all the social sciences except, perhaps, the dismal one.

John Van Maanen, *Tales of the Field*

This book is about how anthropologists, working in areas as diverse as Sri Lanka and the United States, Norway, Trinidad and Japan, have pondered, studied, reflected on and written about the advertising industries that they encountered there. Some are active practitioners in advertising; others are academics who have stepped in, as well as out of, the business. The research methods that they have used, and in some cases still use, are known as fieldwork, and the accounts of their research that they later write are called ethnographies. Through the presentation and analysis of specific case studies, contributors to this book both interpret and allow us to reflect upon the ways in which advertising and marketing consultants increasingly make use of what was once unique to anthropology: so-called 'ethnography.'

More broadly, *Advertising Cultures* aims to inform marketers in business about how anthropologists think of the ways in which they conduct their research – the pitfalls and issues that challenge their discipline – at the same time as it tries to explain to inquisitive academics how and why ethnography has taken off as a consumer-driven methodology in marketing practice. It is the links between anthropology, advertising and marketing, then – in particular, the methods that professionals in each of these fields use to conduct, theorize and write up their research – that are the focus of this Introduction. The underlying questions are: how useful can ethnography be to advertising and marketing professionals? Do the issues that confront academic anthropologists in conducting fieldwork present similar challenges to marketers? And how different are the kinds of 'ethnography' practiced by each group?

Timothy D. Malefyt and *Brian Moeran*

Advertising Cultures

The title of this book may suggest that *Advertising Cultures* is yet another in a long line of books purporting to reveal the 'deep meanings' of advertisements, but often in fact laying bare their writers' various prejudices (occasionally against advertising and its practitioners).[1] However, as will rapidly become clear, this book is concerned primarily with advertising worlds – the people who work in them, the campaigns they produce, the organizations with which they interact. It is in the sense of an organizational world, therefore, that we use the word 'culture' in our title.

Having made this clear, we should perhaps start with a basic definition of what we mean by advertising, then launch into an overview of advertising industries as they function in different parts of the world. In its broadest sense, advertising is the market communication of goods and services of various sellers. Advertising was first conceived as a means of generating demand in a capitalistic system by offering specific information on a product, service, or brand, often in a persuasive format. This traditional view of advertising, to some extent based on Marxist theories of economic exchange, has now been replace by one that is more concerned with advertising's role as a vehicle of social communication. It is in this latter sense that advertising attempts to sell goods, by appealing to consumers through gender identity, celebrity endorsement, romantic imagery, notions of achieving happiness or contentment, and other cultural dimensions not tangibly related to the advertised product or service.[2] At the same time, advertising is not only about social communication, but also about the various networks of cooperative social, personal and financial arrangements among suppliers, clients, advertising personnel, consumers, and so on, that are essential to its operation. It is along these lines that we extend our view of advertising in the present volume.

Any advertising industry consists of a large number of different kinds and sizes of organizations. First there are the media institutions in which advertising is placed: television and radio stations and networks, newspaper and magazine publishers. Many of these – like Time Warner or Bertelsmann – are large conglomerates with global reach. Others are directed at audiences that are extremely local – either in terms of geographical location, or of such criteria as interests and age (many Japanese magazines, for example, appeal to readers whose ages span a mere two to three years). Beside these prominent media organizations, there are others – like transportation companies, those that deal with billboards, Internet companies, and so on – which display advertising and with whose personnel those producing advertising campaigns need to liaise.

Then there are the organizations that pay for the advertising to be produced. These are the clients of those working in the advertising industry, the ones who make the world of advertising go round and round in an endless spiral of marketing images. They may be industrial giants like Toyota or IBM, food and beverage corporations, beauty and cosmetics manufacturers, retail outlets (department stores, supermarkets), service companies (travel agencies, restaurants), purveyors of luxury goods (LVMH, Prada, Gucci), and any other type of company that for one reason or another feels a need to get involved in advertising. Clients may be large or small, global or local, single- or multi-product manufacturers and/or sellers. They tend to be very different from one another, so that their only real connection with the advertising industry and the world of advertising in general is through the fact that they have chosen to advertise.

Finally, there are those organizations which plan and create the advertising that the clients order and that we, as consumers, see and hear (and sometimes smell). The most important of these is the advertising agency. Succinctly put, an advertising agency is an independent service company, consisting of business, marketing and creative people, who develop, prepare and place advertising in advertising media for their clients, the advertisers, who are in search of customers for their goods and services. Agencies thus mediate between three different social groups: industry, media and consumers. They link industry and media by creating new forms for messages about products and services; industry and consumers by developing comprehensive communications campaigns and by providing information about these campaigns; and media and consumers by conducting audience research to enable market segmentation to take place. Traditionally, agencies have been paid a commission for their services (typically 15 per cent of the media cost), although nowadays they are often paid a flat fee. Performance or incentive-based pay is gaining favor among agencies in the US and in other parts of the world as an alternative means for agency compensation. Rather than a set amount, agencies are paid for their services commensurate with their performance in raising purchase consideration or generating actual sales. A recent survey in the US showed that 35 per cent of large agencies (up from 13 per cent in 1991) subscribe to this type of fee structure over the traditional flat fee.[3] This rise is likely to continue as advertising increasingly shifts from traditional media venues of print and broadcast to the more integrated approaches of Internet, PR, direct mail, and event and entertainment marketing. Indeed, this fee structure may also motivate agencies to come up with more innovative communicative strategies for claiming advertising effectiveness, since it is difficult to measure direct correlations between advertising and sales.

Advertising agencies come in all shapes and sizes. The ones that most of us have heard about – like J. Walter Thompson, for example, Saatchi and Saatchi, or Dentsu – are known as 'full-service' agencies. These handle the planning, creation, production and placement of advertising for their clients. They may also handle sales promotion, public relations and other related services as needed by individual advertisers. In short, a full service agency offers its clients a complete range of services beyond the placement and preparation of their advertising.

To carry out this task effectively, however, this kind of agency usually needs to liaise with and subcontract to all kinds of other organizations during the course of producing an advertising campaign. Thus in most advertising industries, we find agencies surrounded by a cluster of creative shops, model and actor agencies, photographic, music and film studios, print shops, production companies, hairstylists, recording studios, Internet and website developers, qualitative and quantitative consumer research suppliers. Some – like a production company – will have their own organizational connections: carpenters to make stage sets for a television campaign, for example, as well as scenario painters and suppliers of anything from dry ice machines to plate glass.

The complex net of social interrelations of the advertising industry can be further seen in the way in which advertising agencies have in recent decades invested in new business opportunities, including merchandizing, telemarketing and e-commerce. They have also driven the commercial sponsorship of sports, art and other cultural activities in the 1980s and 90s, and now look for further opportunities to show their skills in matching their clients' needs for publicity and advertising to the everyday lives of consumers. This development of integrated marketing – which often becomes a kind of 'promotional culture'[4] – has led to agencies participating in all sorts of different areas of the economy. For example, in consultation with television networks, they develop animation programs, supported by product placement and character merchandizing on the part of toy and other manufacturers, on the one hand, and, on the other, arrange marriages between celebrities. In many respects, therefore, advertising agencies may be described as black boxes of cultural continuity and change.

Although agencies differ in the way they are organized, the main functional areas of a full-service agency are: account management (within this function lie the separate functions of account planning and market research); media planning and buying; creative services; and internal services (dealing primarily with finance, personnel, and traffic). They are usually led by a chief executive officer and one or two vice-presidents, who may oversee a board of directors whose members represent different areas of their agency's responsibility.

How do these different areas of responsibility work? When an agency wins a new account or is assigned new business by an existing client, it generally forms a cross-department group, or account team, composed of an account supervisor (supported by account executives), a senior planner who liaises between the account and creative teams, a media buyer, as well as a creative team made up of copywriter and art director with, as necessary, a producer (for television and/or radio commercials). As the chapters by Timothy Malefyt and Brian Moeran in this book show, the account team proceeds along more or less predetermined lines. First, the account planning department works out (often in close conjunction with the client) and solves a marketing problem by conducting new, and making use of previous, research to find out everything it can about its targeted consumers, the product and/or brand advertised, and the relationship between consumer and product. On the basis of answers to a variety of questions, account planners then formulate a strategy that positions the product in relation to targeted consumers and emphasizes the attributes that will appeal to them. From their strategy and research idea they develop typically a one-page creative brief or blueprint from which creatives will implement advertising ideas.

Once the overall marketing strategy and creative brief have been determined and approved they are presented to the agency's creative team, which then works on an appropriate creative strategy, writing copy and preparing rough layouts and storyboards. At the same time, the media buyer works out a media plan that fits the marketing strategy, selecting an appropriate mix of media and preparing a schedule of costs. These three separate plans are then amalgamated into a single package by the account supervisor and presented to the client (which may or may not have been involved during different stages of the agency's preparations). Just how much a client interferes with its agency's work depends very much on the company and personnel involved.

One of the main organizational difficulties facing an account team is that it invariably finds itself having to deal with at least two different audiences whose interests may not be the same. On the one hand, the account planner and creative team focus their attention on how to advertise and sell a product to a particular targeted group of *consumers*. On the other, the account supervisor and his supporting personnel need to liaise between the *client* or advertiser and the agency, and are responsible for conveying the client's marketing needs to their colleagues, as well as for selling their agency's marketing, creative and media plans to the client. Since it is the latter who pays the agency for its services, it may disagree with – even occasionally overrule – the consumer-oriented strategy proposed by the agency's account group. It is thus the account supervisor's job to get the client to agree to his team's proposals, as Malefyt shows in his analysis of a one-day brainstorming session between a New York-based agency and its liquor manufacturer client.

A second organizational difficulty that often emerges in the work of an account group is internal and concerns the different attitudes towards advertising that tend to be held by different people working in an advertising agency. The very *raison d'être* of account planning is to form marketing strategies that at least appear to be based on objective, *scientific* criteria derived from in-depth qualitative and quantitative data, revealing a consumer need that other brands or products are currently not satisfying. These data then have to be transformed into creative images by copywriters and art directors who usually claim to work according to intuitive, *artistic* ideas that may have little actual relationship to the expressed marketing aims. Sometimes conflict between the two types of agency employee occurs and adversely affects the work of the account team which, ideally, needs to blend harmoniously to achieve its client's aims.

A third issue, beyond the functioning of internal dynamics between and among agency and client brand teams, is the finesse with which various agencies from different parts of the world treat conflicts between competing accounts. Whenever an agency wins a new account that conflicts with one already being handled, it has to decide which of the two accounts it wishes to keep. The competing account rule is sociologically interesting because, it ensures two things: first, that there is a continuous circulation of accounts among agencies; and second, that no agency ever becomes excessively large. As a result, by comparison with other industries, the organizations that make up the advertising industry are quite small.[5]

Thus, the advertising industry tends to be highly unstable. Accounts are not fixed in stone. Once handed over to a particular agency, they oblige different kinds of people to come together – from both client and agency sides – to work on a specific problem. As a number of chapters in this book show, this fusion of people involves all kinds of delicate social negotiations and strategies, so that every account is fraught with potential disruption. Agency–client relations may thus come to an end, either because of social difficulties (the account planner cannot get along with the product manager of the client company); or because of incompetence revealed at some stage during the creation of an advertising campaign (creatives refuse to listen to their marketing colleagues' advice); or because of conceptual weakness (a campaign 'bombs'); or because of organizational changes (a product manager is transferred, and her successor adopts a totally different approach to marketing); or because there is an economic downturn and a client's advertising budget is suddenly cut; and so on and so forth, seemingly *ad infinitum*.

As a result, accounts move from one agency to another – circulating in a manner that is not dissimilar from that described so famously by Bronislaw Malinowski in his depiction of the *kula* ring in parts of Melanesia.[6] But precisely because they move, accounts affect the very organization of people in the world of advertising and agencies' ability to employ them. Thus, even in a country like Japan where ideals of 'permanent' employment have been advocated, we find that the advertising industry is characterized by an instability in personnel, as talented copywriters and art directors set up their own creative shops, account planners move with an account from one agency to another, client companies' advertising or product managers find employment in advertising agencies, and so on. The circulation of accounts thus encourages a circulation of people who contribute to the ebb and flow of advertising worlds.

Fieldwork and Ethnography

Having given an outline of the organizational structure of 'advertising cultures,' let us now turn to the methods that anthropologists have used to find out about the world of advertising in such faraway places as India, Sri Lanka, Trinidad and Japan. We wish to pitch the rest of this Introduction at those working in advertising and marketing.

Anthropology has always put great emphasis on fieldwork as the most important way to go about finding out about a society and culture. In this respect, by its very nature, it needs the cooperation of those being studied, which in turn means that personal relations become extremely important to the research process.[7] No doubt, this will ring an immediate bell with those working in advertising and marketing, but just what constitutes 'fieldwork' is sometimes difficult to pinpoint. After all,

> A field study may last for between a few months to two years or longer, and it aims at developing as intimate an understanding as possible of the phenomena investigated. Although there are differences in field methods between different anthropological schools, it is generally agreed that the anthropologist ought to stay in the field long enough for his or her presence to be considered more or less 'natural' by the permanent residents, although he or she will always to some extent remain a stranger.[8]

In other words, fieldwork tends not to be a definition for a method of study so much as an *experience* underlying all understanding of social life.[9] As Danny Miller nicely puts it in his chapter in this book: 'The experience of fieldwork is clearly based upon the muddle in the middle that is also our ordinary experience of life.' This experience is unstructured and is known as 'participant observation.' Usually it is supplemented by various formal data collecting techniques such as structured interviews, statistical sampling and so on. However, the ideal aims of participant observation are that fieldwork be carried out over a relatively long period of time; that it focus on a community of a few hundred people only; and that it take into account every detail of those people's lives and culture as well as the fieldworker's own feelings and perceptions and the nature of relations between fieldworker and informants. In so doing, the fieldworker should get to know every member of that community personally and learn not to be content with generalized information.[10] In short, she should immerse herself as deeply as possible in the lives of those she is observing, so much so that the latter forget that she is there, what she is doing, or why she came in the first place.[11] Doubtless researchers in advertising and marketing will wish that those for (their clients), and on (consumers), whom they conduct their research were so accommodating.

The lack of a 'scientific' definition of fieldwork may be surprising, given its central place in anthropology (and, let us hasten to add, in other academic disciplines like archaeology, geography, sociology and cultural studies), but a number of factors have contributed to its slipperiness and consequent 'mythic elaboration'.[12] First, precisely because fieldwork is an intensely personal experience, it tends to differ from one fieldworker to the next, since each invests a different personality in his or her research. Second, because fieldwork is carried out with a focus on different aspects of social life, from mortuary rites to media organizations by way of race relations – in places as far apart and apparently dissimilar as New Ireland, Mississippi, Hollywood and the Rhodesian Copperbelt[13] – different research topics and locales demand different methods of research.

No wonder, then, that when trying to find out what exactly he should do when carrying out fieldwork, one young anthropologist was advised by his seniors 'not to be a bloody fool,' nor to 'converse with an informant for more than 20 minutes,' 'to take ten grams of quinine every night,' and always to 'behave as a gentleman.'[14] Another anthropologist – this time a woman, Laura Bohannan – fared no better in her search for how best to find the Holy Grail in West Africa:

> The best advice, in the long run, came from the ripe experience of two professors of anthropology. One said: 'Always walk in cheap tennis shoes; the water runs out more quickly.' The other said: 'You'll need more tables than you think.' Both then added, without going into detail, 'Enjoy yourself, and never, never be an embarrassment to the administration.'[15]

Given this lack of clear-cut methodology – together with frequent lack of communicative abilities in the language of the people being studied, and the difficulties that necessarily accompany a fieldworker's being of one gender rather than another – it is perhaps not surprising that fieldwork tends to become idealized (some might say 'fetishized') and participant observation used as a convenient cloak with which to conceal methodological (and, possibly, ethical, as well as personal) shortcomings.[16]

And yet here lies the rub. Although criticized both within and outside anthropology for the authoritative position its proponents have forged for themselves, as well as for assumptions they have sometimes made about the objects of their studies, fieldwork – often referred to as 'ethnography'[17] – has also been appropriated outside anthropology as a means to get at cultural learning.[18] After all, if there is one thing that people who are not anthropologists think they know about anthropology, it is that anthropology is 'the study of culture.'

Now, in fact, these days anthropologists themselves are often a little wary of such a definition of their discipline. One or two, indeed, may become a little nervous when – as experienced by one of the authors of this Introduction – colleagues who are not anthropologists start referring to an anthropologist as 'Mr Culture.' As William Mazzarella points out in his contribution to this book, the culture concept may once have functioned admirably as a means of surveying and mapping human differences in a (quasi-)scientific and essentializing manner. It was this, indeed, that endeared it to advertisers and marketers who may then, as Rita Denny and Patricia Sunderland show, focus on the psychological rather than cultural attributes of consumers. But, these days, anthropologists tend to think that 'all cultures, without a single exception, are systems of the imagination that we are nevertheless taught to accept as real.'[19]

The paradox here is that just as anthropologists appear to be moving away from culture as a useful tool of explanation (especially when used to refer 'broadly to the forms through which people make sense of their lives'),[20] people in the advertising and marketing professions are seizing it ever more strongly in their grasp. Culture is life and life is *very* 'real.' The compelling notion that 'culture' is the invisible glue that holds together the unexplainable behavior of consumers, or that it taps into underlying motivations and needs, or that it can even, at times, stand for the value of the brand, is simply too alluring an ideal for marketers to pass up. True, the strange or alien culture of the 'primitive other' that once underpinned much anthropological research may no longer serve much purpose in an age when the world is perceived – in the eyes of anthropologists, for the most part, wrongly – as being more globally structured in the way that it is administered economically and politically, and more culturally homogeneous in its tastes and lifestyles. Yet this very strangeness, together with the method of studying it, has become a new device by which marketers and advertisers believe that they can observe and 'understand' consumers in contemporary society. In this respect, they are true to the anthropologists' conception of ethnographic work which is triggered by estrangement or defamiliarization.[21]

Just why this should be so is difficult to work out and tends to put those anthropologists who are aware of this interest on their guard. In part, the turn to fieldwork or ethnography in marketing is connected to the cycle of fashion which is itself a part of the endless drive for distinction that characterizes contemporary societies. Individual *people* strive to be different from one another (in how they talk and dress, in what they eat, drink and generally consume, in their work and leisure activities, and so on and so forth). Marketers try to make *products* different from one another for these people (couching such differences in terms of brands). Finally, *organizations* compete with one another to be different (and in the process develop the art of corporate branding and identity). At all three social levels, the development of difference incites change, and change, because it is never seen as stable, becomes subject to fashion.

Put differently, as has been done by Marietta Baba,[22] in a world of global production, there is no sustainable edge that enables companies to succeed, other than by developing and using knowledge and information. Yet, knowledge in one sense is always just out of reach. It is this that drives innovation and propels a company forward. But once attained, knowledge is transformed into information. Easily accessible, it can no longer be guarded and kept as an exclusive benefit for any single business corporation although, as Malefyt points out in relation to a New York advertising agency, people will do their best to control the dissemination of knowledge.

As a result, the human or social factors surrounding the acquisition and transformation of knowledge have become a focal point. Who gets knowledge, by what means and why, and what do they do with it once they have acquired it? These are the kinds of questions that marketers now ask about the purchase and consumption of commodities. Not unnaturally, this interest in the human or social relationships between people and things has led marketers to examine the potential of ethnography as a marketing 'tool.' After all, ethnography is about people.

But how are marketers to find out about such people? Unlike a lot of marketing, 'Anthropology is not a set of questionnaires which are handed over, filled out, and handed back. Most of the anthropologist's time is spent sitting around waiting for informants, doing errands, drinking tea, taking genealogies, mediating fights, being pestered for rides, and vainly attempting small talk.'[23] This may be a slightly exaggerated description of what goes on during fieldwork, and it would probably give a cost conscious advertising executive or product manager who has decided to employ anthropologists like Denny and Sunderland minor heart palpitations were s/he to take this description of ethnographic 'method' at face value. Nevertheless, it is true to say that anthropologists learned long ago that administering surveys and set questions, in the manner practiced by many marketers, only produces answers to what they happen to have asked. It tells them nothing about what has not been asked – which is why anthropologists spend so much time as – in John Sherry's phrase – 'observant participants,' 'sitting around' watching and listening to what is going on about them.

Anthropologists have also learned that what people *say* they do and what they *actually* do are usually very different things. This is why formal interviews in themselves are often unsatisfactory (as Mazzarella wryly notes about informants regurgitating paragraphs from the latest issue of *Campaign* or some such industry literature in answer to his questions). It takes time to get people to open up and reveal things that, for the most part, they prefer to keep away from outside observers. It is only by being around for considerably longer than it takes to conduct a dozen interviews, by becoming a 'part of the scenery' so to speak, that anthropologists are gradually able to build a sense of mutual trust with their informants. It is by 'being there'[24] a lot of the time that a fieldworker learns to spot and take advantage of those moments when people are more, rather than less, likely to talk frankly and honestly about the things that they regard as important in their lives. This is why Miller, for example, believes that methodology in anthropology is an endemic part of the research findings.

For the anthropologist, it is only by 'being there' that the real questions can begin to be asked. And, unlike those of marketing questionnaires which also reveal rather a lot about those asking them, these questions are 'real' because they make sense to the anthropologist's informants. As Marianne Lien suggests in her contribution, it is sheer ignorance that allows the anthropologist to ask questions about things that her informants take for granted, thereby unsettling what seems to them self-evident. This does not mean, however, that the answers that emerge are definitive 'truths.' As mentioned above, so far as the fieldworker is concerned, all data about cultural facts, as well as the facts themselves, are interpretations. In terms of marketing, these interpretations exist for marketers, for their informants, *and* for their clients. They are all caught up in webs of meaning that they themselves spin (and advertising people are masters of spin) and 'facts' as such do not exist (at least, not in the sense that they are usually taken to exist by business people everywhere). Somehow the world of one has to be translated for the world of the other, and this is the task besetting both fieldworker and marketer.

Precisely because each deals with issues of interpretation and translation, we might also argue that, just as for the anthropologist there is no 'primitive,' in marketing there is no 'consumer.' There are simply other consumers, living other lives – even for the product manager of a food company in Norway who could only say that he had 'an overall knowledge of the Norwegian food market.'[25] In spite of the reams of data that marketers have produced about consumers, therefore, as anthropologists we would agree with Paul Dresch and Wendy James that in social terms 'most of human life around the globe is a blank space.'[26]

This is why fieldwork – in the sense in which it has been developed within the discipline of anthropology – is so important, and why what an anthropologist would regard as the quick-fix marketing approach, with its necessary focus on problem solution, is so unsatisfactory and, ultimately, self-defeating. At least, the problems tend not to be 'solved' in the longer term, although the marketers stay in business as a result, because, so long as their methods remain as they are, new 'problems' always and inevitably arise.

The irony here is that marketers today face exactly the same problems with their research methodology that anthropologists faced one hundred years ago. Anthropology has not always been characterized by fieldwork's long *durée*. In its early days, it, too, consisted of distanced observations and unsubstantiated conclusions – usually based on brief interviews with 'natives' conducted on the deck of a passing ship or the verandah of a local mission station. Like the marketer today, the anthropologist was an inquirer, and it took a move into the center of the village to change not just the primary locus of inquiry, but the theoretical orientation to which those working in the discipline have now become accustomed.[27]

So, long-term fieldwork may seem to involve too leisurely a time frame for marketers living in a world of rushed projects and deadline after urgent deadline. They might ask what an anthropologist can achieve in twelve months that they cannot do in twelve days. What indeed! Certainly it is not impossible to do contracted research – especially group research – in shorter spaces of time. But it is only by staying somewhere over an extended period of time and listening to what people tell you as an anthropologist that you can begin to grasp what the 'problems' might be and what, therefore, you are looking to analyze and explain. Only then will your questions become pertinent.[28] If this kind of approach were practiced by those doing marketing research, they would be able to move from observation to participation, from formality to informality, from mere enactment to both enactment and embodiment. In short, it would bring about the kind of theoretical reorientation of which marketing is badly in need and for which marketers themselves are searching in their souls.

Those who doubt this proposition have only to read through the chapters in this book. True, the anthropologists whose work is represented here are not looking at consumers but at those working in advertising industries around the world. But the conclusions they draw, the analyses they provide and the levels of self-reflection that enter into their work may be seen as exemplary models for marketers to follow in their studies of consumers.

Advertising and Anthropology

Now let us turn to issues that are of interest to both advertisers and anthropologists. Although the ways information are ultimately employed by these two groups of researchers in studying collectivities of people may be different, there are striking similarities in methods, motivations and aims that we might pause to consider here. These similarities include such varied facets as comparison, interpretation, methodology, and the natures of the audiences studied, as well as of the professional worlds in which these groups operate.

1. Both advertising executives and anthropologists (the latter often in strange surroundings) try to make sense of what does not immediately make sense, and pass on their understandings to others. They are, in Steven Kemper's phrase, 'folk ethnographers.'

2. Before carrying out their research in the field, both advertisers and anthropologists need to learn about those whom they are going to study. As Moeran points out in his chapter, an agency's orientation regarding its client's marketing strategy, problems and aims is akin to an anthropologist reading around a particular subject before conducting fieldwork. It is this background knowledge that permits both groups to formulate hypotheses – about the nature of exchange, about values or consumption practices – which they then test in the field by talking to people who are labeled 'informants' or 'consumers.' They constantly seek new ways to answer age-old questions, and therefore are open to new descriptive theories about the nature of human behavior.[29] Ideally, they compare their findings with those of previous studies.

3. Both professional groups make 'a zigzag movement between the observation of facts and theoretical reasoning, where new facts modify the theory and (modified) theory accounts for the facts.' Both also impose 'ordering patterns and regularities onto the observed material, and . . . depend on [their] own theoretical abstractions in order to do so. The challenge lies in saying something significant about culture and social life through these abstractions.'[30]

4. Whether presented as brief, bullet-point reports or extended monographs, the ethnographies of both advertisers and anthropologists are driven by experience, politically mediated (in that they reveal one person's or group's power to represent another), historically situated, and shaped by specific traditions of their respective professions – including narrative and rhetorical conventions.[31]

5. Advertising agencies and anthropologists make a living from writing up the results of their research and presenting it to others – corporate clients or academic peers – who in one way or another vet their work. Their analyses – and the advertisements and commercials they produce – are interpretive acts that decode one set of people for another. In this sense, both advertisers and anthropologists are cultural intermediaries who study others for other others.

6. People in the advertising profession and anthropologists are usually separated from their different publics by the fact that each group has its own assumptions, disciplinary practices and language (in plain terms, jargon). Moreover, as Kemper points out, both tend to spend more time talking to and interacting with others in their professional community than with the 'general public' whom they would claim to represent.[32] In this respect, they are often eyed askance by those outside their professions. Having to peer into realms of social action that are alien to their own groups and gathering information on them, instils an impression of adventure for some and intrusive voyeurism for others.

7. Both advertising executives and anthropologists tend to 'present a front of hard assurance, of findings as "results." Even the description of method is usually *ex post facto*.'[33] These findings are then fed back to reinforce or modify existing systems of beliefs for both groups, whether as systems of power and resistance, or beliefs about brand values.

8. Each professional group operates in an organizational world that makes the carrying out of ethnographic research competitive. Advertising executives usually have to make presentations to clients; anthropologists submit written proposals to research foundations and other funding bodies. In this sense, both have to make a successful pitch in order for the research to go ahead. Advertising executives are

like ethnographers in that both 'make a living by convincing clients that they understand how the natives think.'[34] In both worlds, there is a tendency for success to breed further success. One successful presentation for an account often leads to other accounts; one successful grant application often leads to further funding.

9. Both anthropologists and advertising executives pay surface attention to the idea of 'culture' which, as we have seen, is 'akin to a black hole that allows no light to escape.'[35] In the end, however, both groups of professionals are more concerned with the social interaction, beliefs and values surrounding the relation between people and things in a society. Advertisers tend to focus on how people *use*, and should use, products in the narrow confines of sales and consumption, and what motivates them to continue to do so. For their part, anthropologists examine how those same products fit into a wider scheme of social organization and belief systems.

10. However, as Mazzarella points out, the important thing about both advertising professionals and anthropologists seeking to understand 'culture' is that 'their work necessarily causes them to intervene in areas far beyond the strictly defined boundaries of their technical expertise.' Ironically though, given their extremely limited public audience, it is only anthropologists who have felt the need to take responsibility for the cultural ramifications of the work that they do. Advertising people, whose work is far more widely disseminated, have tended to limit their view of ethics to questions which 'are generally internal to the credibility of individual advertising campaigns, interpreted as tools for selling particular products.'

So, if there are similarities between these two professional groups, there are also important differences. Those outlined below involve research orientation, team-work, immediacy, intervention, media and technology.

1. Ethnography is used by advertising professionals as a means towards action-oriented results. Since 'ideas and insights are as much part of the marketplace as are more material consumer goods'[36] advertisers and marketers take results gleaned from ethnographic studies and treat them as material 'facts,' which are then turned into communication objectives, brand directives and target market imperatives. The effect of this is to imply a certain cause and effect lineality, using a system of knowledge aimed at achieving specific ends. This is not generally so of fieldwork as practiced by academics, although it *is* true of applied anthropology.

2. The anthropologist is a generalist who *works on her own*. She usually selects a topic of interest, reads around that topic before heading off to 'the field' where she spends a certain length of time observing and participating in local lives and then returns home to sift her data and write up a report (article, book) for an academic

audience. All of this is done without much input from others, apart from a PhD supervisor or friendly colleagues in a department seminar.

Those working in advertising, however, are specialists (in account planning, market analysis, copywriting, visual design, and so on) who *work as a team*. The 'object' of the consumer is constructed from shared information shaped by any number of individuals and teams of people who do field research, carry out analyses, dream up visual ideas, write copy, and find the best combination of media in which to place the finished results. And all the time, information about what is going on during the construction of a campaign is being relayed to the client who gives continuous feedback on what they think is more and less appropriate to the task in hand.

As a result, far more discussion and negotiation, as well as the use of inter-personal skills, go on among advertising professionals in the preparation of a campaign than they do for a lone anthropologist writing a paper or monograph. In anthropology, feedback can be solicited by means of seminar paper presentations at different universities, but ultimately changes are required only when a work is submitted to a journal or publisher and a blind review process involving not more than three persons 'in the field.' In advertising, the constant exchange of inform-ation between different specialists within an agency, as well as between agency and client and subcontracted organizations, means that an advertising campaign is continuously being tinkered with, moved in one direction rather than another, then back again, before reaching an acceptable form. Whereas the anthropologist can, at the end, proudly point to her work and say: 'This is mine,' nobody can legitimately lay claim to ownership of an ad campaign.

3. Public reaction to the work of anthropologists and advertisers is very different. If anthropologists 'write' culture, as Kemper points out, advertising *produces* it.[37] What advertising executives say about different kinds of people, and the images with which they endow them, are found in advertising campaigns that are then watched, read and listened to by those very same people. This can lead to instant discussion and debate of a kind that does not usually arise from publication of anthropological works.[38] Ultimately for advertisers, reactions to an advertising campaign are evaluated by quantitative tracking data that measure consumer awareness, interest, opinion, consideration, and actual sales figures. This type of public reaction has real implications for the success or failure of a client's product manager, an advertising account, or even the agency itself in terms of continued employment with a particular client. In other words, there are real-life con-sequences for how the work of advertisers stirs, or fails to stir, public response.

4. In the way that advertising must be responsive to an ever changing public and the sometimes fickle demands of its client, it is temporal and transitory. Advertising

can be seasonal, event-specific (e.g., public elections, award shows), regionally or territorially based, alert to product advances and apologetic of failures, attuned to scandals or successes of public officials running for office, as well as to more gradual shifts in target market demographics, or sudden changes in a nation's emotional climate (such as after the events of 11 September in the US). In this regard advertising negotiates a sense of time, place and circumstance (as Kemper shows in this volume between representations of the local and the national). This means that the cultural texts which advertising produces are often (intentionally and unintentionally) quick to go out of date and become irrelevant, compared to those accounts of anthropologists which aspire to be more lasting and definitive.

5. Then there is a difference in what or whom they choose to study. Anthropologists are more or less free in this regard. For advertisers, on the other hand, there are fewer choices, since what and whom they study tend to be predicated on the latest trends in marketing (for example, grass-roots marketing, the affluent class, young urban hipsters).[39] These, in turn, cause other advertisers to jump on the proverbial competitive bandwagon.

6. A major premise underlying fieldwork in both anthropology and marketing is that what people think and how they behave are *not invented*, but *reflected* in the final study. Yet the ethnographic knowledge developed by advertising agencies tends to be cutting-edge, sophisticated, and more aware of current developments in society than is that of most anthropologists. It is this immediate relevance, perhaps, that leads advertising executives to feel the need on occasion to *create* social divisions in a market. They may justify themselves by arguing that yuppies, guppies, generation X, early adopters, or other demographic targets that came into common parlance in the English-speaking world during the last two decades of the twentieth century, are 'out there' and visible, but their visibility is precisely because of their construction by advertisers in the first place.[40]

At the same time, we also need to note that during the processes of constructing an advertising campaign, each of those involved (from account executives to creatives) can construct the consumer into an object, if only to a slight degree, for his or her own purposes. At any given point, information can be managed to achieve certain ends – like, for example, making consumer feedback more palatable to a client. There is thus often an incentive among those working in the advertising profession to shape and direct consumer information, rather than maintain their own reflective representations of someone or something 'out there.'

Since consumer research is backed by a client's financial resources – resources that typically far exceed those of the lone academic anthropologist (even the favored few funded by research grants), advertisers' fieldwork research typically sources its consumer information from a variety of locations for any given study.

Getting a broad 'read' on consumer behavior involves sampling a diverse range of consumers in multiple market locations across a nation, rather than focusing on a single, more or less remote village or tribe. In this sense, the kind of fieldwork research practiced by advertisers may be one step ahead of that undertaken by anthropologists since it already carries out what has been termed 'multiple site research.'[41]

7. There are also differences between anthropologists and advertising professionals in the scope, breadth and presentation of the work itself. While the media through which an anthropologist publishes are typically limited to paper and oral presentations for a select academic audience, advertising people tend to create multidimensional works that span a number of different media – both in their creation and distribution. As Barbara Olsen points out in her contribution to this volume, an advertising campaign is not necessarily limited to print or broadcast advertisements. It may also involve point-of-purchase stand-ups or in-store displays to attract consumers. In other words, ad campaigns take on in their various forms of representation a contextual multidimensionality that anthropological works typically lack.

In addition, there is a tendency for marketers to employ the latest technology not only in the production of their ad campaigns, but also when gathering information on consumers. For example, professional grade video recorders, miniature clip-on microphones, hired professional cameramen are often taken by researchers conducting fieldwork, or 'ethnographic,' interviews. Information gleaned is then often sent back immediately to the client by means of the latest internet technology (internet streaming video, for instance) or Fed-Exed overnight.

8. By comparison with what goes on in advertising and marketing, anthropological fieldwork is neither labor- nor capital-intensive. Ethnography as done by anthropologists may be time-consuming, but it has the immense practical advantage of being cheap.

Ethical Dilemmas

One of the major issues facing all of us all of the time, especially when we are employed in professions that are primarily concerned with the dissemination of information and knowledge is that of ethics – an issue also raised by Baba in her Afterword. We have already broached this topic in discussing the cultural ramifications of the parallel work done by anthropologists and advertising professionals. Now it is time to ask: What are and what should be the relations between those who profess to be 'expert' and those whom their expertise is all about and from whom they gained their expertise in the first place?

One of the things that has come to worry anthropologists a lot during the past two decades is the relation of power that exists between ethnographer and informant. For a long time, precisely because they studied 'primitive' peoples in isolated parts of the world, anthropologists could say more or less what they thought, without any serious objections being made by those whose lives were made famous. This was partly because fieldwork was often conducted in colonial situations; partly because of the state of informants' education systems, literacy and foreign (primarily English) language ability; and partly because of the lack of development of communications and information technology. Nowadays, however, anthropologists are no longer able to 'study down' with such ease and often have to obtain informants' – at least, tacit – approval before publishing anything about them.

In this respect, anthropology has edged closer to existing realities in the advertising world, where people are employed by agencies to go out and conduct ethnographic research on a selected 'group' of consumers, but find themselves in a precarious situation with regard to reporting on what they learn 'in the field.' Perhaps it is to justify the uses to which they put their knowledge that advertisers typically pay informants for their time (although this is not unknown in anthropological fieldwork where, typically, gifts are handed over).[42] Making the exchange of information a form of economic transaction changes not only the nature of the relationship between researcher and informant, but – in the eyes of the advertiser, at least – the nature of how that information may then be used.

At the same time, the development of advertising and other industries in 'first world' societies has been accompanied by the parallel (though usually later) development of norms regarding consumer 'rights.' This means that consumers in the United States, for example, who are interviewed in their homes or brought together in focus group discussions are told that the information that they have given will not be broadcast in any manner or form without their expressed written consent. In other words, there are in the US (as well as most parts of Europe and some other parts of the world) legal safeguards that limit what advertisers may or may not do with the information obtained. If they were to air anything, they would almost certainly be obliged to get permission from their informants, and even have them sign a waver in exchange for extra royalties. Although academics in general are nowadays asked to sign forms relating to such ethical issues as the use of informants or live animal experiments, in general anthropologists do not pay people prior to publishing the information that they have learned from them.

But neither advertising nor anthropology is *only* concerned with studying down. The issue of power relations is also present in their 'studying up.'[43] There are two social arenas where this occurs. First, as Moeran soon learned when writing up his data after a year's fieldwork in a Japanese advertising agency, an anthropologist can come up against the power of a corporation which wishes to censor those parts of an academic discourse that are not to its liking.[44] In this respect, advertising agencies themselves have it fairly easy when doing research on consumers who, for the most part, do not have institutionally-backed means of redress.

However, agencies *do* have to face their clients . . . almost every day. This is the second arena where power relations come into play. Precisely because it is the client who hands over the money that enables an agency to carry out its work and continue to prosper, advertising executives have to ensure that the client is 'always happy.' This client–agency relationship inevitably affects decisions made during the course of preparing an advertising campaign.

This relationship spreads its tentacles into all areas of an advertising executive's work. For example, should a copywriter who does not smoke, who avoids 'secondary smoking' at all times, and who believes that tobacco companies have a lot to answer for in terms of their perceived moral irresponsibility towards consumers, work on a new cigarette campaign when asked to do so by his creative director? After all, he owes allegiance to his agency, as well as to the agency's client. And should the creative director then fire the copywriter for refusing to cooperate on the campaign proposal? Similar sorts of questions can be raised about advertising political campaigns, environmental issues, and automobiles among other goods and services.

Suppose a copywriter *does* decide to ignore the fact that, beside the environmental damage they cause, automobiles are also usually responsible for killing more people every year in the United States and most parts of Europe than is anything else. What does he do, as a man, when he realizes that the client's market analysis calls for a sexist ad campaign that suggests that the convertible 'model' in question is a man's mistress (to revert to an old case study)?[45] Does he then call into question the creative director's gender bias, revealed in the latter's decision to put him on this particular job, rather than one of the women copywriters employed by his agency? How far can he go in upsetting the internal hierarchy of his organization, and the external hierarchy between agency and client?

Then there is the matter of paying consumers for their information. This is something some anthropologists have done and still do, but it does raise other ethical issues. For example, when and when not should money be used as a form of recompense? In Japan, for example, gifts are preferred, since it is generally believed that time given to a researcher cannot properly be measured in monetary terms. In the United States, however, this does not necessarily work. A growing trend in market research there is to study affluent consumers, and pay them for their time (Malefyt is employed in advertising for a luxury brand). But this then raises another ethical problem, in that the incentive money paid to wealthy respondents could better be given to those who really need it.

But then comes the realization that getting to know consumers in depth through ethnography is not really about *knowing* them – except in terms of their consumptive relations to products and brands. After all, as Lien points out, most products are 'constructed' with a *future* consumer in mind. In other words, the affluent are more attractive to marketers than are those with less disposable income precisely because of the former's tendency, or at least potential, to spend three times more on both luxury and everyday goods. And affluent people also appeal to marketers because they usually belong to elite groups of one kind or another, and so influence others in their consumption patterns through their social and cultural capital.

These are the sorts of ethical problems that business people face every day. Many are indeed aware of them, but not many – we suggest – are able to resolve them satisfactorily. For their part, anthropologists can escape this confrontation with everyday ethical problems because they are outside the 'big, wide world,' safely cocooned in an intellectual environment. It is true that they have ethical problems of their own (regarding plagiarism, for example, or the sexual harassment of students), but for the most part they can afford to step back and reflect before plunging into their work, then step back and reflect once more. For better and for worse, in its urge to move ever forward, business does not allow this to happen.

The power given to, or taken by, people to say particular things in certain situations is very important in this discussion of ethical issues. So far, we have talked of the institutional constraints on people to follow a particular line, to remain with 'the herd.' There are, of course, some who do decide to speak out against what they perceive as unethical – like the senior civil servant who blew the whistle on the EU Commission in the autumn of 2001, or the *Washington Post* reporters who slowly but surely uncovered the Watergate 'affair' that led to the resignation of former president Nixon. For the most part, however, individuals and corporations want to avoid trouble . . . at all costs. There is 'too much at stake' – a stake where people can be burned for their indiscretions. This is as true of the world of academia as it is of the field of business. People try to avoid stepping out of line, in how they look, in what they say, in almost everything they do. Corporate clients, indeed corporations in general, are terrified of 'negative publicity' – to themselves, their brands, their profitability, even, occasionally, their employees. 'Political correctness' is rampant everywhere, which may explain why ethics is a growing concern. As more and more companies become aware of the liabilities arising from unethical behavior, they have begun to hire 'ethics officers' to oversee their operations – even if, for the most part, the latter are more concerned with protecting their employer's vested interests than with being in tune with consumer demands.[46] It would seem that we need a practical ethics for the practice of ethics.

Managing Fieldwork

So far, we have outlined the practice of 'fieldwork' or ethnography as regarded by – possibly purist – anthropologists, before proceeding to look at similarities and differences between anthropologists and members of the advertising profession. It is now time to look in a little more detail at the current status of ethnography in business: that is to say, at how advertisers and marketers use ethnography as a research tool. What significant differences are there between the use of ethnography by anthropologists and the use of ethnography in business? And how do these differences affect the ways in which advertising professionals continue to practice their work?

As noted earlier, anthropologists typically use ethnography as a means towards understanding the people they study. In the world of business, however, ethnography is specifically aimed at achieving action-oriented results. In advertising and marketing, therefore, the sense is that one has to be able to move forward, towards some definable, actionable end. It may at times seem as if those concerned actively look for – even invent – a problem in order to find a matching solution that then justifies their existence as advertising or marketing professionals. In this respect, we might suspect them of absorbing ethnography into their occupational sphere in the same way that business generally has absorbed other types of disciplines that began to study it. Be that as it may, what we need to be aware of is the fact that business almost always transforms that which it adopts into a managed project.

This is very much the case with fieldwork practiced by advertising and marketing professionals. The process of ethnographic research is closely managed, so that the idea of the intrepid anthropologist venturing out alone and unmonitored with notepad and pencil in hand becomes almost surreal. Modern methods of fieldwork in business often support several members of a party conducting research in homes, restaurants, supermarkets, on street corners, or wherever consumers are consuming, along with appropriate video camcorders and tape recorders to help those concerned better manage the process. Indeed, the ethnographer's basic recording tools have been modified by business to include the latest in micro-cassette tape recorders, digital video equipment and professional videographers, as well as the usual written notes and observations made by fieldworkers. Moreover, consumers are not just filmed on tape. The tapes themselves are professionally remixed, shortened and edited to create a more actionable image of the consumer for the final report to the client.

The very introduction of such controlled measures may – to some extent, justifiably – raise the hackles of conventional academic anthropologists, who are continuously confronted and have to struggle with the issue of representation in the ethnographic encounter. In particular, they are concerned with how their presence affects the quality of the information they gain from their informant(s), so that they seek to minimise, as much as possible, the effects of their intrusion. What they try to avoid is having respondents 'perform' as well as 'inform.' Yet, by introducing filming techniques and by including multiple interviewers, marketers affect consumer behavior in a manner that encourages, perhaps, the kind of performance that the academic anthropologist tries to avoid. Thus, consumers may feel they have to smile or nod their heads to show appreciation for what the interviewer is saying or asking. They may even do things that they would not normally do, precisely because of the presence of a video camera.

Compounding this dilemma, we see increased pressure from corporate clients to achieve quicker turnaround time in analysis and presentation of results. The corporate ethnographer is not allowed a lengthy period of time to sift through material and reflect on data, as academic anthropologists without stringent dead-lines do, since final results are often demanded for presentation a week or two after fieldwork ends. In other words, the ethnographic enterprise practiced by business not only witnesses an invasion of space with the camera, but also an erasure of time by the analyst.

What, then, are the effects of shortened analytical time and the inclusion of the client's penetrating gaze on the ethnographic encounter? In relinquishing their previously exclusive stance as arbiters of knowledge, anthropologists in the marketing field have unwittingly contributed to an increase in the amount of commentary coming from their clients. This is because there is more consumer experience available to the client who then becomes an associated witness to the research in question. New and faster ways by which ethnographers record and represent the consumer not only provide the client with more, readily visible materials, but also afford corporate marketers even greater opportunity to react to them. This in itself means that clients are able to take control and manage the ethnographic process. In other words, while professionalism and authority are still part of the scene, the locus of authority has shifted from the anthropologist as professional recorder to professionalism in recording equipment.

This shift from human researcher to research technology has also enabled a transfer of power and control from researcher hired to carry out a project to the organization financing the project itself. That is to say, modern methods of data gathering have created out of the ethnographic encounter an unavoidable partner in the client. At issue is the fact that clients evaluate the ethnographic interview in terms of their own marketing objectives, unaware of the contextual rapport that the interviewer may have established with the respondent. During a week of fieldwork, recorded tapes are typically translated from the fieldworker's video recording machine into VHS format, whereupon they are then sent overnight to clients. A roomful of client members typically views and critiques not just the content and quality of the tapes, but also the style and line of questioning carried out by the ethnographer herself. Typically, everyone wants a say. Even junior client members voice their concerns – not necessarily to add brilliant additions or insights to the review, but to establish their savvy and marketing acumen in front of their corporate bosses. While the pictured consumer provides a way of making the strange familiar, the digitized video image is also a way of presenting the consumer neatly packaged as a brand to the client. And as a brand, how the consumer is then represented in advertising allows the client full freedom and justification in commenting on and criticising those representations.[47]

In assuming the role of in-home voyeur, the ethnographer's camera is reminiscent of another favorite research method used by marketers: the focus group. After all, the camera frame offers a similar type of backroom region where the client can comfortably observe the consumer from a safe, unobtrusive distance. In the tradition of the focus group format, all conversations on film are framed within a timed, spatial context, with clear boundaries of beginning and end, and underlying rules of comportment. In this way, the videotaped ethnographic encounter incorporates a similar 'observe and control' ideology to that of the focus group setting. As is the case with other forms of exhibition, such as those in museums and world's fairs, the transfer of humans from the privacy of one sphere (in this case, the home) to an arena of public display conveys an unmistakable message of power over the subjects in question.[48] Ethnography in this way becomes subsumed under the business model of management so that even the respondents are subject to rules of comportment – a far cry, indeed, from the idea of informal and unstructured discussions that are the partial aim of academic anthropologists' participant-observation. And if respondents do not say the 'right' things at first, the researcher can always go back to 'probe further,' and altogether ignore what has been previously recorded.

So how should professional anthropologists react when the corporate client who hires them becomes part of the ethnographic encounter? This condition increasingly presents a new reality for anthropologists who work in the field of marketing, as ethnographic consultants Sunderland and Denny may attest, and as Olsen describes in her account of how she conducted in-store research for a small New York-based agency. One problem for anthropologists working with corporations – besides that of the managed methodology of ethnography – lies in the theoretical approaches that marketers typically take.

While advertisers attempt to manage ethnography as a tool to read consumer culture better, business ethnography in general tends to be driven by prevalent models about what makes up human motivation. Thus, Sunderland and Denny note that psychological models prevail as dominant models by which marketers evaluate their consumers. Abraham Maslow and his hierarchy of needs, Eric Ericson's theory of the progression of life-stages, Freud's psychoanalytic model of unconscious tendencies towards sex and aggression, as well as quadripartite models of binary tensions from structuralism, are popular models of choice among marketers today. They are all used for their simplicity of design, as well as for their logical cause-and-effect relations, which allow marketers to position their brands and those of competitors relative to one another. In his contribution to this volume, Malefyt describes how some of the models that are used to position consumers and brands are in themselves reflective of the relations between client and agency.

Another of the psychological models – that of personality in culture – has been derived from anthropology. For decades now, business has been looking for certain key psychological drivers that separate what marketers see as 'emotional' from 'rationalistic' motives in consumption behavior. As a result, the kind of study of emotion in culture that began in American anthropology, and was highlighted in the work of Ruth Benedict, has come to be almost fetishized in marketing. By taking a 'deep' view of the lives of consumers, marketers believe that they can bypass more rational and calculated responses, of the kind they encounter in focus groups, and thereby get to a deeper, more emotional level of understanding. They are convinced that people act in more naturalistic ways, whether in the home or out on the streets, and that by observing them they can get past rational barriers to consumption and learn more about people's 'true' emotional motives. This idea of the emotional motive they then tie into the equity of the brand.

But, whether making use of consumer emotions and personality, Maslow's hierarchy of needs, or a structural analysis that uncovers 'tensions' in buying decisions, marketers always assume some kind of objective reality in what they are seeking, rather than take issue with interpretations of the kind of consumer behavior that they are evaluating. So far as they are concerned, as Mazzarella points out, consumer preferences are not constructed; they are simply 'there' to be discovered. From a marketing standpoint, people are supposed to be driven by needs, wants, and desires that can be fulfilled by buying and using a particular product. The task of marketers, then, is to seek out, appropriate, and then match the particular consumer need with the correct product or brand benefit. And 'ethnography' is used as a tool to ferret out those needs. Thus, while the aims and substance of fieldwork may these days differ, fieldwork still remains very much a holy grail for anthropologists and marketers alike.

Advertising Anthropology

In the final section of this Introduction, let us briefly introduce the chapters in this book and focus briefly on some other common points of interest not discussed so far. The first two chapters in this book are broadly concerned with the relations between the global and the local, as they are acted out in the neighboring societies of Sri Lanka and India. In the first, Steven Kemper uses the analogy of advertisers as folk ethnographers to reflect upon how to think about Sri Lankan society. As an anthropologist, should he continue to think of it in strictly anthropological terms as being 'shaped by local religious, kinship, caste and land tenure systems'? Or should he, perhaps, adopt the advertising executive's view of Sri Lanka as an advertising-driven consumer society populated by different market 'segments'? Such questions lead him to look at how different advertising agencies adopt different strategies when creating their ad campaigns, and often use 'local culture' as a marketing tool to sell *advertising*, rather than commodities themselves (a point, incidentally, that is repeated in later chapters on advertising in India, Trinidad, and Japan). His argument is that advertising – in Sri Lanka at least – moves culture beyond local differences by presenting 'zones of display' that are neither local nor global – 'near enough to be recognizable, distant enough to be worthy of desire.' In this way, the advertising business in general often creates images that run counter to a national government's appeal to particularistic, even chauvinist, local values.

This point is taken up by William Mazzarella who continues the globalization theme in his discussion of advertising in India. His initial aim in conducting fieldwork among Bombay advertising professionals was to study how global brands are translated for local markets and given a certain 'Indianness.' Advertising thus becomes a form of cultural mediation in its assemblage of images. Once again, we find that advertising agencies act as cultural brokers as they tell their clients what is and is not 'Indian' and thereby legitimate their existence. And once again we find transnational clients finding it hard to beat the 'locals,' since they are trashed for their 'value arrogance' if they fail to consider their consumers' 'Indianness,' and are seen to be racially arrogant if they do not treat those same 'Indian' consumers like everyone else in the world.

Mazzarella uses his fieldwork experiences to question his role as an anthropologist studying urban English-language advertising in a country where the vast majority of people cannot understand it, or afford to buy the products it promotes. Painfully, he compares the rarified (and, of course, cool conditioned) air of the advertising agency office in which he sat all day with the sultry, teeming Bombay streets through which he made his way home every evening. Wryly, he notes the circularity of the information given him, as well as the reified idiom of a marketing discourse that gave nothing away beyond the smooth exterior of the advertising world in which he moved. Such fieldwork is tough; it is isolating; it can break your will unless, like Mazzarella, you take it by the horns.

The following two chapters reveal different facets of the workings of advertising industries in two rather different parts of the world. Daniel Miller offers three case studies – moving from the production to the consumption of different kinds of soft drinks in Trinidad – as part of his broader 'radical empiricist' stance that only microcosm fieldwork can produce macrocosm theory. That theory, outlined here, concerns the relation between economy and culture. In the first study, we see how unspoken assumptions framed meetings between an advertising agency and its client, on the one hand, and between different members of the agency's account team, on the other, and ultimately affected the cultural content of the campaign for a soft drink relaunch. In the second, the intended sexual meaning of an ad campaign for a soya milk product is totally rejected and reinterpreted by consumers, thereby allowing Miller to reflect upon the processes by which cultural norms can be formed *vis-à-vis* commodities. In the third, for 'a black sweet drink from Trinidad,' Miller points out how people all over the world have been able to turn Coca-Cola into something essentially local and different, and argues that transnational companies themselves tend to adopt different business strategies in different countries.

He also argues that local advertising agencies, as well as local branches of global advertising agencies, have invested a lot of time and energy in persuading transnational clients that Trinidad is a 'special' market. As a result, in contra-distinction to advertising in Sri Lanka as described by Kemper, much Trinidadian advertising is unashamedly 'local' in its use of images. Such cultural differences, however, are simultaneously used to create economic differences that allow a local advertising industry to flourish (often at the expense of global agencies).

In the fourth chapter, Brian Moeran makes use of a case study in which he actively participated to discuss the production of a proposed advertising campaign. In so doing, he picks up on a rather different form of globalization – one that is not initiated in the West, but spreads from East Asia. Here we have a Japanese advertising agency's presentation to its Japanese client of an advertising campaign directed at German and North American consumers. The problem facing agency personnel was to fathom how the client's key decision-makers would interpret particular sets of images as 'European,' 'American,' or 'Japanese.' Like those involved in the Trinidadian soft drink relaunch described by Miller, they had to anticipate interpretive processes, on the one hand, and, on the other, to understand the social processes that went on in their client's corporation. Globalization ends up being as much about interpersonal relations between individuals representing different corporations, therefore, as about the strategic expansion of those corp-orations themselves.

In the end, the images presented by the agency to its prospective client con-stituted a visual shorthand for specific places, dramas and meanings. Moeran argues that the media have little choice about how they disseminate cultural stereotypes and image clichés, because of the way in which their content is limited in terms of space and time. They thereby create a global stylistic continuity, in which common differences – in Japan, as in Sri Lanka, Trinidad and India, created by local advertising industries – are readily understood by local audiences all over the world.

Barbara Olsen is also concerned with how an advertising campaign gets off the ground. In her fascinating 'narrative ethnography' of a marketing problem facing a major brassiere manufacturer in the United States, Olsen argues that 'it is the consumer who decides and forces marketers to become the change agents of history.' Her focus is on how the small New York agency in which she used to work was hired by its client, Warner's, to increase its share of the market. Assigned, with two other young women, to handle the account, Olsen found herself doing all kinds of fieldwork – from one-to-one interviews (far more productive, she says, than focus groups) to department store sales floor observation. She also found herself having to face issues of gender, sexuality and class at almost every turn along the tortuous path to success.[49]

One strength of this chapter is Olsen's demonstration that an effective advertising campaign is not limited to broadcast or print media, but often achieves success through other diverse marketing channels, such as in-store displays and point-of-purchase promotions.[50] Once the agency realized that it was targeting not one but three groups of people – the store buyer and retail clerk, as well as the consumer – it had to prepare three different types of sales promotion. But it was in the client's own showroom, where bras were placed on hangers for store buyers to see and feel, that the successful concept of customer self-service was born.

In Chapter 6, Timothy Malefyt also focuses on the carefully staged social interaction that goes on between advertising agencies and their clients, as the former prepare ads for the public domain. Using as his case study a liquor brainstorming session, he examines the processes by which members of an American agency read and adjust their behavior to maximize personal relations with their corporate client. He also demonstrates the ways in which psychological models of the consumer and brand are created and managed by the agency to mirror relations between agency and client.

Although the stated aim of the workshop is to allow the agency to gain an understanding of its client's consumer, brand and competition, the real aim is to build what Malefyt calls 'relations of affinity' – and ethnography is 'a purposeful tool' used in this process. An agency also builds relations of affinity with a client through the mutual expression of a language style that is based on metaphors of warfare to show their togetherness *vis-à-vis* consumers.[51] In addition, the agency uses simple market models, like Maslow's hierarchy of needs, not because it believes that they in any way provide satisfactory explanations of consumer behavior, but because they are simple enough to facilitate discussion and interaction with the client. This, then, is the real purpose of ethnography. But the implication of this is that, unlike Olsen's conclusion from her case study, consumers do not seem to have much influence on what goes into an advertising campaign, but often get sidelined by the more important social interaction that goes on between an advertising agency and its corporate client.

In Chapter 7, Marianne Lien presents an account of marketing and advertising from the client's perspective, as she describes and analyzes the challenges of modern food manufacturing affecting a product manager in a Norwegian food company. Here the focus is on the material content of the product – the taste, texture and packaging of a convenience frozen food range called Bon Appetit – on the one hand, and its visual and symbolic representation through advertising and a television commercial, on the other. It is the challenges provoked by the dialectic between practice and knowledge that leads marketers in general into 'loops, reversals, and dead ends' when it comes to decision-making and action. In other words, marketing is far more self-conscious and reflexive than idealized models of the profession suggest.

The fact that, in Norway, convenience foods have been associated by consumers with 'foods of foreign origin' (like Italian pasta dishes, chop suey, and beef Stroganoff) takes Lien into a discussion of the familiar and the foreign, and so brings us full circle to how marketers and consumers interpret national images – this time through 'imagined cuisines.' She argues convincingly that every time a locally defined image of the exotic (consisting of a careful balance of familiarity and significance) is disseminated by means of a successful food product, it contributes to a process of routinization that forces product managers to search for other, still unspoiled, imagined cuisines. Ultimately, this would seem to lead to an 'imagined globalization' as more and more different and remote parts of the world are brought into marketing representations.

In the final chapter, Patricia Sunderland and Rita Denny ask what the role of culture is in ethnographic practices. As anthropologists plying their trade as research consultants, they find themselves in a quandary. Anthropology may be in the process of becoming 'in vogue,' but their clients have little idea what the discipline or word actually connotes. Instead, they have found that it is *psychology* that is the overarching theoretical paradigm in market research and anthropologists are called on to carry out ethnography to find out what people think of themselves, rather than to provide a cultural analysis of brands, products or services in everyday life. Not surprisingly, Sunderland and Denny find themselves occasionally talking right past their client, who cannot – or will not – understand the problems affecting both the selection of respondents and the analysis of fieldwork results. In the end, in spite of all the talk of 'culture' in business, it is psychological, not cultural, analysis that is demanded.

This is, of course, a paradox. How can 'ethnography,' which focuses on cultural – and, Europeans would quickly add, social – relations, continue to be used by advertising and marketing professionals, who are still delving into the 'mind' and 'psyche' of *the* consumer? Sunderland and Denny hint that the problem may be particularly 'American.' People in the United States, including anthropologists and marketers, seem to have a cultural 'predilection for the psychological.'

But if that predilection is then foisted, by means of marketing theories dominated by Americans, onto the rest of the world, then we are witnessing a far more subtle form of global hegemony. In other words, we are being invited to look beyond the globalization of multinational corporations and media images and – like Lien, though in a slightly different way – to join battle with the globalization of *ideas*.[52] What tactics, then, should we adopt as anthropologists who are also advertising professionals and/or academics? How do *we* now play the game of distinction and branding that is demanded in the market of ideas?

These are the kinds of issues that, as anthropologists working in or doing research on advertising, we need to resolve. And for this we will need a lot of resolution. After all, the processes of advertising are convoluted and opaque; yet its marketing mechanisms and advertising images thoroughly pervasive. As anthropologists, we cannot afford *not* to get to grips with them. The same holds good for the advertising industry. Anthropology potentially provides it with such incisive dissections of social processes and cultural norms that advertising and marketing professionals cannot afford *not* to use it properly. If we have any advice to give, it is to socialize advertising industries into advertising anthropology.

Notes

1. e.g. Williamson (1978); O'Barr (1994).
2. Jhally (1996: 6).
3. *Advertising Age*, (4 June 2001), p. 1.
4. Wernick (1991).
5. Moeran (2000).
6. Malinowski (1961 [1922]).
7. Riesman in his Foreword to Bowen (1964: xi–xii).
8. Eriksen (1995: 14).
9. Van Maanen (1988: 3).
10. As propagated by W.H.R. Rivers, the Cambridge anthropologist, in 1913 (quoted in Stocking 1983: 92).
11. Interesting reflections on the different kinds of material gleaned from informants through, first, interviews and then, participant observation can be found in Powdermaker (1967: 155–82).
12. Stocking (1983: 70). George Stocking (1983: 80) also points out that the term 'field work' was introduced into British anthropology at the very beginning of the twentieth century by Alfred Haddon who borrowed it from 'the discourse of field naturalists.'
13. These examples in fact represent the fieldwork interests and locations of a single anthropologist, Hortense Powdermaker (1967).

14. Advice given to Evans-Pritchard (later Professor of Social Anthropology at Oxford University) by Bronislaw Malinowski, Edward Westermarck, Charles Seligman and Alfred Haddon (in Eriksen 1995: 16).
15. Bowen (1964: 4).
16. Eriksen (1995: 16).
17. e.g. Osborne (2002: 29). Strictly speaking, ethnography is the writing up of fieldwork research.
18. Comaroff (1992: 7).
19. Read (1980: x).
20. Rosaldo (1993: 26).
21. Marcus (1998: 16).
22. Baba (2001).
23. Rabinow (1977: 154).
24. Watson (1999).
25. Rabinow (1977: 150–1).
26. Dresch and James (2000: 10).
27. Stocking (1983: 93).
28. Cf. Baumann (1988: 229); Dresch and James (2000: 14).
29. This is, perhaps, one reason why marketers have become interested in the idea of culture and in the practice of 'ethnography' as a new way to understand human consumption.
30. Ericksen (1995: 18).
31. See Van Maanen (1988: 4–7).
32. Cf. Kemper (2001: 7–8).
33. Bowen (1964: xviii).
34. Kemper (2001: 4), from whom this quote is taken, argues that this is what *differentiates* advertising executives from anthropologists. We ourselves believe, however, that the latter *do* spend a lot of time and energy on convincing their colleagues that they are 'expert' in a particular society and culture and that they derive their living therefrom. Kemper also points to the institutional factors that differentiate advertising from anthropology. Again, while the competition and the move of personnel among agencies may be more obvious and intense in the advertising industry, it is by no means absent in the academic world.
35. Van Maanen (1988: 3).
36. Bendix (1997: 226)
37. On writing culture, see Clifford and Marcus (1986). We might add, however, that by exoticising a particular people in their writings, anthropologists have sometimes themselves 'produced' a culture, or at least an understanding thereof.
38. Exceptions include Margaret Mead in the United States and, more recently, Nigel Barley in the United Kingdom. The fact that anthropologists increasingly

study people 'at home,' however, means that their work is, perhaps, more likely to be picked up and discussed.

39. In his chapter in this book, Steven Kemper suggests that there is a tendency in Sri Lanka for the direction of ethnographic interest to move from village to town to city in the case of anthropology, whereas advertising moves in the opposite direction.

40. Kemper (2001: 3–5).

41. Marcus (1986). This is not to say, however, that we ourselves agree with George Marcus's (1998) outline of, and arguments in favor of, multi-sited fieldwork as a methodology.

42. Powdermaker (1967).

43. Nader (1969).

44. Moeran (1996). Happily, the disagreement between advertising agency and anthropologist was resolved informally in the latter's favor.

45. Packard (1981: 77–8).

46. Zipkin (2000).

47. We should note that by allowing the consumer to become 'branded' by clients, marketers have in fact contributed to an ongoing process by which not just products but business organizations and celebrities are also branded (see Moeran 1996: 278–80).

48. Bennett (1994).

49. Olsen's observation about how marketers tread warily around social boundaries, and are reluctant to blur status categories, echoes earlier discussions of cultural stereotypes.

50. It is success in such below-the-line activities that often, as in this case, leads to above-the-line advertising in the four main media of newspapers, television, magazines and radio (cf. Moeran 2001: 286–7).

51. Marianne Lien (1996) also comments on the use of war metaphors among marketers.

52. Arjun Appadurai (1990) has touched upon this issue with the notion of 'ideoscapes' in global flows.

References

Appadurai, Arjun 1990 'Disjuncture and difference in the global cultural economy'. *Public Culture*, 2 (2): 1–24.

Baba, Marietta 2001 Discussant in 'Outside the academy walls: Placing anthropology in the world of business', invited session, 2001 American Anthropological Association, 100th Annual Meeting, Washington, DC.

Baumann, Gert 1988 'Village fieldwork overseas versus urban research at home,' *Journal of the Anthropological Society of Oxford*, 19: 225–32.

Bennett, Tony 1994 'The exhibitionary complex,' in N. Dirks, G. Eley and S. Ortner (eds) *Culture/Power/History: A Reader in Contemporary Social Theory*, pp. 123–54, Princeton, NJ: Princeton University Press.

Bendix, Regina 1997 *In Search of Authenticity*, Madison, WI: University of Wisconsin Press.

Bowen, Elenore Smith 1964 *Return to Laughter: An Anthropological Novel*, New York: Doubleday.

Clifford, James and George Marcus (eds) 1986 *Writing Culture: The Poetics and Politics of Ethnography*, Berkeley: University of California Press.

Comaroff, John and Jean 1992 *Ethnography and the Historical Imagination*, Boulder, CO: Westview.

Dresch, Paul and Wendy James 2000 'Introduction: Fieldwork and the passage of time,' in P. Dresch, W. James and D. Parkin (eds) *Anthropologists in a Wider World*, pp. 1–25. Oxford: Berghahn.

Eriksen, Thomas Hylland 1995 *Small Places, Large Issues: An Introduction to Social and Cultural Anthropology*, London: Pluto.

Goffman, Erving 1976 *Gender Advertisements*, Cambridge, MA: Harvard University Press.

Jhally, Sut 1996 'Advertising,' in Adam Kuper and Jessica Kuper (eds) *The Social Science Encyclopedia*, pp. 6–7, London: Routledge.

Kemper, Steven 2001 *Buying and Believing: Sri Lankan Advertising and Consumers in a Transnational World*, Chicago: University of Chicago Press.

Lien, Marianne 1996 *Marketing and Modernity*, Oxford: Berg.

Malinowski, Bronislaw 1961 [1922] *Argonauts of the Western Pacific*, London: E.P. Dutton.

Marcus, George 1986 'Contemporary problems of ethnography in the modern world system,' in J. Clifford and G. Marcus (eds) *Writing Culture: The Poetics and Politics of Ethnography*, pp. 165–93, Berkeley: University of California Press.

—— 1998 *Ethnography Through Thick and Thin*, Princeton, NJ: Princeton University Press.

McCracken, Grant 1989 'Who is the celebrity endorser?: Cultural foundations of the endorsement process,' *Journal of Consumer Research*, 16(12): 310–21.

Moeran, Brian 1996 *A Japanese Advertising Agency: An Anthropology of Media and Markets*, London: Curzon.

—— 2000 'The split account system and Japan's advertising industry,' *International Journal of Advertising*, 19 (2): 185–200.

—— 2001 'Promoting culture: The work of a Japanese advertising agency,' in B. Moeran (ed.) *Asian Media Productions*, pp. 270–91, London: Curzon.

Nader, Laura 1969 'Up the anthropologist,' in D. Hymes (ed.) *Reinventing Anthropology*, New York: Pantheon.

Neff, Jack 2001 'Feeling the squeeze: out of commission: Traditional pay plans are dead. The compensation conflict lives on,' *Advertising Age*, p. 1.

O'Barr, William 1994 *Culture and the Ad: Exploring Otherness in the World of Advertising*, Boulder, CO: Westview.

Osborne, Lawrence 2002 'Consuming rituals of the suburban tribe,' *New York Times Magazine*, 13 January, pp. 28–31.

Packard, Vance 1981 *The Hidden Persuaders*, Harmondsworth: Pelican.

Powdermaker, Hortense 1967 *Stranger and Friend: The Way of an Anthropologist*, London: Secker & Warburg.

Rabinow, Paul 1977 *Fieldwork in Morocco*, Berkeley: University of California Press.

Read, Kenneth 1980 *The High Valley*, New York: Columbia University Press.

Rosaldo, Renato 1993 *Culture and Truth: The Remaking of Social Analysis*, London: Routledge.

Stocking, George 1983 'Fieldwork in British anthropology,' in G. Stocking (ed.) *Observers Observed: Essays on Ethnographic Fieldwork*, pp. 70–120, Madison, WI: University of Wisconsin Press.

Van Maanen, John 1988 *Tales Of The Field: On Writing Ethnography*, Chicago: University of Chicago Press.

Watson, C.W. (ed.) 1999 *Being There: Fieldwork in Anthropology*, London: Pluto.

Wernick, Andrew 1991 *Promotional Culture: Advertising, Ideology and Symbolic Expression*, London: Sage.

Williamson, Judith 1978 *Decoding Advertisements: Ideology and Meaning in Advertising*, London: Marion Boyars.

Zipkin, Amy 2000 'Getting religion on corporate ethics,' *The New York Times*, 18 October, pp. C10.

–1–

How Advertising Makes its Object
Steven Kemper

Ask anyone to reflect on his or her own society, and they will produce a folk ethnography. To this extent, everyone is an ethnographer, not because human beings routinely stand back and reflect on the nature of their society but because every person has tacit knowledge and the ready-to-hand skills that allow him, let's say, to rise on certain occasions and remain seated on others. It is this knowledge or skill that the ethnographer seeks to understand and, when he does, what he produces is simply a worked-up version of what the actor entertained more naturally. While there is more to ethnographic analysis than gaining access to the mental states of one's informants, the equivalence of actors' understandings and ethnographic ones is a defining mark of anthropology as a discipline.

If every human being is a folk ethnographer by default, anthropologists and advertising executives are ethnographers in the strict sense of the word. In different ways both are trained as such, and both get paid for making claims about how the natives think.[1] In the case of advertising, agencies compete with one another by claiming better knowledge of how that thinking will affect a particular product or service. Addressing a prospective client, an executive musters the equivalent of ethnographic authority, that hard-to-define sense that the person speaking knows. Logical similarities aside, the two professions are becoming interdependent in everyday practice. As Mazzarella points out (this volume), where agencies once hired psychologists, they now advertise for anthropologists and insert them into agencies as 'future planners.'[2]

Anthropologists have encountered a crisis of confidence over the last two decades or so, questioning whether the idea of meaning, much less the concept of culture, can allow anthropologists to make claims about other kinds of people. At roughly the same time, the culture idea has drifted into popular discourse, and advertising executives nowadays speak of culture as a way to talk about consumption as a social phenomenon (as opposed to a purely psychological one). Business constraints steer advertising executives away from the worst excesses implied by the idea. To make a plausible pitch, executives need to stay current in a way most ethnographers, who eventually have to leave their fieldwork sites, cannot. Concentrating on demographic complexities provides a second advantage. Having to attend to markets within markets militates against the temptation to understand a society as a single entity. Advertising executives might in principle have knowledge of the natives that is not only sophisticated but also less prone to the essentialism and ahistoricism – 'these people have an essence; they are irremediably and always one way and not another' – of which ethnographic accounts have been accused.

My interest in the advertising business came from contemplating the analogy between anthropological and advertising practice, and it led me to think that here was a way to learn something new about Sri Lankan society. Why not ask people who have a professional interest in understanding that society just what they know about it? Anthropologists interested in Sri Lanka have understood it as a society shaped by local religious, kinship, caste, and land tenure systems. More recently, they have emphasized new expressions of Buddhism, ethnic violence, and the historical memory. These interests have created a picture of Sri Lanka that is admirable but incomplete. Advertising people are interested in the same society pictured in different terms. For them, Sri Lanka is a society of consumers. It fans out from Colombo and divides neatly into two groups – the middle class, typically English-speaking and living in Colombo, and those who live in provincial cities and villages.

Much has been made of ethnographic work as a task that produces texts.[3] Instead of assuming that the intellectually-central parts of the endeavor are participant observation, interviewing, and their default value, 'being there,' anthropological theorists two decades ago began to focus on the way ethnography gets written. They insisted that the way anthropological knowledge is reduced to journal, lecture, and book form is a constitutive act and deserving of scrutiny. By this recent standard, ethnographers have another characteristic in common with account managers, copywriters, and other creative people in the advertising business. Nonetheless, while anthropologists produce ethnographic texts, the texts which advertising people produce – a thirty-second commercial qualifies as a 'text' just as much as a book – create another kind of knowledge.[4]

The ethnographic study of Sri Lanka begins with Seligmann's early twentieth century account of the island's only aboriginal people, the Väddas, and that focus on the primitive, the traditional, and the unspoilt set the course.[5] By the 1950s and 60s – when Leach, Tambiah, and Obeyesekere began their work – ethnographic interest had settled on village life. Only recently, and then haltingly, has it looked to urban settings, modernity, and transnational processes in the island. In other words, anthropological research on Sri Lanka started out in a way that could be criticized as exoticizing or orientalizing. Advertising could be criticized for contrary sins. Its focus fell first on a small, Westernized elite living mainly in Colombo. Advertisements, framed in English, and often featuring line drawings of European faces and places, treated those consumers as 'brown Englishmen' given to the tastes and values – even through the 1960s and 70s – of Victorian England.

For the first two-thirds of the twentieth century, advertising ignored the great majority of Sri Lankans. Over the last third, advertising and ethnography moved in opposite directions – ethnography spread from village to town; advertising from the capital city to the hinterlands.

If anthropology is understood as 'writing' culture, what advertising 'writes' ends up producing culture. When ethnographers construct a picture of the remote parts and peoples of Sri Lanka as exotic, they too create culture. But when advertising does so, the Sri Lankans who view advertisements start to inhabit the cultural forms pictured in those advertisements in a way that is direct and powerful. Although producing culture is an unintended result of motives that are commercial and not representational, this byproduct has great importance for people's self-understandings. Newspapers and periodical literature link the members of a society in an 'imagined community,' their regularity, demotic focus, and world-making qualities joining people who have no face-to-face experience of fellow readers in a league of anonymous equals.[6] Television pushes these effects much further, joining viewers in an electronic community made stronger by higher levels of both synchronicity and visual power. While newspapers, radio, and television entertain and inform, the advertisements that drive these media carry existential force that can overpower other forms of content. Advertisements create this force by converting commodities into 'libidinal images of themselves,' placing goods and services in 'zones of display' that motivate desire and fear.[7]

The proposition that advertising like ethnography 'writes' culture, like all metaphors, has its limits. Advertising executives play the role of ethnographer with real disadvantages. Unlike the solitary ethnographer's work, advertising is produced by many hands, and, as Malefyt shows (this volume), competing interests influence that product in surprising ways.[8] As part of an urban-dwelling middle class, executives have negligible contact with people who live in villages. Executives invariably speak English as their first language and transact business in English (most Sri Lankans do neither). Advertising executives have the Westernized tastes and interests that characterize 'brown Englishmen' all across South Asia.[9] Disproportionate numbers of them come from minority communities. Many are Burghers, that is, the European or Eurasian descendants of Dutch colonists, and others are Sinhala or Tamil Christians. And whatever their ethnic origins, advertising executives are cosmopolitan people, keeping them at a remove from most Sri Lankans. The social distance that separates the people of the advertising profession from their public may be no greater in Sri Lanka than in many postcolonial countries, but that distance reinscribes in their everyday lives the distinctions between foreign and local, the modern and the traditional that figure prominently in advertising texts.

Moreover advertising does not simply 'write' culture because it does more than provide information about products and address consumers. When anthropologists advocate for the rights of, let's say, indigenous people, those communities have a sense of their own identity. When advertising executives use the word 'segment,' they employ it not as a noun but a verb. To segment a market is to create a market segment, not merely respond to an existing one.[10] As in the expression 'young urban professionals,' segmenting a market begins with an act of phrase-making. Something more is required to turn fictive communities into communities of consumption. Advertising cannot create that segment without inventing tropes of gender, ethnicity, class, and locality that cause consumers to identify with the people and practices depicted in advertisements.

In so doing, advertising executives create new and often startling images of the people who read advertisements and watch commercials. They are hardly the only source of images of Sri Lankan society people encounter, and those images are reinterpreted as they are read.[11] But whatever individuals make of them, advertising representations of Sri Lankan society have become a way in which people acquire a sense of place or locality, and thus of themselves. If figures of the modern show Sri Lankans how to be less like themselves, figures of the local show them how to be more Sri Lankan. Given the social distance that separates the people who make advertisements from the people who consume them, figures of the local can be as alien as figures of the modern. Whether advertising deterritorializes the imagination or domesticates it, it follows the same trajectory. Exhorting, advising, and sometimes merely picturing, advertising has no reason to exist if it cannot move people towards something new.

Proposing an advertising campaign to prospective clients, advertising executives need to know more than the people who constitute their market. As Brian Moeran's chapter makes clear, they also need to understand the predispositions of the clients seated across the room.[12] For an advertising executive, closing the deal requires a set of symbolic interactional skills that allow her to win the confidence of clients who come to that encounter with the full range of human peculiarities. I intend to show that advertising executives must also make similar calculations about competing advertising firms and the way they serve the local market of business enterprises. They must negotiate a layered and complex context that includes clients, other firms, and local consumers. Making its way through this tangle of calculations weighs on the kind of advertisements a firm produces and in turn on the way advertising makes its object.

The Local Landscape

The history of the Sri Lankan advertising industry has been shaped by its small market, proximity to a much larger one to the north, and postcolonial context. The first agencies appeared in the 1950s representing products such as Horlicks and

Biia Essence of Chicken. The large oil companies that sold their products in Sri Lanka had advertising campaigns developed in India, and when transnational advertising firms – J. Walter Thompson and Bozell were pioneers – came along, they were run by offices in Bombay. By the late 1950s, the transnational firms had opened offices in Colombo and were soon joined by a variety of local firms. SWRD Bandaranaike and his wife, Sirimavo, (who succeeded him after his assassination) dominated Sri Lankan politics until the late 1970s, and their governments imposed import restrictions and price controls, both of which had predictable effects on advertising revenues. But the unchanging characteristic of the local advertising market was demographic. Advertising, in newsprint but also on commercial radio from the 1950s, kept its gaze on an urban-dwelling, Western-oriented middle class.

Change came in 1977 when J.R. Jayewardene became prime minister and opened up an economy dominated by state industries and import restrictions, saying 'Let the robber barons come!' As trade and consumption picked up, advertising revenues rose and the number of agencies tripled, reaching over 100. At the same moment the Japanese government offered Sri Lanka facilities for television broadcasting, a gift with striking implications for both ordinary people and the advertising industry. For agencies it meant both another medium in which to place advertisements and the need to develop the technical skills to produce television commercials. It created a much larger audience to address. Easy credit arrangements for purchasing televisions and an expanding network of broadcast towers brought villages in Sri Lanka within reach of television signals. Newer forms of media do more than complement older forms. Often they change the relationship between older forms and their publics. In this sense television transformed both its viewers and other media, for its ability to transcend the limits of language and literacy gives television the power to shape the imaginative work of print and radio.[13] Whatever place newspaper reading had played in provincial towns and villages, now the nation state would be linked in an electronic union of unseen and silent others, the 'people' made witness to their collective life as represented in the daily flow of news, entertainment, and advertising.

For good reason, then, advertising agencies began to speak of advertising 'in the local idiom.' What they meant by that expression was everything from framing advertisements in Sinhala (although the emphasis on locality has not to this day produced much Sinhala language advertising, and even less Tamil) to constructing advertisements that showed respect for local sensitivities. Print advertisements of the 1950s and 60s would have been hard put to offend those feelings because they seldom engaged local culture at all. Television's capacity for greater expressiveness, its visuality, and its intrusiveness – a family will often turn their television on in the morning and keep it on for the rest of the day – brought the local decency issue to the fore. So did showing commercials made elsewhere on television, for advertisements filmed in Singapore often acquire power they lacked originally to make Sri Lankans uneasy. At this historical juncture – roughly the late 1970s – the advertising business became self-consciously ethnographic.

In most cases, what makes foreign commodities engaging for some people and off-putting for others is not the commodity but the context in which it is presented. As the twentieth century drew to its close, the temptation grew for advertising firms to place commodities in 'zones of display' both provocative in tone and realistic in construction – a luxurious locale, a situation where men and women are brought into close contact, the surface, color, and form of the human body (most often the female body). Many Sri Lankan viewers would be offended by romantic contact between men and women on television, but they would also be discomforted by a child who talks behind her mother's back, sharing a secret with television viewers. In one advertisement a little girl says her mother gives her milk because it is nutritious. She drinks it because she likes it. Winking at the camera, she says in Sinhala, 'Don't tell Mommy.' As innocent as the secret-sharing appears to a Western audience, viewers in Sri Lanka thought the scene challenged parental authority, and the government responded by pulling it from the airwaves.

With the coming of television, the largest accounts, most global accounts, and the largest fraction of the advertising business's revenues, continued to be fixed on English-language advertising. Yet the expanding range of broadcast signals meant that viewers in the hinterlands were now privy to television advertisements even when not always addressed to them. Television established a visual regime that brought various markets into a single world. Advertising executives began to construct advertisements in a way that made consumption available to rural consumers as well as urban ones, the young women who began to have incomes because of their work in a variety of free-trade zones, and students who read English although it had not been their first language. At the same time, television became the nation state's way of educating 'the people,' teaching, celebrating, and signaling consent to a 'libidinal economy reinserted into the material economy.'[14] With the hard-to-overlook exception of the Tamil north and east, the nation began to form a single market.

Advertising addresses its public by way of the local idiom in both global advertising campaigns and more local ones. The reinterpretation of a global campaign constitutes one example of advertising done in the local idiom, but there is a more local form of local idiom advertising, and it amounts to a much larger share of advertising revenues. These 'local idiom' advertisements take local products and services and put them in the most convenient place, the local context. This kind of local idiom advertising appears in several forms: when advertising agencies – both global and local – attempt to position local products (as in the case of locally-made cream crackers competing with foreign equivalents), link up consumers in the countryside with those in the city (surely the default-value motivation of most marketing schemes), or domesticate a product that has a long entanglement with colonial power and practices (of which banking is the leading example). All call on creative directors to find means to create a specifically local kind of subjectivity.

The contrast between commodities advertised in 'zones of display' that emphasize their foreignness, expense, or aspirational horizon and commodities constructed 'in the local idiom' constitutes a major choice for advertising firms and their clients. What makes this distinction still more consequential is that governments care about it as much as advertising firms. Where colonialism shifts the focus in traditional societies – and the chief source of symbolic production – from the cosmo-magical relationship between human beings and the supernatural to the relationship between European officials and the local elite, postcolonial circumstances shift it again to the relationship between the national government and the most ordinary of people, citizens. A fundamental task for the state nowadays in postcolonial societies is protecting its citizens against foreign commerce and culture. As a result, when an advertising firm thinks of positioning a commodity in an innovative way, it must consider the reaction of government as much as clients and consumers. Only a few decades ago, the leaders of postcolonial states were Westernizers. These days they defend television viewers against the West.

Given their history, function, and business model, most commodities fall on one side or the other of the distinction between the global and local. Some, such as banking products, can be constructed on either side. An agency can advertise a global bank by emphasizing its technology and global reach, extolling it for its strengths. Another bank, global or local, can be dropped into a localizing 'zone of display,' to suggest that the bank is a friendly institution because it is a local one (it might be foreign but acts like a local business). Each of those tropes brings other associations. That which is foreign – whether a product manufactured elsewhere or a local product placed in a foreign 'zone of display' – is linked to modernity, urban-life, European faces and places, and levels of material comfort unknown to most people in one of the world's twenty poorest countries. That which is local is linked to tradition, village life, Sinhala culture, and frugality. There are class referents here as well, for foreign products are invariably upmarket, and local products are not. Korean cement can be marketed at a Rs. 5 premium per bag for exactly that reason.

Against local competition, the transnational firms have major advantages – larger organizations and better resources (from in-house production teams to professional training for staff). Doing business with Grant McCann-Erickson, J. Walter Thompson, or Lintas offers local clients the prestige that goes with being served by the same agency that handles global clients. And prestige counts in the advertising business: when a creative director I know in Colombo established his own agency, he created a fictional nameplate for it. Thus a man named

Rajapakse established an agency which he named Williams, Fletcher, and Stoltz. His assumption was that Western founders would lend credibility and the appearance of being a going concern to a business he ran from his apartment.

Local agencies compete by claiming better knowledge of the local market, while trading on social proximity to local clients, and lower, sometimes much lower, cost. Dealing with some clients, those virtues go a long way. Smaller advertising firms make a living by servicing as few as two or three accounts, and they maintain those accounts by way of family ties or long-standing social relationships with their clients. A few of the larger local firms and local agencies with a nominal connection to a global franchise such as Ogilvy & Mather can compete with the transnationals for important local clients. Smaller firms survive by offering extraordinary service. Even though his product is cheaper than the competition, let's say, a businessman finds that his cash registers are not selling. His advertising man does impromptu market research, driving around town and asking shopkeepers along the way why they are not interested in an efficient machine at a reasonable price. The advertising executive returns to his client and tells him that the last thing small merchants want is a cash register of any kind. Register tapes leave a trail of paper that subjects the shopkeeper to having to pay taxes.

For their part, transnational agencies make a localizing promise of their own: we can 'think globally, and execute locally' by exploiting our organizational advantage, while recognizing the need to approach local markets with the same ethnographic skill that local agencies claim for themselves. Based on this view, they replace the product-oriented thinking of local agencies – 'here is a product, now let's see who will buy it' – with market research that can locate needs and preferences waiting to be addressed.[15] Heeding the market, the transnational firms insist, is equally important for both cosmopolitan advertisements and those constructed in the local idiom. Market research makes it possible to understand how these two notions play off class factors in specific cases, for both kinds of advertisements carry symbolic loads that reference class as much as residence.

A Transnational Firm in a Sri Lankan Context

Of a number of women who occupy senior positions in large advertising firms, Lilamani Dias is the best known. Having started her career as an account executive at J. Walter Thompson (JWT), she became a principal of the firm and served as president of the local professional organization. In the process she earned a reputation in the business as a creative person with the ability to construct highly effective advertisements. She had been recommended to me for her knowledge of the domestic market. When I first met her, I expected to hear a lot about 'local idiom' or 'Sinhala idiom' advertising.[16] She did indeed use those expressions in response to questions that prompted them, but when she recounted the advertising campaigns she liked best, she chose advertisements that put commodities in modern 'zones of display' or ones that transcended the global–local distinction altogether. Her background at JWT made that orientation not altogether surprising, but reference to 'the local idiom' has become a piety of advertising discourse, and I expected her at least to honor the expression when talking to a Westerner. I also assumed that exploiting the 'local idiom' would be essential for bringing her new firm into a market already crowded in the late 1990s with other transnational firms.

What she emphasized instead were 'trailblazing' advertisements, ones that do innovative things with little reference to the way most Sri Lankan consumers live. She spoke derisively of an advertising campaign she found 'villagey.' But more to the point, when I asked her to define 'local idiom' advertising, she characterized it by saying that Sri Lankans were different from Indonesians. Indonesians will spend money on beauty products; Sri Lankans will spend their money on the same toothpaste product people in Indonesia buy for, let's say, creating an attractive smile only if it's advertised for its healthful benefits, let's say, preventing cavities. To that extent, 'local idiom' advertising is simply advertising that understands its market, not advertising that addresses Sri Lankans as Sri Lankans. When Sinhala chauvinists use the expression *jatika cintanaya* (local thought or culture), they mean it in a narrow, mythologized sense – after four centuries of European domination, Sinhalas are people obliged to return to their own ways.[17] For Dias, respecting local culture means approaching the Sri Lankan market in terms of its sociological characteristics.

Sometimes the 'modern' enters advertising discourse for reasons purely strategic, as in the case of the two best-selling analgesics in Sri Lanka, Panadol and Dispirin. When JWT relaunched Panadol in the late 1980s, the firm positioned it as modern. Advertisements from this time focus on various individuals, who recommend the painkiller for reasons that follow the logic of modernity. Each is dressed in the clothing of a modern profession – an airline pilot, a project engineer, a medical student – and each is identified by name, itself an innovation, and one that introduces a measure of both individualism and everyday-ness previously absent in Sri Lankan advertising.[18] All say that they haven't the time for the pain – reiterating Carly Simon's 1974 song of the same name – and emphasize Panadol's use as preventive (as opposed to the way villagers I lived with in the 1970s used analgesics – by sending someone down to a local shop long after the headache had set in).

Dispirin had been the market leader for a long time before Panadol took away most of its market share, although in village markets it remained the dominant painkiller. Its agency decided to respond to Panadol's success with a series of commercials that featured villagers in caricatured form speaking colloquial Sinhala. Dias found the village models 'ugly' and the pitch demeaning to Sri

Lankans. Because JWT had grabbed the high-ground of modernity, it was not clear how Dispirin's agency could respond in any way other than following the road not already taken. Hired as a consultant, Dias advised replacing the 'villagey' types with modern-looking people inserted in a village setting, people who could plausibly speak of Dispirin's modern qualities. Dispirin is faster-acting than Panadol (which is paracetamol), but it is also easy on the stomach, she told her clients. Where Sinhalas had long thought of Western medicines as fast but harsh, under her hand Dispirin became the product – Western, local, hybrid? – that was fast but free of side effects. And modernity in a thirty-second dramatization moved into the village.

After a long career at JWT, Dias found herself in a conflict of interest when she married an Englishman who worked at Lever Brothers – because of the threat to the agency's independence created by Lever's association with JWT in Sri Lanka. She resigned and became a consultant, but by the late 1990s she saw the possibility of establishing a local office of Lintas. This offered her a chance to enjoy the benefits of a connection with a global firm, run her own show, and become an equity partner in the local firm. The problem was finding clients. She began with some advantages – her reputation as a creative director and a lifetime of social connections. She could solicit accounts from the growing number of local businesses made possible by two decades of economic liberalization, and in principle she could use the 'local idiom' notion itself to create a brand identity. The firm could set itself apart as a global enterprise with a woman at the helm who fully understood how to reach the generality of Sri Lankans.

Once she had located vacant space in a residential part of Colombo, she publicized the new firm in a series of print advertisements. Those advertisements urged prospective customers to 'come sit beneath the mango tree, and we will puzzle out your future.' Because her office space had formerly been a private home, there actually was a mango tree in the atrium, although no one was likely to leave the air-conditioned comfort of the building to sit there. But the tagline's jussive mood evoked both a relationship of equality and concern – 'we will work out your future' – and the cooling, indigenizing shadow of a mango tree under which to formulate those plans. In no time at all she was employing some 100 people, and the firm had secured accounts with local and foreign corporations.

Just as the Lintas office was coming into its own, JWT launched a television commercial that used the 'local idiom' in a form considerably stronger than most 'local idiom' advertisements. A global firm that typically had sold either transnational products such as Lever's or represented local corporations selling products constructed in ways that emphasized their modernity and sophistication, JWT started to position Laojee tea by putting it in a Sinhala context. It is too much to say that the innovation was shocking, but it caught viewers unprepared. Anandatissa de Alwis had made a radio commercial three decades earlier organized around a taxi driver. He is asked why he uses a Dagenite battery and responds in colloquial Sinhala. When a gentleman comes to the curb and hails a cab, he knows he must rush to the spot. A reliable battery – he says in language people use all the time but had never heard on radio – is essential for swooping down on the customer before another taxi does so.

The Dagenite commercial featured a working man, not the kind of person who gets moved around the city in a taxi (and who ordinarily shows up in advertisements), and those class references were given voice by the everyday language the man spoke, their effect made stronger because his words appeared in a 'zone of display' where a more formal Sinhala dominates. Who better than a taxi driver to appreciate the value of a battery that starts at once? The commercial made de Alwis' career, and people in the advertising business nowadays cite it as the paradigm example of 'local idiom' advertising and smile over de Alwis' ingenuity. But the most instructive aspect of this radio commercial is that virtually no one followed suit, exploiting a working-class model or colloquial Sinhala, in the following thirty years. The great majority of advertisements on radio, television, and in print use more formal language and feature models who show no signs of manual labor.

The Laojee tea commercial recalled de Alwis' work, focusing on an attractive young woman at a boarding house who is seen serving food and drink to a dining table full of young men. They kid and cajole her until she decides to offer them Laojee tea. At once she starts to look lovelier and happier, and they respond with less ragging. The commercial's local idiom character depends on the colloquial language spoken by the actors against the lilting background of a well-known tune 'Rosa.' The young woman's smile, a slight wiggle of the hips, and baila music (popular music of Portuguese origin) give the spot a borderline form of provocation. No one would read the setting as a village context. It is a boarding house, located somewhere in a major Sri Lankan city or its outskirts. But the everyday language and the ambience of the setting gives the commercial a distinctly local and downmarket – if not a 'villagey' – quality. Its Chinese name notwithstanding, Laojee is itself a downmarket product with a 'local' feel. The advertisement found its public, winning several advertising awards, and Lipton Laojee enjoyed a percentage jump in sales reaching double digits.

JWT could make a commercial with a 'village' resonance; Dias did not think her firm could. JWT had hegemony in the local market and an association with so many foreign brands that no amount of colloquialism could change people's thinking about the agency. Who knew anything about Lintas? The firm's name itself had no foreign associations (or local ones for that matter). Despite its global reach and many up-scale accounts elsewhere, Lintas was new in Sri Lanka and its character as amorphous as a new commodity. Dias needed to avoid the association with the 'local' in the strong sense of the word because village Sri Lanka (and the products villagers prefer) carries a distinctly 'down-market' quality. For a new agency, these are not associations to be cultivated. She would have to position her firm pretty much like the other advertising firms that dominate the market, at least if she wanted to attract the large accounts essential for making her firm a success.

Their differences notwithstanding, Sinhalas and Tamils have common expectations about the proper behavior and, even more so, the chastity of young women. Families' worst fears fix on their daughters acquiring a reputation as promiscuous. Such a reputation is disastrous for a young woman's marriage prospects, and it takes her family's status down with it. As a consequence, few commodities pose as many problems for advertising as cosmetics (although sanitary napkins and condoms have their challenges).[19] For many young women using scent or pressed powder – themselves relatively innocuous cosmetics – requires smuggling them into their bedrooms and applying them outside of their homes.

For advertising firms and manufacturers, the potential for increasing cosmetic sales is hard to resist. The proliferation of free-trade zones has put discretionary income in the hands of young women who work there. The problem is that these women live at home under the authority of their parents, and their fathers in particular view cosmetics in terms not of self-expression but promiscuity. Simply trying to localize cosmetics or naturalize them has its own problems because they cannot be inserted into a village 'zone of display' without alienating their principal market, young urban women who cannot identify with village life. Finding terms of address that transcend local forms of difference frustrates creative directors the world over. The problem is still more challenging in postcolonial societies where local identity categories carry serious moral weight and political importance.

Dias's solution lay in what she called the 'sidevi' look – modern enough to reach urban women, innocent enough to keep a village woman's father from objecting when he discovers his daughter's wearing scent or pressed powder. And that innovation created a natural imaginary featuring models who bear no discernible signs of either the urban or the rural. She created the 'sidevi' look ingeniously and indirectly, focusing the camera on facial close-ups, flowers, flames, and women whose appearance is attractive but unmarked by signs of either village or city life. That approach will not work with cosmetics such as lipstick, rouge, and eyeliner indelibly associated with prostitution and harder to recuperate. But it renders scent and powder as innocent as they can be made in a Sri Lankan setting, and fit for domestic use.

Creating the 'sidevi' look represented an attempt to domesticate the global apparatus of beauty, establishing a local community of consumption that ran from city to village. Scent, nail polish, and pressed powder today; lipstick and rouge sometime in the future. There had been Sri Lankan advertisements forty years ago that ignored the urban–rural dichotomy by focusing on Western models. Dias found another way to transcend that dichotomy, focusing on models who were Sri

Lankan in an unmarked, generic way. In so doing, she created a generically Sri Lankan woman, a woman without ties to the local topography of ethnicity and place.

Under the Mango Tree

Television addresses more people than newspapers reach, but communicating with that audience requires new tools:

> Given the limited purchasing power of most Indian consumers and advertisers' own orientation to urban middle-class 'people like us' (or PLUS), we cannot take for granted the existence on television of an aesthetic acceptable to popular audiences. It is only with the recent establishment of national television that it has become economically – and aesthetically – viable to address larger publics. Until this time, it was assumed that 'creative' input was required chiefly for the premium market, which is predominantly a minority Anglophone population. With market liberalization, the advertising industry in India has begun investing in the cultivation of more indigenous, regionally inflected tastes.[20]

Absent the regional factor that complicates the task in India, Rajagopal's characterization fits the Sri Lankan case without further qualification. In both cases, the advertising business looks out at an economy where most consumers have limited amounts of discretionary income, a premium market located in colonial cities that loom over the rest of the society, and a society where the English language carries great prestige but limited range. The argument that in India television raises the possibility of addressing a community of consumers – much larger and generally poorer than the English-speaking urban-dwelling audience of the last one hundred years – also strikes a chord with what I know about Sri Lanka. But what to make of the notion that television might provide an 'aesthetic acceptable to popular audiences' or in my terms advertising framed in the 'local idiom?'

Several realities make it difficult for advertising to find such an aesthetic, and others make even looking for one unlikely. The most obvious constraints are the location of a disproportionate number of upmarket consumers in a few urban settings, and the social and economic connections that tie advertising executives to the companies that seek to advertise upscale commodities. In markets such as Sri Lanka, creating a popular aesthetic, advertising products in a way that features village life, and exploiting actors who look like ordinary people are not strategies with obvious potential. The demographics make addressing village Sri Lanka attractive, for the island is not nearly as urban as most developing countries, and parts of the countryside have newly-won prosperity. But the class aspirations – for villagers as much as urban-dwelling people – make addressing people in terms of popular aesthetics, at least popular aesthetics narrowly defined, less compelling than advertisements that speak to their hopes and long-term strategies. What is clearly acceptable to Buddhist consumers is the evocation of the Buddhist past, settled out in the great relic mounds and artifacts of the ancient cities of northern Sri Lanka. Whether such scenes mean anything positive to Tamils is a matter that confronts anyone's attempt to find a popular aesthetic.

By emphasizing the symbolic interactionist context in which advertising camp-aigns are pitched, Moeran points to another factor. Selling an advertising campaign requires knowing not only which consumers, if properly addressed, might buy that commodity. It also requires knowing both the social structure of the client's firm and what the client himself assumes about the commodity and the consumers – Europeans and Americans in Moeran's case – he wants to reach. In the Japanese case, clients bring to the table their own 'occidentalized' conceptions of the West, and any campaign that seeks to persuade such clients that the advertising firm has a strategy to address a Western audience needs to do so by way of the clients' understanding of what Germans and Americans are like. If advertising produces a simulacrum of local culture, it also trafficks in simulacra of foreign cultures.

Still another force is the relationship between an advertising firm and its competitors. Establishing a new advertising firm requires less attention to local consumers than to local clients. When someone such as Lilamani Dias speaks of the 'local idiom,' she does so in a way shaped more by the need to sell advertising than to sell commodities. Lintas found itself in no position to organize a campaign in the localizing, popular, Sinhalized way JWT had done (at least on one occasion). Its newness to the market, its natural affinity for multinational accounts, and the taste of its founder – all incline towards 'trailblazing' and spectacular work, but not towards communicating with the people of Sri Lanka in terms of an 'aesthetic acceptable to popular audiences.'

A national communication policy might insist on media communications that speak to a national public in a way that presumes and encourages the expression of local culture, but the advertising business everywhere resists government control. The Venezuelan case represents an example of a state trying to bring advertising practice within the control of a state-controlled media policy designed to promote 'endogenous cultural development.'[21] As one would expect, advertising firms have resisted such controls, and the weakness of government in such places makes doing so easy enough. The more moderate course – the state insists on local ownership of advertising firms and local production of advertising work – assumes that locals making advertising will produce a popular aesthetic. The cases of Brazil and Malaysia suggests the perils of so doing.[22] As in Sri Lanka, there are social structural and economic forces that drive the aesthetic upwards, fixing the focus of advertising on consumers with substantial discretionary incomes, These effects are increased by the aspirational quality of many of advertising's productions. These factors do not make for rational communication.[23]

This upward movement is understandable in the context of both the hegemony of multinational firms in the global economy and the cosmopolitan character of the people who produce advertisements, not to say those who buy a disproportionate share of the big-ticket commodities they sell. But the allusive distinctions of class – especially in the way class interacts with village and town – aggravate the process through which local advertising systems move into the world system (as Sri Lanka did after the election of 1977 when J.R. Jayewardene opened the economy to foreign commodities and television broadcasting). When Western (or east Asian) commodities reach faraway places they are fitted to the local scheme of things. This requires the creation of an aesthetic that is neither Western nor popular.

Recall the case I mentioned earlier – the contrast between village and town aesthetics picked up by the advertising campaigns of Panadol and Dispirin. Panadol began to sell its product as modern yet local, as reliable as traditional Sinhala medicine, despite the fact that the analgesic's origins were as Western as the song which dominated the advertisement. The song appeared on Carly Simon's 1974 album *Hotcakes* and by the early 1980s had become a tag line for an Excedrin commercial on American television. By the late 1980s the same tag line was heard in Sri Lanka to sell Panadol to consumers as the 'modern' alternative to Dispirin. A melodic aphorism circulates across the world. It starts out as a refrain in a popular song, becoming the tag line for a Western analgesic in Western markets, and then a tag line for another analgesic in a south Asian society. In its original context 'not having time for the pain' means not lingering over a relationship gone sour; in the Sri Lankan commercial, it celebrates a modern attitude towards physical pain, treating it with a preventive agent and getting on with life.

Advertising charges the material world with the electricity of desire, but it also libidinizes other materialities such as local physiognomy. The human face is prettified in a way that puts it just beyond the reach of ordinary people. In places such as Sri Lanka, Singapore, Thailand and Malaysia, that is, in places where the difference between local faces and foreign ones is marked or where the difference between various kinds of local faces carries political and economic importance, the use of pan-Asian models in print and electronic advertisements functions in this.[24] Advertising has traditionally put beauty just beyond touch by representing local standards of what constitutes attractiveness in pure form. Pan-Asian faces do something more by globalizing Sri Lankan standards of beauty, transcribing 'fragments of local knowledges within a wider orbit of intelligibility.'[25]

As Lilamani Dias's work suggests, advertising – again in places where the distinction between local and global is marked – transcribes local knowledge in a second way. It takes local culture and moves it beyond the matrix of local differences – global and local, town and village, Sinhala and Tamil – not rendering it foreign, but familiar enough to resonate without referencing any particular venue, village or town. That advertising has ideological effects is not news. Nor is it news that advertising provides consumers with a sentimental education that challenges local standards of propriety, beauty, and rationality. But communication between the advertising business – libidinizing culture, bleaching it of particularity below the level of the nation state – and its public works at cross-purposes with the campaign speeches of politicians increasingly driven to address local communities with appeals that are particularistic and sometimes chauvinistic. No one would claim that advertising represents the better angels of our soul, but it is only fair to say this much. Commercial interest frequently ignores minority communities, but it finds no advantage in demagoguery.

Advertising firms both local and global participate in this project of bleaching models of their ethnic and regional characteristics. Dias's firm invites clients to sit beneath a mango tree not because local people do much of that and not because an account executive will ever sit there with a client. It is a localizing notion, and more inviting than 'come into my air-conditioned office, take a chair, and we will think out your future.' It is also a localizing trope without any local referent just like local faces bleached of all ethnic character. I am tempted to say that the one thing Sri Lankan advertising is not about is Sri Lanka. But it is fairer to conclude that the one thing that Sri Lankan advertising is not about is the anthropologist's Sri Lanka, understood in high particularity founded on closely examined cases. Instead advertising creates a simulacrum of Sri Lanka. And that contradictory bargain – striking images of the local, motivated by references that resonate with nothing particular in the local context – defines the cultural forms that issue from advertising texts, near enough to be recognizable, distant enough to be worthy of desire or fear.

A group of Ogilvy & Mather 'future planners' function in a way that is properly ethnographic, leaving their New York offices and watching consumers use commodities in more natural settings. Later these commercial ethnographers look for discrepancies between consumers' own representations about those commodities and how they relate to them in their everyday lives. That knowledge allows Ogilvy & Mather to distinguish their clients' products from the competition, for the sake of inserting those commodities in 'zones of display' which pick up on the micropractices that make people depend on certain commodities (for reasons a psychologist would probably never discover). David Ogilvy had been trained as a pollster; 'in the deadly-serious business of advertising' today his descendants take their inquiries into the field.[26]

Whether advertising ethnography gets at those tacit assumptions and subtle practices, whether firms construct advertisements accordingly, and whether consumers pick up on culture rewritten as advertising copy, responding to clues they themselves have provided – all are open to question. Assuming a positive answer to all three of these issues, one could imagine a future where advertising ethnography constitutes part of a feedback loop so skillfully constructed that advertising firms completely master the mysteries of consumption. In the world we actually inhabit the great majority of advertising firms never bother with either psychologists or anthropologists (and I cannot vouch for how seriously such people are taken ultimately at Ogilvy & Mather).

This volume reveals a variety of forces that weigh on the process by which advertisements are made, and these forces complicate the role played by either ethnographic or psychological knowledge. They also mitigate the fear that advertising will play a role in creating a world of homogeneity, technocratic regimes, and overorganized societies. In places such as Sri Lanka, advertising people talk of a vernacular kind of ethnographic competence, but even 'local idiom' advertising produces advertisements not much different from the competition. Multinational firms, local ones, firms that advertise their knowledge of local realities, firms that tout their ability to make world-class advertisements all make advertisements organized around a simulacrum of Sri Lanka. The world's societies may not be rushing towards convergence and sameness, but to the extent that local societies look at, and listen to, advertisements they encounter another kind of homogeneity. As a profession directly involved in moving commodities and culture around the world, advertising does most of its work at the level of the nation state – not the globe and not the complex contours of local life – representing human experience with more uniformity than local society knew previously. If rootedness in place and time is increasingly at risk in today's world, that risk comes as much from the way local actors – in this case, advertising firms – pursue their interests as from commodities and culture arriving from afar.

Notes

1. Keith Basso (1979) organizes his study of Western Apache joking behavior around the argument that ethnographers are not the only people who do ethnography. The Apache would probably not recognize their jokes as a 'microsociological analysis' as Basso asserts they are (p. 17). Advertising executives are folk ethnographers in a more systematic and self-conscious way – they speak in terms very much like 'microsociological analysis.'
2. 'Critical publicity/public criticism: Reflections on fieldwork in the Bombay ad world,' in this volume.
3. Marcus and Fischer (1986), and Clifford and Marcus (1986) are the paradigm sources.
4. The idea that human action can be approached as a text ready for interpretation comes ultimately from the tradition of Biblical hermeneutics. Paul Ricoeur

points out the possibility of extending the text idea from writing to social action (1981: 197–221).

5. Seligmann and Seligmann (1911).
6. Anderson (1983).
7. I have taken the 'zone of display' idea from Greenblatt (1990: 161–3).
8. Malefyt, 'Models, metaphors and client relations: The negotiated meaning of advertising,' in this volume.
9. There were as many sorts of 'brown Englishmen as there were regions and historical moments during the colonial encounter in south Asia. But the paradigm is surely the development of the Bengali middle class. A good treatment of the interaction of England and India can be found in Peter van der Veer (1999: 3–43).
10. Tedlow (1990).
11. De Certeau (1984).
12. 'Imagining and imaging the other: Japanese advertising international,' in this volume.
13. Rajagopal (1998: 15). An American example of this process would be the way newspapers take on many of the visual conventions of television after television becomes the dominant channel of communication. *USA Today* is a prime example. Its vending boxes on city streets even look like television sets.
14. Ibid. (1998: 16).
15. Goldstein (1989: 61).
16. But for a few exceptions, Sri Lankans with demonstrably Tamil characteristics do not figure in Sri Lankan advertising. As a consequence, Sinhala faces have become synonymous with Sri Lankan faces. The contrast with Malaysia – where government policy has required the presence of Chinese and Indians as well as Malays – is striking. See Kemper (2001: 44–73).
17. Kemper (1991: 105–60).
18. It is hard to find ordinary Sri Lankans willing to recommend any product in a public context, people resisting on the grounds that such behavior is inappropriate. Media figures and beauty queens have no such reluctance. When they endorse a product, they do so – indeed they must do so – as themselves: as, let's say, Rosie Senanayake, and not as *a* celebrity. In this context, Anderson's rethinking work on nationalism is to the point. He contrasts the unbounded and unenumerated seriality of newspapers and the bounded and enumerated seriality he links to governmentality. The contribution of advertising to the experience of nationalism depends on seriality of both kinds, from the depiction of unbounded tropes – *a* peasant, *a* housewife – to bounded ones such as a celebrity endorsement. See Anderson (1998: 1176–33). When advertisements identify – an airline pilot named, let's say, Sarath Fernando – they convert regular people into quotidian celebrities.

19. Both require discretion. Advertised on television, sanitary napkins and condoms are constructed as 'medicine' to allow parents to deflect questions from children. I once encountered a Colombo shopkeeper who kept sanitary napkins on his shelf wrapped in newspaper to prevent casual customers from being offended.
20. Rajagopal (2001: 91–2).
21. Mattelart (1983: 117–21).
22. Ibid. (1983: 137–8).
23. For a discussion of the analysis of communicative utterances, see Habermas (1981: 75–101).
24. Although exactly what the category (and its equivalents such as Eurasian) entails differs across markets, pan-Asian models (as the term is used in Southeast Asia) are people with complicated genetic backgrounds, making them look a little like all Asians–although more handsome or beautiful than most – and not quite like any, Kemper (2001: 44–73). Thailand provides another case where Eurasian models have come to dominate the local fashion, entertainment and advertising industries (Seth Mydans 2002).
25. Rajagopal (1998: 16).
26. Frank (1997: 46).

References

Anderson, Benedict 1983 *Imagined Communities*, London: Verso.
—— 1998 'Nationalism, identity, and the world-in-motion: On the logic of seriality,' in Pheng Cheah and Bruce Robbins (eds) *Cosmopolitics: Thinking and Feeling Beyond the Nation*, Minneapolis: University of Minnesota Press.
Basso, Keith 1979 *Portraits of 'The Whiteman,'* Cambridge: Cambridge University Press.
Clifford, James and George E. Marcus (eds) 1986 *Writing Culture: The Poetics and Politics of Ethnography*, Berkeley: University of California Press.
De Certeau, Michel 1984 *The Practices of Everyday Life*, trans. by Steven Rendall, Berkeley: University of California Press.
Frank, Thomas 1997 *The Conquest of Cool*, Chicago: University of Chicago Press.
Goldstein, Carl 1989 'The selling of Asia,' *Far Eastern Economic Review*, 29 June, pp. 60–1.
Greenblatt, Stephen J. 1990 *Learning to Curse*, London: Routledge.
Habermas, Jurgen 1981 *The Theory of Communicative Action*, trans. by Thomas McCarthy, Boston: Beacon Press.
Kemper, Steven 1991 *The Presence of the Past: Chronicles, Politics and Culture in Sinhala Life*, Ithaca: Cornell University Press.

—— 2001 *Buying and Believing*: *Sri Lankan Advertising and Consumers in a Transnational World*, Chicago: University of Chicago Press.

Marcus, George E. and Michael M.J. Fischer 1986 *Anthropology as Cultural Critique: An Experimental Moment in the Human Sciences*, Chicago: University of Chicago Press.

Mattelart, Armand 1983 *Transnationals and the Third World*, South Hadley, MA: Bergin & Garvey.

Mydans, Seth 2002 'On blue-eyed Thais flaunt your Western genes,' *New York Times*, 29 August.

Rajagopal, Arvind 1998 'Advertising, politics and the sentimental education of the Indian consumer,' *Visual Anthropology Review*, 14 (2): 14–31.

—— 2001 'The violence of commodity aesthetics,' *Social Text*, 19 (3): 91–113.

Ricoeur, Paul 1981 *Hermeneutics and the Human Sciences*, trans. by John B. Thompson, Cambridge: Cambridge University Press.

Seligmann, C.G. and Brenda Seligmann 1911 *The Veddas,* Cambridge: Cambridge University Press.

Tedlow, Richard S. 1990 *New and Improved: the Story of Mass Marketing in America*, New York: Basic Books.

Van der Veer, Peter 1999 'The moral state: Religion, nation and empire in Victorian Britain and British India,' in Van der Veer and Hartmut Lehmann (eds) *Nation and Religion: Perspectives on Europe and Asia*, Princeton, Princeton University Press.

Critical Publicity/Public Criticism: Reflections on Fieldwork in the Bombay Ad World
William Mazzarella

My tiny Premier taxi shudders to a halt at the Mahalaxmi traffic lights. Immediately, a group of boy hawkers, wearing tattered shorts, efficiently fans out among the lines of waiting cars, searching for likely customers. The midday sun is oppressive and a cloud of exhaust fumes is already hanging over the junction. The boy who finds me is clutching a couple of books carefully wrapped in transparent plastic. 'Deepak Chopra, sah! One hundred rupees only, sah!' The books, which are in English, are titled: The way of the wizard: twenty spiritual lessons for creating the life you want. *I remember how, about a year earlier, I had seen the millionaire New Age guru Chopra on American public television, peddling yuppie mysticism to an earnestly reverent audience. More recently, I had come across Chopra in the Indian press arguing that the cause of poverty was an individual inability to realize 'wealth consciousness.' Asked by a journalist whether he was ready for* sanyas [renunciation], *the urbane doctor replied: 'Renunciation is in the consciousness. If I think myself into anonymity, that would be* sanyas *for me. I long for it but it won't happen tomorrow.' The traffic suddenly lurches forward, and the hawkers scurry back to their traffic island.*

Introduction

Advertising and anthropology have never been more closely allied than today. Agencies, who used to show a marked preference for psychologists, now routinely advertise for anthropologists to fill slots with ambitiously devised titles like 'future planner.' Anthropologists, in their turn, are delightedly discovering that some of their erstwhile models of culture (particularly the old structuralist ones) suddenly seem to have all sorts of commercial applications. This, it seems to me, is an occasion for both fascination and foreboding. I write this essay out of the conviction that this marriage, apparently made in heaven, cries out for critique. By 'critique' I do not necessarily mean an oppositional commentary. Rather, I intend a rigorous analysis of the conditions and implications – both formal and ethical – of a particular set of beliefs or practices.

Such a critique, even in the rudimentary form offered here, will necessarily take us far beyond the relatively narrow confines of advertising and anthropology as professional practices. It will require us to situate the alliance between anthropology and advertising in relation to the worldwide ascendance of consumerism as a model of social participation (one dimension of what is generally known as 'neo-liberalism'). At a time when citizenship is everywhere being re-imagined as consumption, advertising is one of the key sites at which normative visions of social life are expressed and explored. And in an age of globalization, culture – that hoary terrain – has returned as one of the key idioms of this exploration.

But this is not just a critique of the advertising business. It is equally and reciprocally an exploration of what it might mean to 'do' an ethnography of such an institution. I went to Bombay, India, in the late 1990s to study the production of advertising in the context of globalizing consumerism. I soon became aware of several contradictions or tensions in this practice. Initially, as I discuss below, I assumed that these contradictions had to do with the apparent mismatch between the smug plenitude of advertising images and the prosaic struggles of life in the city. However, I came to understand the project of advertising as less self-contained, more internally contradictory, and – most importantly – as necessarily engaged, *beyond the volition of its practitioners*, in the politics of everyday life.

Relevance and Doubt

In the beginning of my fieldwork in Bombay, I had a kind of mantra. Whenever someone asked me what I was doing, I would say I was studying advertising and globalization in India. On the face of it, my timing was good. Facing a dire foreign exchange crisis in the summer of 1991, the recently installed Congress government of P. V. Narasimha Rao had pushed through a series of reforms intended to 'liberalize' the Indian economy. The Nehruvian dream, it seemed, was finally being dismantled: after four decades of import substitution and government licensing, foreign investment was now ardently being courted. Most of the pro-liberalization lobby argued that the reforms could not be sectorally selective, that India would have to take, as the phrase had it, the potato chips along with the computer chips. By the mid-1990s, a host of foreign consumer brands were jostling for space on Indian shop shelves, and the Indian advertising business was going through a period of explosive expansion.[1]

Given this context, my mantra seemed eminently intelligible to many of the people that I approached in the Bombay business world. At the same time, and for the same reasons, my interest in the cultural politics of Indian advertising fared less well with other local constituencies. Many of my intellectual and activist inter-locutors responded with barely disguised contempt, or with polite boredom. Was not the advertising business, they asked, simply a refuge for overprivileged, overpaid, overgrown children; faddish corporate fops with nary a care for the travails of the 'common man?'[2] Did I think I would learn anything about the 'real' India from these people? Why was I bothering with urban English-medium advert-ising that the vast majority of the country's population could not understand, made for goods that they would never be able to buy? Finally, was there not something rather unsound about my own position, a researcher on a generous American grant, hanging out with a socialite elite, in a city where most people didn't even have a solid roof over their heads? Returning home from these encounters, I would try to buck myself up with the thought that these objections were only a symptom of an ossified and outdated notion of political relevance, one that, to its own detriment, refused to take into account the crucial mediating functions of commercial imaging in contemporary public culture.[3] Still, the criticisms continued to gnaw at me; the disjunctures they pointed to just seemed so visible, so palpable.

Some of it was obvious and empirical, the stuff of countless magazine articles on the contradictions besetting economic liberalization in India: most of all, the yawning gap between the sudden availability of shiny new consumer goods and the miserable condition of much basic infrastructure. Microwave ovens were becoming available to some, but it was almost comically difficult to procure a reliable supply of cooking gas. Cable television and mobile telephony were readily available (the former, in particular, for relatively little money), but getting a basic terrestrial telephone connection required an exasperating amount of bribery and months of tireless effort. Fancy imported cars gleamed in shop windows, but roads were so poorly maintained and so overcrowded that attempting to drive was often hardly worth the aggravation.

This general scenario, familiar enough as a gloss on life in many 'Third World' cities, found a direct parallel in my own daily experience of doing fieldwork. This was particularly true of the first few months of my research, when I was spending my days inside the Bombay office of a transnational advertising agency network, trying to do what we anthropologists stubbornly but rather vaguely call 'participant observation.' Each time I left the air-conditioned office of the ad agency where I was doing my fieldwork, I felt a small shock. During the day, the space within the four walls of the office, with its computers, its cubicles, its conference rooms and its fax machines, had served as a kind of simulacrum of the smooth-edged world of the ads that were being produced there: all executive resolve, sharp angles, and globalized rhetoric. But in the evening, I would step directly into a warren of mid-town Bombay streets, crowded with human and animal bodies, packed with transactions, noises, and smells of all kinds, a realm of highly embodied and personalized exchanges. From street-corner entrepreneurs to the violent power politics of the Bombay drug and movie mafia, this was a world radically different from – and yet imaginatively imbricated in – the immaculate capitalism of the billboards.

In fact, I found myself buffeted between a consciousness of contradiction and an even more disturbing intimation of *continuity* between the hypo-abled bodies of the dispossessed and the hyper-abled, cellphone-toting billboard bodies, looming over me from their backlit perches. At first I had predictably enough interpreted the constant spectacle of suffering and mutilation at Bombay's road junctions as a kind of opposite to the ingratiating language of advertising. My liberal visitor's inevitable guilt and revulsion had in some obscure way still been tempered by a (certainly equally misplaced) social realist ethos of balance and perspective; a categorical separation between 'authentic' suffering and 'staged' advertising. But soon my mind started playing tricks on these complacent categories. One night, a list of advertising principles that I had copied down that day in a newspaper archive seemed, with a sickening logic, equally to apply to the advertising executive and to the person behind the arm that was being extended into the back seat of my scooter rickshaw: '1) draw attention; 2) arouse immediate interest; 3) impart information as quickly as possible; 4) convince viewer/reader; 5) induce action.'

Transparency and Opacity: A New Sense of 'The Field'

Many of my initial conversations with Bombay ad people did little to dispel my anxiety. As an anthropologist professionally socialized to look for the telling detail, the unexpected articulation, I found myself increasingly frustrated with the quality of my interviews. Given that I was studying a group of professionals whose livelihood depended on impression management, it was perhaps hardly surprising that the overt content of many of these initial conversations seemed less than spontaneous. Qualitatively, their statements shared something with the way that ads are often illuminated: full on and depthless, with the attention focused on hyper-realistic tactile surface detail at the expense of shadow and perspective.

And then there was the circularity of the information that I was able to glean. On the way home from my appointments, perusing a local business magazine on the commuter train, I would often find my precious interview material duplicated almost verbatim in one current article or another. As an ethnographic observer, hungry for an 'inside' perspective, it was particularly unnerving suddenly to perceive myself as the last in a long line of journalists.

Initially I was naïve enough to expect that some sense of the contradictions involved in the work of advertising in India would emerge spontaneously in the course of my interviews, that my informants would somehow 'own up,' in a confessional mode, to the ethical dilemmas with which I assumed they were wrestling. But of course many of my informants responded like the agency boss who leaned contentedly back in his chair when I asked him how he felt about the changes brought about by the economic reforms of the previous few years. Puffing on a cigar, he beamed:

> I feel extremely good! There is not universal agreement, but there is certainly a swing in favor of free commerce, which I believe is going to be critical to the economic development of the country. Seven or eight years ago, if you had asked the man in the street, he would probably still have been anti-business. But now people are beginning to understand.

At this point, the conversation would segue into a familiar and impersonal litany: the advantages of competition, 'the Indian consumer's' dawning brand consciousness, the residual agonies of government 'red-tapism,' 'ad-hocism,' and 'authorityism.'

On the one hand, like any ethnographer, I was a meddling visitor in a world that was quite obviously in many ways distinct from the one that I would call home. On the other, my informants and I were also, in each others' eyes, occupants of specific professional categories – 'ad man,' 'academic' – that were translatable (if not fully equivalent) across our respective lifeworlds. With the handful of informants who gradually became personal friends, these categories became less important. But in more formal situations, such as when conducting interview appointments, I frequently found that this apparent categorical transparency in practice produced a kind of opacity. As senior members of a global business elite speaking to a junior member of a global academic elite, many of these informants chose to address me in a reified idiom – marketing discourse – that acknowledged our mutual standing yet, to my initial frustration, appeared to give nothing away.

The obverse of this more or less smooth exterior was, in a sense, just as predictable: late-night despair, after one too many drinks. At a crowded bar, a young copywriter from one of the big agencies morosely warned me that dangerous things were happening to India. The United States were just the latest neo-imperialist installment in a long line of pretenders. 'I'm just scared of a white world,' he said. So how did he reconcile his views with his job, I wondered. 'I'm a fucking hypocrite,' he shot back, 'the lowest of the low.' He then spoke sentimentally of quitting the ad business and becoming a documentary filmmaker working in the slums, showing people 'the real India.' Later, disconsolately stepping across cracks and rumpled figures on the pavement, he muttered: 'Everything's advertised . . . this shirt I'm wearing which is sold to me in a shop that's advertised by a man who's advertised.' We made an earnest date to meet the following afternoon and visit that pre-eminent site of urban authenticity – approved and certified as such by no less an authority than the *Lonely Planet* guide – the slums at Dharavi. But when I called the next day, the copywriter's sister informed me that he had left for the day to play cricket.

Soon enough I found myself ensconced in the Bombay office of a transnational agency network, and the tenor of these early encounters gave way to an immersion in the day-to-day process of advertising production. I became more attuned to the pragmatic worlds of my informants, and I began to work out how to bring into concrete focus the large-scale theoretical abstractions that I had carried with me to India ('the cultural politics of globalization' etc.). It was a necessary, and ethnographically reassuring, first step.

But looking back I realize that my concern to situate my study at a particular 'site' also drove me down a blind alley. In my pursuit of the 'real reality' of Indian advertising practice, I spent a great deal of time chasing processes and practices that I imagined to be just around the next corner, behind a closed office door, articulated in a meeting to which I had not been invited. At the same time, my sense of the disconnection between the minutiae of life in the agency and the world outside its doors grew steadily more oppressive.

What I was struggling to envision was a different, more complex sense of the field in which I was doing fieldwork. Here, the contradictions were not between what the advertising business did and what went on in some other realm, some 'real world' of the streets. Rather they were internal to a wider field, a field which included all these places and moments as nodes, nodes at which the public circulation of images and discourses took on temporary forms – in advertisements, to be sure, but also in political rhetoric, on television, in everyday conversation, in public debate.

Certainly, in retrospect I can enumerate my research strategies, such as they were, according to conventional labels. I did 'participant observation' for several months in the agency. I did 'interviews' with practitioners all over the city. And I did 'archival research,' both of primary source materials and of magazines and newspapers. But such a list captures very little of the peculiar and shifting shape of 'the field' as it took shape around me. Increasingly, I saw myself exploring a kind of dynamic force-field, a space of circulation comprising a series of sites that were public, private, and ambiguously located along the continuum. I literally imagined myself following images and texts as they moved through this field. Sometimes they would disappear from view altogether; at other times, they would pop up simultaneously and confusingly at multiple locations – on billboards, in magazine articles, in casual conversations. Sometimes they appeared in surprising combinations; often, their *avataras* came across as heavily overdetermined. Always, I had the sense that I was trying to inhabit and understand (*not* overview) a kind of totality, but one that was open-ended and part of larger routings and collisions that were taking place far beyond Bombay.

Culture and Accountability

> To speak of culture was always contrary to culture. Culture as a common denominator
> already contains in embryo that schematization and process of cataloging and classif-
> ication which brings culture within the sphere of administration.
>
> Horkheimer and Adorno, 'The Culture Industry'

I mentioned above that there was, in the beginning of my time in the field, a kind
of surface affinity between what I said I was doing and what my agency informants
said they were doing. In other words, my project was expressible in terms that
echoed those of marketing thought. When I was applying for research money,
during the year before I went to India, I framed my project as a study of the
Bombay ad business as a point of cultural mediation in a time of globalization. The
core questions – which I found resonated very closely with what some of my
agency informants, particularly in account planning and brand strategy functions,
were thinking – included: how were global brands being translated for local
markets? What sorts of 'Indianness' emerged and were perpetuated in the process?
How did the business, in its dealings with multinational clients, manage the need
to insist that Indian consumers were both Indian *consumers* – that is, hungry for all
the accessories of a globally-defined middle-class life – and *Indian* consumers –
that is, consumers whose hearts and minds could only be reached by respecting
their cultural particularity (see Kemper's chapter in this volume for reflections that
are both geographically and conceptually adjacent)?

Both my agency informants and I were asking these questions in a context
where cultural identity and cultural difference had suddenly become both big
business and good governance. In politics (and within those fractions of academia
who understand themselves in part as governmental consultants), optimists spoke
of multiculturalism and pessimists of the clash of civilizations. In business the
globalization of consumer markets had made possible, if not inevitable, the rise of
culturally sensitive marketing.

As an anthropologist working in the late 1990s, my 'take' on this context was,
however, radically different from those of my informants. Indeed, since the 1980s,
the affinity between the grand old culture concept and the taxonomic needs of
globalizing bureaucracies and consultancies had given rise to a great deal of
concern in the discipline. Initially, this unease was in the main expressed as a crisis
of representation, as an anguished desire for a mode of ethnographic writing that
would not essentialize its objects.[4] Then, as 'globalization' moved to the forefront
of the anthropological agenda in the early 1990s, attention also started turning
more squarely towards the cultural politics of transnational corporations and quasi-
governmental organizations.[5]

The apparent convergence between advertising people and anthropologists over the culture concept has been used to make an ideological claim on both sides. The claim is that both parties are really doing the same thing: that is, discovering an underlying and already-existing cultural order.[6] What is avoided here is any consideration of the multiple mediations – advertising and marketing among them – that serve to rework and reproduce what we think of as culture and cultural difference.[7] After all, one of the central articles of faith in marketing is that marketers do not invent or impose consumer preferences; rather they track pre-existing and objective empirical consumer information by means of research, the better to respond to real consumer needs. With the globalization of consumer markets, the culture concept became one of the most important ways in which this stance was maintained, for what could be more deeply embedded in consumer psyches, more resistant to arbitrary tampering, than culturally grounded consumer preference?

For me, the uncomfortable upshot of all this was that, to the extent that my presence in the agency made any structural sense at all, it was as a potential purveyor of essentialized cultural knowledge. This assumption was not, most of the time, squarely spoken. Nevertheless, it put me in an awkward position: in order to fulfill this expectation I would have had to abandon the question that interested me most, namely, how did advertising itself work as a mode of cultural production? I well remember the look of mounting alarm on the face of one of my agency hosts during an early discussion of my research plans, as he began to sense my interest in turning the ethnographic lens upon *his* practices rather than on those of the official objects of marketing and anthropological research alike: 'ordinary people,' a.k.a. 'consumers' in all their cultural peculiarity. To his great credit, and with his boss' approval, he nevertheless just let me get on with it.

Whether the ethnographic eye turns towards the internal workings of an agency, or whether it looks outwards towards the public fields through which advertisements circulate, I would suggest that we owe it to advertising to do what nowadays it least expects us to: to take it seriously. Just as we should not placidly accede to the fiction that advertising simply responds to consumers' desires, so we should not peremptorily dismiss it as fraudulent. Its languages – whether we like it or not – are our languages, its spaces are our spaces. What we need to do is to examine how and why advertising intervenes in these languages and spaces.

One way to move into such an examination is to think about the cultural politics of advertising images in formal terms. Once we accept that such images are neither 'mirrors' of society (in Stephen Fox's phrase), nor radically detached from the social worlds through which they circulate, then the way is open to thinking about how these images become part of what Daniel Miller (1997) has called 'projects of value.' Projects of value are more or less successful attempts, by individuals and institutions, to generate value and meaning out of the elements of public culture –

images, discourses, signs. The practice of advertising is one such project of value (or rather an institutional assemblage of many such projects of value). And, I would argue it is an exceptionally important one. Not because what advertising people do with images matters more than what other people do with images, but because the practice of advertising is so deeply implicated in the general contemporary movement towards both the 'marketization' of public life and the 'imagification' of the market.

In its relation to this general movement, advertising could be described as a 'hegemonic' project; its spokespeople and its institutions certainly enjoy a certain sway around the world today. But it is crucial to recognize that advertising is not watertight, that its basic building blocks (images and texts) will not, as it were, 'sit still' for any length of time. The poetry and potency of images and texts will always exceed and trouble the instrumental limits of any given agenda – commercial, disciplinary, or subversive. This is because they are already embedded in social life, which is to say that they are riddled with all the dense encumbrances of history, experience, and identification.

At the same time, this is not just a story about the impossibility of fixed meanings or authoritative claims in advertising. Rather, the densely social resonances of these images and texts give them the quality of a kind of symbolic commons (one might perhaps call this 'culture') that cannot but impose certain obligations on their users. To the extent that advertising draws upon a common symbolic and affective account, as it were, it becomes entangled in a kind of ethical debt. Ostensibly, the repayment resides in the form of the functional satisfaction that the advertised object promises. But in fact the equivalence is misleading, because, in addition to the exchange of cash for commodity, a symbolic investment is taking place on the part of consumers (and of producers) of advertising. This is an investment in an imaginary domain that far exceeds the unique selling propositions of individual goods. Most generally, this is an investment in happiness, transcendence, self-transformation, a Good Life for individuals and collectivities.

To the extent that the figure of the consumer-citizen takes over from earlier kinds of approved political subjectivities – the subject of the nation, the subject of development – the burden of these absolutes comes to rest upon its creators' shoulders: the advertising business, street-side philosopher of the consumerist dispensation. In the face of this impossible responsibility, the claim of marketing ideology – that advertising is merely a response to actually existing society – is understandable. Furthermore, it is not wrong in its disavowal; the materials on which advertisements are built *are* collective, because they are social. What is disguised here is that the advertising business is necessarily *also* professionally constrained to proclaim proprietary expertise in the public deployment of these materials. Otherwise, there would be no reason – other than the simple conveyance of 'information' – for the advertising business to exist.

William Mazzarella

I spoke earlier of my unease, in the field, over the tension between what I perceived to be the smooth surfaces of the language of advertising and the palpable struggles of urban life in Bombay. Moving beyond the confines of the agency walls, thinking increasingly of the larger public field inhabited and transformed by advertising, I came to see how deeply the claims and practices of the business, far from being irrelevant to 'the common man', had become caught in the contradictions of a society imagined in the image of consumption.

Liberalization and Globalization: Predicament and Opportunity

The peculiar social formation known as mass consumerism achieved public and political prominence in India in the early- to mid-1980s. At this stage it was still largely an internal affair; the avalanche of foreign brands and transnational satellite television stations would not descend until 1991. From the beginning, consumerism was touted as a kind of sensuous antidote to the castrating agency of state planning, with its peculiarly bureaucratized rhetoric of austerity. Advertising was crucial to the selling of the consumerist dispensation. This was not simply because it made consumers aware of goods, but – more profoundly – because the advertising business, particularly through the rapidly expanding medium of television, promoted its services as an authentic and direct engagement with the embodied needs of Indians at large. The tactile quality of commodity images could, apparently, reanimate the self-realizing energies that years of political exhortation had shriveled. At the same time, the newly imported discipline of marketing promised to extend the mobilization of the consuming populace beyond the elite Anglophone enclaves with which, until then, most advertising had been identified. In this way, consumerist seductions strove towards a populist legitimation.

But this equation was also internally contradictory. Many of the products and images that were the most important examples of the ad industry's power to mobilize collective aspirations were, by definition, upscale and aimed at relatively exclusive market segments. The paradox was, in turn, mediated by the claim that far from being elitist, such 'aspirational' imagery merely granted *all* Indians the pride of an equal right of desire. Again the isolationism and shoddiness of the planned economy were attacked: now Indians would be free to dream world-class dreams. As a prominent Bombay copywriter told me:

I have always believed that it is not that the beggar on the road dreams of being the most well-off beggar. He has the right to dream of being a king. So he dreams of being a king, I dream of being a king. So everyone wants the sun and the moon and the stars. It's not that people dream in segments – that I will only dream this much because I am here. Everyone has the right to dream.

Of course, the fact that the Indian ad business was making these kinds of claims in a public cultural context where doing something about the extreme poverty of half the population had become a mainstay of political legitimacy made the proposition both more striking and more difficult to support.

The tension between an urban consuming elite and the poverty of the rural 'masses' was a classic figure of post-Independence Indian politics. To some extent, the advocates of consumerism in India pointed towards the rapid expansion of a new 'middle class' as a possible amelioration of this polarized field. But if the middle classes were, on one level, the mainstay of the consumerist apologia, they were also, in a different way, a problem quite as vexing as that of the poor. The green revolution of the 1960s, the new entrepreneurial dynamism of the 1970s, and the new money pouring out of the Persian Gulf between the oil crisis in 1973 and the onset of the Gulf War in 1990 had given rise to a new class of 'vernacular rich;' wealthy businessmen, farmers and traders who did not share the habitus of the older, English-medium elite. Here was a vast market for upscale and expensive products, and an enormous reservoir of that crucial fuel for marketing: aspiration. But many corporations and the advertising agencies that represented them were deeply torn between a wish to appeal to these *arriviste* classes and a deep-seated reluctance to be identified with such imagery.

The copywriter had assured me that consumers didn't dream in segments. But sometimes, I found, it was nevertheless still desirable for them to dream in nations. Alongside the 'Hinduization' of national politics, the globalization of markets had brought the question of Indian cultural identity/integrity back into public focus in the mid-1990s.[8] With the dramatic influx of foreign brands into India after 1991, the local advertising and marketing industries found that their existing task of coordinating locally relevant images and narratives was now cross-cut by a new axis: the mediation of the local and the global. However, the new situation also brought a fresh contradiction to these relationships, a kind of crisis of value: many of the brand images that had seemed so desirable when they were largely out of reach lost much of their luster now that they had become readily available. My executive informants, who found themselves caught between global clients who expected them to add value to their products and local consumers who seemed all too indifferent, produced an apparently paradoxical discourse. The structure of the discourse wasn't new – it recapitulated the tension at the heart of two centuries' worth of Indian experiments with modernity.

On the one hand, my informants loudly berated their foreign clients for their 'value arrogance': did they not realize that Indian consumers needed to be addressed in ways that respected their essential cultural specificity? On the other hand, these same executives had nothing but scorn for the apparently condescending way in which many transnationals had tried to 'Indianize' their advertising or their products: did Indians not deserve the same quality as everyone else? Either way, the transnationals were trashed for their neo-imperialistic assumptions.

Of course, these executives knew full well which side their bread was buttered on, and they managed to salvage for themselves a highly strategic role. Positioning themselves as expert brokers between the ambitions of their clients and the cultural inscrutability of Indian consumers, they turned what had initially been a profound crisis of value into a virtuoso display of legitimation. Rhetorically, they now appeared as a new kind of popular hero: defending Indian cultural integrity against transnational imperialism. The measure of this magic was that globalized consumerism, of all things, was suddenly being presented as the guarantor of Indian cultural revitalization.

At the same time, this legitimating discourse was necessary precisely because my informants' predicament was so volatile. The legitimacy of the advertising business has always and everywhere rested upon the claim that the industry brings together a uniquely intuitive understanding of concrete images with a rationalizing and panoptic marketing expertise. As the advertising business, and the media through which it operates, become increasingly global in scope, so national culture becomes one of the key idioms through which it may claim local expertise *vis-à-vis* its clients. By the same token, executive claims to exclusive expertise are more than ever threatened from above as well as from below. Against global standardization by distant corporate headquarters advertisers must argue local specificity. But against upstart local illuminations, they must equally argue the priority of global standards of quality and coordination.

Efficiency and Intensity

These and other structural tensions, which on the surface might appear to be matters internal to marketing, took on a far wider political significance. This was partly because the legitimation of mass consumerism necessarily involved claims about human nature, social life, and the possibilities of communication writ large. But it was also a result of the fact that these claims were increasingly gaining mainstream acceptance outside of the business world.

For decades, the Indian private sector had routinely railed against the communicative strategies of the Indian state.[9] But starting in the mid-1980s, and in conjunction with the dramatic spread of commercial television in India, commercial marketing expertise started gaining a new authority in some influential political circles. Parties, religion, and the nation-state itself were being branded and these brands were increasingly being mobilized as parts of comprehensive multimedia marketing strategies.[10] The more the business moved into the limelight, the more it was expected to provide a model not just for selling products but for communication *tout court*. The upshot of this was that the advertising business found itself in an impossible situation, precisely *because* its tenaciously nurtured dream was finally coming true.

As I have argued elsewhere, it was often in conversations about the genre known as 'public service advertising' that the tensions became most tangible. Many advertising people would speak passionately and eloquently to me of the 'electric' power of their art, a power to effect social change far beyond the capacity of existing political initiatives.[11] If public service campaigns had often fallen short of their aims, I was told, it was because of the failure of government to hold up its end of the deal, to ensure the requisite infrastructure.[12] And yet my conversations with Bombay ad people about public service advertising often concluded in a diminuendo: the grand generic claims that practitioners often made about the transformative power of advertising, particularly in a 'developing society,' gave way to a sober reflection on the limited compass of isolated efforts, as if the deployment of advertising campaigns were analogous to individual actions.

The small victories that trickle-down might bring sat uneasily alongside the libidinally charged visual incantations of the billboards. As one creative star (who had received awards for his own public service work) reflected:

There is an effort going on. What's Lever spending its time on today? It's trying to find a market to replace those sticks for cleaning your teeth in the villages. I'm not saying that the industry is socialistic in its thinking. But in its process of exploring newer markets, it will have to go with the needs which will help improve the lifestyles of the people . . . The process will happen. I don't think [the industry] has any intention anywhere in the world to work towards a social cause. But if you're progressive in your market expansion also, in your *own* agenda, it's bound to have some impact on making lives a little better. If I had an ambition that my car should shine every morning, that's my own agenda. And so I find a boy sitting out there and I say 'hey listen, I give you ten rupees a month, you're begging out here, come and shine my car spick and span every morning.' With my own motive I've actually generated something somewhere . . . But I guess, as the economy grows, at least some good things can happen. Some bad things will also happen, but some good things will also happen. There will be exploitation of labour, but then there will be labour to begin with [laughs]! There is no labour! There is an unemployed guy who gets employed and *then* he gets exploited [laughs]! I think there is a sense of responsibility that you need to have. I'm not saying that I'm any Mahatma Gandhi, but if you again go back to the basic premise 'respect your audience,' whether it would be a Mercedes buyer or whether it be a chap who's going to buy a branded salt, you'll have to respect your audience.

This cautious realism has the ring of a modestly sensible proposal, so much so that we are prone to forget, for a moment, how much of an advertisement has nothing to do with the kind of functional considerations at play here. The sub-category of public service advertising, by addressing precisely those issues that are conventionally deemed to be the object of 'development' (literacy, birth control, agricultural practices) performs two ideological functions. First, it helps to legitimize advertising *per se* in terms of aims that are widely held to be ethically desirable within the official discourse of the developmentalist state. Second, it encourages the impression that there is a smooth continuity between these aims and those of mass consumerism more generally. By implication, and sometimes by overt argument, the backlit images of cellphone-toting executives are understood to reside on a continuum that also includes government-sponsored messages about fertilizer.[13]

In other words, the political legitimation of advertising takes place in a zone of 'development' concerns. But the other end of the continuum, the imagescape of cellphones and jumbo televisions, where in fact advertising does most of its work, is not considered to be political – except in a purely negative way by those who (like the activists I referred to above) would dismiss it as irrelevant. There is thus a desperate need to fill this lacuna with a concerted analysis of the cultural politics of advertising practice. And it is in just such an analysis that I see the most fruitful engagement between advertising professionals and anthropologists.

Critical Publicity

I borrow the term 'critical publicity' from Jurgen Habermas,[14] who used it to refer to a (perhaps idealized) kind of public debate that would be free of the debilitating distortions of commercial interests. I do not share Habermas' privileging of discourse over images; my discussion so far should have made it clear that it is precisely the relation between the two that we need to explore. But I do think that it is crucial that we continue to carve out spaces of conversation that are minimally constrained by corporate balance sheets.

The really important parallel between anthropologists and advertising professionals is not that they both seek to understand something called 'culture.' Rather, it is that they are both engaged in public cultural practices. The question is what they might be in a position to teach each other. There is an irony in the fact that it is anthropologists, whose works have such limited circulation, that have gone to such great lengths to explore their own responsibilities *vis-à-vis* a politics of representation. Advertising professionals, on the other hand, operate the most comprehensive mechanism of public cultural intervention ever invented, but have generally interpreted the question of responsibility quite narrowly. The habitual language of 'industry standards' and 'self-regulation' restricts consideration of the impact of advertising to questions of 'fairness,' 'content' and 'truth;' in short, to parameters that are generally internal to the credibility of individual campaigns, understood as tools for selling particular products.

But advertising is of course never just about the products it dramatizes. Nor is its content limited to propositional claims. The ways in which images, sounds, and text come together in advertising cannot be evaluated separately from some sense of the wider resonances, projects and responses that those elements are imbricated in, in situations and settings that may at first sight seem quite distant from the ostensible aims of a given campaign.

It is true that the advertising business, in one of its public guises, likes to see itself as the trickster inside the business machine (just as anthropologists sometimes like to see themselves as jesters at the court of social science). It prides itself upon a certain unconventionality, a commitment to 'pushing the envelope' and 'lateral thinking.' It is not uncommon to find ad people including phrases like 'When the world zigs, you should zag' in their mission statements and client pitches.[15] But for all the talk of 'thinking outside the box,' this thinking must still take place *within* a literal box, a box marked 'Dove,' or 'Ray-Ban,' or 'Videocon,' a box defined at its base by the inexorable bottom line.

The advertising business, like any business, encourages and rewards only the sort of critical reflection that is likely to be profitable within the terms of the enterprise, defined instrumentally. But to say that workers in the business are not rewarded for the kind of reflexivity that calls the accepted borders of the enterprise into question is not to say that they do not regularly, often agonizingly, engage in just this kind of reflexivity. To be sure, most of the executives and creatives that I knew in Bombay loved the adrenalin rush (and the incomparable salaries) that came with the job. But as we have seen, they would also regularly turn despondent about what some of them saw as a kind of gilded cage. The walls of this cage defined, ultimately, a relation of impotence: between the circumscribed and impoverished rationality of professional practice on the inside, and, beyond, the fearsomely complex public travels of the images themselves, for which no single set of actors could reasonably be expected to take full responsibility. No wonder that the outcome of the despondency was so often cynical anger, ironic detachment, or defensive boosterism.

But the impotence goes both ways. Built into so many of the calls for anthropology to be 'publicly engaged' or 'relevant' is the notion of a radical separation between an Ivory Tower – within which a rarefied 'life of the mind' seeks refuge from the crush of the street – and a World of Business, in which all is cut-throat instrumentality. It is this kind of binarism that leads to the idea that the relevance of what academics do depends on dragging hapless professors, blinking like moles in the sunlight, into the so-called Real World. By the same token, it is this kind of binarism that encourages those who work in business to believe that public debate is a kind of inessential good, a luxury, or – worst of all – 'politics.' Both anthropology and advertising are endeavours that cannot help but overflow their own borders. For that reason, they both point to the possibility of critical engagements that would problematize the boundaries of 'expertise' – and, above all, of that most cultural of measures of value, 'utility' – that help to police our public conversations.

Some will object that it is to be expected that concerns for profitability and efficiency will come first for those who do not enjoy the eccentric and luxurious working conditions of research campuses. By extension, one might ask, what room, in the everyday running of a business, can there be for a pesky anthropologist who is not directly focused upon contributing to the bottom line? My response must be to insist again that advertising is, at heart, a public cultural intervention at least as much as it is a business venture. In fact, it is a business venture *because* it is a public cultural intervention. And until this fact is taken seriously – which means giving both sides of the equation equal priority – we will be stuck with the kinds of experiential, ethical and political disjunctures that I have outlined here.

Acknowledgments

The research upon which this essay is based was made possible by the generosity of the Social Science Research Council and the American Institute of Indian Studies. For critical commentaries, I am indebted to Jennifer Cole, Keith Hart, Timothy Malefyt, John McCreery, Brian Moeran, Barbara Olsen, Kimberly Wright, and to the participants in seminars at Sarai in Delhi and The Mumbai Study Group in Bombay.

Notes

1. Measurements of the size of the advertising industry worldwide tend to be calculated in terms of 'capitalized billings,' in other words, the amount of money that the agencies charge their clients. Since only a fraction of this money actually ends up with the agency, such figures give a rather inflated impression of financial clout. Nevertheless, the expansion of the Indian ad business in the period 1980–2000 was nothing short of astonishing. (I have adjusted the following rupee amounts according to historically relevant exchange rates.) Sarna (1982, a and b) suggests that the industry grew from 37.38 crores of rupees in 1975 (US$ 44 million) to 89.11 crores in 1980 (US$ 111.4 million).

An OBM Media Bulletin from 1983 is more boosterish, figuring 236 crores for 1980 (US$ 295 million) and 296.9 crores for 1982 (US$ 312.5 million). Karlekar (1986) offers 200 crores for 1981 (US$ 232.5 million) and 400 crores by 1986 (US$ 317.5 million). Some impression of the exponential growth that followed can be gained from figures cited in Jeffrey (2000: 58), according to which the business grew from 930.9 crores in 1990–91 (US$ 423 million) to 5,331 crores in 1997–98 (US$ 1.4 billion), at an average rate of growth of 30 per cent a year. Steven Kemper notes that there were 93 advertising agencies in Bombay in 1960 and 425 by 1988 (Kemper 2001: 35).

2. It would be interesting to compare and contrast the twin discursive reifications in Indian public discourse, 'the consumer' and its older counterpart, 'the common man.' Both are, of course, habitually and strategically deployed as shorthand for distinct versions of 'the public interest.'

3. Jawaharlal Nehru himself, the first prime minister of independent India, had railed against consumerism in his seminal text, *The Discovery of India*:

> With all its splendid manifestations and real achievements, we have created a civilization which has something counterfeit about it. We eat ersatz food produced with the help of ersatz fertilizers; we indulge in ersatz emotions, and our human relations seldom go below the superficial plane. The advertiser is one of the symbols of our age with his continuous and raucous attempts to delude us and dull our powers of perception and induce us to buy unnecessary and even harmful products. (Nehru 1948 [1946]: 469)

4. The watershed text here is Clifford and Marcus (1986). The issue has generated a bewilderingly vast literature, both inside and outside of anthropology. For further musings on the problems – and the uses – of essentialism, see Spivak (1988) and Hutnyk (2000). For a set of reflections on the fates of the culture concept, some years after the initial moment of crisis, see Ortner (1999).

5. In some respects, though, earlier anthropological attention to the cultural politics of tourism had prefigured this concern. For inaugural statements, see MacCannell (1976) and Graburn (1976).

6. In anthropology, the locus classicus of this argument is Sahlins (1976: Chapter 5). Sahlins' position here must be understood in the context of its time, as a culturalist polemic against naively materialist explanations. Since then, however, his general argument has been thoroughly domesticated by marketing theory and consumer behavior research, the better to present cultural preferences as 'given' and thus exonerate the culture industries from critique.

7. In his acerbic way, Theodor Adorno reflected on how elements of consumer culture are often justified with reference to a quasi-anthropological notion of tradition: 'High-pressure publicity and continuous plugging to institutionalise some obnoxious type does not make the type a sacred symbol of folklore. Many

considerations of an apparently anthropological nature today tend only to veil objectionable trends, as though they were of an ethnological, quasi-natural character' (Adorno 1954: 233).

8. Rajagopal (2000) offers a compelling meditation on the affinity between the rise of a televisual Hindu nationalism and the ideology of consumerist liberalization in India.

9. Manufacturers and advertising agencies had also frequently sought to collaborate with and consult for state projects. As I describe elsewhere (Mazzarella in press: Chapter 3), these collaborations tended to heighten the mutual suspicions of both sides.

10. In a sense, of course, the 'branding' of these entities has an ancient history. Sovereigns and subsequently political parties, polities cosmic and secular have always used identifying and emotively charged insignia. In post-independence India, advertising sporadically intersected with politics. The pro-business Swatantra Party brought in flamboyant Bombay creative Kersy Katrak to work on its campaign in 1966; Katrak went on to work on promotional materials for the opposition Janata Party in 1977 and 1980. The decisive consolidation of the relationship between full-service marketing and national politics came in 1984, when Rediffusion took charge of the Congress Party's campaign and Trikaya handled the communications of the opposing BJP. This is not to say that the transition has been smooth. In fact, one of the points made by several commentators is that the increasing marketization of Indian politics tends to marginalize older, perhaps more rigorous, forms of grass-roots political mobilization (Rajagopal 2000; Brosius 1999).

11. See Mazzarella (2001, in press).

12. In a sense, the isolation of public service advertising *per se* is misleading, since, according to the ethos of mass consumerism, *all* advertising is a kind of public service. That is to say, it claims to facilitate the realization of a better society. I thank Shuddhabrata Sengupta for raising this point.

13. The words of Gurcharan Das, former head of Procter & Gamble India, and long-time commentator on the Indian business scene, neatly express this implication:

> In a country like India, which has poor communications, the farmer has a right to know about the latest pump that has been invented by Batliboi. He can know about this pump in the most efficient manner through advertising . . . In an information-starved country like India, advertising . . . is also socially desirable. It is an important means to inculcate socially beneficial behaviour such as family planning and dowry abolition, conservation of energy, preservation of wildlife and forests, and living in communal harmony . . . The most unfortunate consequence of the advertising tax disallowance is that advertisers have had to cut off the already

slender connection of the countryside with the modern world, depriving rural areas of the opportunity to share in the benefits of the twentieth century, which include consumer products. This is almost as bad as depriving them of the right to free speech and the right to vote. (*Economic Scene* 1983)

14. Habermas (1989 [1962]).
15. This particular motto was delivered by British creative star John Hegarty on a visit to India in 1998.

References

Adorno, T. 1954 'How to look at television,' *Quarterly of Film, Radio and Television*, 8 (3).

Brosius, C. 1999 'Is this the real thing? Packaging cultural nationalism,' in C. Brosius and M. Butcher (eds) *Image Journeys: Audio-Visual Media and Cultural Change in India*, London: Sage.

Clifford, J. and G. Marcus 1986 *Writing Culture: The Poetics and Politics of Ethnography*, Berkeley: University of California Press.

Economic Scene 1983 'Spotlight: It's an ad world,' 1 December.

Fox, S. 1990 [1984] *The Mirror Makers: A History of American Advertising*, London: Heinemann.

Graburn, N. (ed.) 1976 *Ethnic and Tourist Arts: Cultural Expressions from the Fourth World*, Berkeley: University of California Press.

Habermas, J. 1989 [1962] *The Structural Transformation of the Public Sphere: an Inquiry into a Category of Bourgeois Society*, Cambridge, MA: MIT Press.

Horkheimer, Max and Theodor Adorno 1972 [1944] 'The culture industry: enlightenment as mass deception,' in Horkheimer and Adorno, *Dialectic of Enlightenment*, New York: Continuum.

Hutnyk, J. 2000 *Critique of Exotica: Music, Politics and the Culture Industry*, London: Pluto.

Jeffrey, R. 2000 *India's Newspaper Revolution: Capitalism, Politics and the Indian-Language Press 1977–1999*, New York: St Martin's.

Karlekar, H. 1986 'The great advertising boom,' *Indian Express*, 11 September.

Kemper, S. 2001 *Buying and Believing: Sri Lankan Advertising and Consumers in a Transnational World*, Chicago: University of Chicago Press.

MacCannell, D. 1976 *The Tourist: A New Theory of the Leisure Class*, New York: Schocken.

Mazzarella, W. 2001 'Citizens have sex, consumers make love: Marketing Kama-Sutra condoms in Bombay,' in B. Moeran (ed.) *Asian Media Productions*, London: Curzon.

—— (in press) *Shoveling Smoke: Advertising and Globalization in Contemporary India*, Durham: Duke University Press.

Miller, D. 1997 *Capitalism: an Ethnographic Approach*, Oxford: Berg.

Nehru, J. 1948 [1946] *The Discovery of India*, Seattle, WA: Signet.

Ortner, S. (ed.) 1999 *The Fate of 'Culture': Geertz and Beyond*, Berkeley: University of California Press.

Rajagopal, A. 2000 *Politics After Television: Hindu Nationalism and the Reshaping of the Public in India*, Cambridge: Cambridge University Press.

Sahlins, M. 1976 *Culture and Practical Reason*, Chicago: University of Chicago Press.

Sarna, S R. 1982a 'A study of expenditure by various industries,' *Business Standard*, 24 August.

—— 1982b 'The top ten spenders,' *Business Standard*, 25 August.

Spivak, G. 1988 'Can the subaltern speak?,' in C. Nelson and L. Grossberg (eds) *Marxism and the Interpretation of Culture*, Urbana: University of Illinois Press.

-3-

Advertising, Production and Consumption as Cultural Economy
Daniel Miller

This paper consists mainly of three case studies of the soft drink industry in Trinidad: The first focuses on an advertising campaign for a soft drink, the second on the advertising and consumption of Supligen – a soya-based drink, and the third on the production and consumption of Coca-Cola. Prior to presenting these case-studies I will briefly consider the methodological stance this work represents, in many ways a quite conservative sense of the merits of ethnography. I then turn to the theoretical debate that it raises which is that posed by recent attempts to rethink what we mean by the idea of a cultural economy. Finally, the case studies serve as demonstrations of the stance described.

The Methodology of Radical Empiricism

The sense of anthropology conveyed by this discussion is probably about as unfashionable as it is possible to be. I would characterize my approach as analyt-ical, structural, and holistic. Ethnographically the approach is based on participant observation within one site, at a time when anthropology favors multi-sited fieldwork. It is empathetic seeking to see things from the point of view of those observed, but analytically it does not identify the interests and reasons behind what informants do with what they say or the reasons they give. In general 'cause' as a phenomenon in this work tends to be viewed as structural rather than personal, largely the effect of contradictions within the institutions which to a great extent determine what people do. This is because I believe such structural contradictions are indeed the dominant cause of most human activity. While such an approach was fashionable during the 1980s when structuralist and Marxist approaches held sway it is at variance with much contemporary anthropology. Although language and intentionality are a part of what I study, I consider them limited in their ability to answer the question 'why' something happened. My interest is resolutely in social phenomena, hardly ever in individuals per se. My anthropology is primarily directed to the question of what it is that makes people, rather than what it is that people make. This is to my mind entirely compatible with an empathetic and moral concern for the experience of what it is to be those people.

Furthermore this work strives towards a context defined as holistic. That is in order to understand advertising I would prefer to broaden the foundation for this task in as many directions as possible. This material comes from the book *Capitalism: An Ethnographic Approach*[1] in which the two chapters on advertising appear after studies concerned with production and prior to studies concerned with retail and consumption. Context also involves the background of the people who work in advertising, including aspects such as gender and ethnicity. Had I had the space I would have considered factors such as education, class and the effect of dominant discourses in business studies literature. I did in fact look at the influences of foreign TV and international advertising fashions and styles upon them. But many contemporary anthropologists again see this understanding of context as a simplistic dualism and the pretension to holism is particularly derided.

This approach then goes strongly against the contemporary grain. Yet I would argue it may lay some claims to be part of what I hope would be a larger radicalism. For one thing I was brought up in an academic tradition in which radicalism was largely expressed through theory; there was a genuine sense that new approaches such as structuralism and Marxism really changed the way one thought about the world. But over time these became static, and it seemed to me increasingly that theory in anthropology was more like a fashion industry. That if at a given period you did not refer to postmodernism, or postcolonialism, or cite the right sources then your work was somehow suspect. Instead we followed what might be termed 'acceptable forms of radicalism.' More and more I felt that the true radicalism was highly empirical, because there was such a discrepancy between the models and theories by which the world was being described and what might be learnt from patient qualitative analysis of the phenomena being theorized that the way to shake up complacency in academia was through their study. Under this 'radical empiricism' it was the microcosm of ethnography that had to become the foundation on which to build the macrocosm of theory. Needless to say I have little respect for most psychologists or economists, since to my mind their overly emphatic insistence on being empirical is based on defensiveness because it is the one thing they rarely are. They never seem to study 'real world' situations in their actual complexity. Thus economists rarely study actual economies. Qualitative participant observation has the advantage of being empirically rich while involving an awareness of the falsity of claims either to subjectivism or objectivism, since the experience of fieldwork is clearly based upon the muddle in the middle that is also our ordinary experience of life.

The word muddle is not a bad place to start when describing the actual experience of ethnography, my own attempts to study advertising being more a case of muddling through than providing a model for methodology. I tried to follow particular campaigns, and after a while I realized that the structure of the industry generated certain types such as 'creatives' and 'account managers' that needed to be fully encompassed. But methodology in anthropology is part of the research findings. That is to say after a while I started to sense the specificity of the Trinidadian situation, that, in a small island, gossip works differently and public knowledge about companies works differently and therefore I had to work differently. I continually changed how I worked as I began to learn what it was I was working on. This is why I always tell my students that in anthropology consistent methodology is bad methodology, because we don't even know what we are studying until we have nearly finished studying it. If I was to pick out two things from my experience in Trinidad that I felt were worth passing on as advice they would be these. First I tried to remain unimportant and discrete and to arrive too early. As a result workers and executives would keep me waiting a very long time in their offices, and couldn't be bothered to change what they were doing or saying because of my presence. I found that what I happened to overhear going on during these waiting times was often more valuable than the meeting I was officially supposed to cover. Second I never accepted advertisers' own assessments of the meaning and impact of anything they did. I always spent time with communities of consumers to find out what they thought they were seeing and its consequence. This is because on the whole advertisers do not know what it is they have created, in the sense that the way in which consumers sitting in front of a TV read adverts is often astonishingly different from anything they had assumed, but they rarely bother to find this out by participating themselves in such everyday consumption. Even in anthropology I have the sense that most studies of advertising fail to follow through to this aspect of their studies.

The Problem of Cultural Economy

This emphasis upon ethnography corresponds to a current debate within anthropological and sociological theory over what has been called cultural economy of which advertising may be considered a clear example. The term 'cultural economy' is suitable since in general this debate lies between those who see a phenomenon such as advertising as a meeting point or mixture of two distinct forms that may be termed 'culture' and 'economy' and those who use an institution such as this to combat such dualisms. The distinction is often subtle. To take one of the most influential recent theorists Bruno Latour[2] does his work amount to the study of a bringing together of science and society (of which economy and culture would be subcategories) or does it start from the hybridity of forces that challenge the original dualism? For example, one of his co-workers Michel Callon[3] has recently argued with respect to the case of the market that he is working to undermine the duality of culture and economy, while I have argued that in practice he tends to reinforce it.[4] Some works, such as that of Sayer and Ray,[5] seem quite clear that common sense shows there are actual economic forces such as markets and that while these may interact with culture they are distinct from it.

Slater[6] provides a study of advertising campaigns for Johnson's Baby Oil and Energen crispbread that demonstrates clearly how misleading it is to think of advertising as just some kind of cultural intrusion into commercial and economic activity. Rather the very concepts of 'market' and of 'product' that advertising has to work with are just as inseparably cultural phenomena. The key in competition is often rivalry over the promotion of different structures of markets, which are quite distinct from the models of both market and competition within markets that are assumed within economics. In practice the sense we have of both product and consumption is inseparable from the structure of the market and the strategy of advertising that goes with it. Market structure and advertising strategy are not givens but alternatives that are fought over. I have made a similar point with respect to the concept of value: in most transactions price is not a disembedded abstraction that permits calculation, but rather tends to be reduced to a qualitative form where it can be placed in the general mix of consideration along with other qualitative forms.[7] Not surprisingly this approach meshes well with the holistic pretensions of ethnography.

What I take from these latter approaches is the importance of studying advertising itself. That in effect people who regard the world as having distinct worlds of the economic and the cultural are talking as though advertising didn't exist, and that advertising demonstrates how inaccurate the languages of various disciplines that rest upon such a dualism have become. Both the history[8] and the ethnography of advertising demonstrate that culture and economy are not separate or interwoven spheres, but rather economic activity is merely one form of cultural activity. In the case studies that follow I want to go further. The first study considers the internal dynamics of advertising agencies, the second and third consider consumption and production. The intention is to suggest that if all economic activity is best studied as cultural practice, then this is going to be just as true for the study of production as it is for the study of advertising. In short by emphasizing advertising in the anthropological study we are in danger of persuading people that advertising is a 'cultural' activity as opposed to a more 'economic' activity such as production. By contrast I want to argue that the case made here with regard to cultural economy is just as true for production or markets as it is for advertising itself.

Case Study One – Structural Tensions Within Advertising

Much of the ethnographic study of advertising in my and others work consists of participating in the development of particular campaigns, sitting in on meetings between agency and client, between account managers and creatives and going drinking after the meeting to find out what they think in private as opposed to what they say to each other. I want to focus upon one such meeting between creatives and account managers (AM) from the agency and product manager (PM) and marketing director from the client. These were companies with a good track record of working together, but there were critical internal social dynamics, including the desire of a fairly junior product manager to prove himself in the presence of a fairly senior marketing director.

The meeting was based on the decision to relaunch a drink, both in itself and as part of a range, through a twenty-second television advert for the drink and a thirty-second advert for the range. The total advertising budget was approximately US$ 20,000. The presentation by the product manager started with issues concerning the financial health of the country and then the company, but soon became concerned with the problem of the client's competitor company which had created a situation in which it was suggested 'if I could drop my price by even fifteen per cent, which would make it significant to the consumer, I have to double the amount of volume to make up and there is no way you can sell double the volume.'

This was followed by a generally upbeat description of the kind of advert the product had in mind. There was a constant rhetoric of warfare in relation to the competition: 'I am quite prepared to wipe them off the market prematurely'; 'I want to be seen as what I am, the leader.' He ended by saying that 'we want the packaging to look so appealing and the advertising to be so stupendous that people just go like zombies and buy this product.' The presentation was full of bravado envisaging exciting scenes and glamorous images: 'If you drop a woman there, dark tan, can see the pores of her skin . . . I want a scene that sucks you in. Romance in a real way, that people can touch.'

The next meeting was within the agency where the creatives presented a storyboard based on a quite different issue, a new way in which the package was to be opened. There were various comic playlets with the ending that only . . . could pull it off. This proposal was crushingly derided by the account manager who suggested it was far too people-oriented and what was required was an emphasis upon the product attributes. The creatives retreated in confusion, one complaining 'I wish we had known that this is what they wanted before, from the very start, because we wouldn't have wasted all this time at all', and then stating 'I really thought that, ok it is a new product and image right, and it is supposed to be original and creative.'

So within a short time I had been presented with three extremely different perceptions of what ought to be going on. What underscored this result was that it was not just the anthropologist who was trying to understand the unspoken assumptions that frame such encounters. The reason the account manager ridiculed his creatives was in part what he saw as their failure to decode the initial meeting properly. It should have been clear to them that all that bravado had nothing to do with the actual campaign but was a performance aimed at impressing the marketing manager. It was a ritual they needed to sit through, but one which was not to be taken seriously. It should have been 'obvious' that the advert was a launch ad which was primarily concerned with presenting the new image of the packages and the attributes of the drink itself, in particular, with reference to the 'problem' of taste and bubbliness. They should have known to ignore the entire content of the PM's presentation.

Such encounters are actually quite common in advertising agencies, and reflect the structural fault between creatives and account managers who constantly struggle for relative authority. The former need to claim that it is creative and exciting adverts that sell products, the latter assume it is emphasis on product itself and brand that ultimately counts. As Moeran points out (1993: 88) many of the rituals of advertising such as presentations to clients 'are part and parcel of the processes that serve to define and maintain the advertising community as a whole.' At one point the creative said 'that's very very limiting', to which the account manager replied: 'It is the confines under which you are working. That is the difference between fine art and graphic art right, it would be nice not to have confines but that is the real role . . . just treat my product strongly, my branding and my product attributes.' In their muttered asides the creatives confirmed amongst themselves their prejudices about account managers who have no concept of how advertising could actually work.

What is interesting about such arguments is their possible consequences. In this case what had been established was a trajectory of constraint which helps account for the final advert produced by the campaign. The advertising agency saw itself as being 'mature' enough to read between the lines of the brief and prepare an advert which was true to the unspoken 'realities' of the commercial context. They assumed that this meant that, despite everything said to them in the brief, a highly cautious conservative approach was called for, given the precarious situation of the brand. As was suggested in a later conversation with me, 'when you hear that what they want is something slick with a calypso you know you have to keep translating as you go along.' As meetings progressed the internal conversations become more 'honest' about the wider context to this campaign. The agency had a sense that it was dealing with a poorer product than that of the rival company: 'you have a perception of a flat horrible tasting product to deal with. OK, you have that perception, it exists. They are being beaten out of the market to the point that they had to withdraw two, and if this continues they will have to discontinue.' Such statements were based on the company's own research which showed a clear preference for the rival's drink, on the grounds that it was sweeter, more bubbly and thicker and for technical reasons this was likely to remain true for a while. So the 'subtext' to their brief was the necessity to address the problem that although efforts had been made to improve the product's bubbliness, marketing research showed that the drink still did not match its main rival.

What was happening was that the agency, in its desire to excavate one message and ignore another in deciding what the company 'really' wanted, may have overcompensated. Subsequent meetings resulted in an increasingly bland and decontextualized advert. As the marketing manager noted later on in the campaign, 'I said sharpen the product a bit more, but now we have taken away everything else and only have product alone.' Conservatism in the context of creating an advert takes the form of complete concentration on the product itself and its brand name and form as opposed to relating the product to a given context. But it took more than the meetings so far described for this to happen. There was at least one further stage of further decontextualization to go through. The next meeting was a presentation by the agency to the client which, of course, made no mention of the previous conflict. Instead it provided the result of a compromise, which retained some inclusion of person and context in the proposed advert.

The proposal was to place the drink within a 'lazy Sunday morning.' This might be viewed as a consumption context suggesting to the viewer an appropriate time for drinking a product with this flavor. But the creatives clearly saw this as rather less specific in its impact. Rather it was a way of objectifying the concept of 'flavor' itself. At one point someone said: 'Sunday morning is not a time but a mood, a character. You know just as you hear certain types of music on Sunday morning, classical music' – 'and religious music' chimed in another voice. Everyone laughed. The point was made by the joke. Religious music would have really meant Sunday morning, as opposed to the mood symbolized by that time which is what the creatives wanted to evoke. The discussion used the concrete case to deal with more general semiotic issues. When one opined 'You can't create a mood without a situation', the reply was 'but sometimes you don't need to describe the situation. For example, if you were to open on a Sunday morning, it could be a Sunday morning because it's not a workaday, the person not rushing nowhere, relaxing, so I am drinking . . . on a lazy Sunday morning.'

Later on in this meeting an executive noted that with the recession actual Sunday mornings rarely fitted the image being discussed. The unemployed were not working on weekdays and even those in work might be hustling to find some further ways of making money on Sundays. The reply was that 'that doesn't go on in reality but this product could help you feel that way.' In other words, the drink would help at least evoke a temporary sense of something desired but largely lost. The client's PM could see a further problem as he noted 'I would not say *lazy* Sunday, I find that a negative, something like laid back or inactive but not lazy.'

This illustrates how advertising operates within the schema of what Schudson[9] called capitalist realism. This is a realism that is not based on veracity to the outside world as in showing a typical person drinking in a typical fashion. Rather this is a realism constituted by the long-term role of advertising in constructing a genre within which commodities are supposed to be part of a kind of hyper-real idealized world of consumption.

The discussion that took place in the meeting was covering ground that has been increasingly the focal point of academic discussions about the nature of the semiotic relationship. This is not surprising since many of these ideas were first formulated in the critique of advertising, and later became a major part of the training of advertising personnel. For example, at one point an executive referred to an article he had seen in a magazine about the advertising industry looking to future trends: 'I found that where he said ads were going, I remember their script because he said the ads that were moving your brand was a feeling it wasn't a product, but I didn't agree with it. I don't want to risk this, it is something new. I don't want to totally eradicate what you had before.' The creatives, however, were keen to relate the strategy to such trends since they might thereby salvage some status-enhancing discourse from the realities of their constraints. They may have been refused the more overt creative advert, but they could argue that this degree of decontextualization was in line with a more subtle form of suggestive mood/flavor construction that was now in favor. What had started as a constraint (i.e. the emphasis upon the product) was being re-termed as something 'sexy.'

From the perspective of the client the move to decontextualization was fine if argued to be a strategy to concentrate on branding and product image. But they became nervous if told that this was actually some kind of new wave attempt to create what academics have termed 'a postmodern decoupling of the sign from the signified.' Once again the creatives' desire to feel good about what they were doing could eventually turn others against them. But this was only part of what was involved in considering an advert as a semiotic form. The problem was that the company could not control the order of evocation between sign and signified. There was the possibility that the viewer would see the product as itself captured by the context of this mood creation so that desire for the product would be reduced to the specificity of the particular time evoked (and by implication the consumer would restrict their drinking to those occasions). As one executive put it: 'everytime you put in a setting you are going to fix consumption time or pattern or occasion. If it was a soccer match you could say fixes it with sport. You said you didn't want setting, wanted it in the middle of nowhere.' The fear now was that reference to Sunday morning would not be read as a mood but would limit consumption to actual Sunday mornings. Within the general climate of caution this lack of confidence in their ability to control the semiotic direction of their own images was enough to sink the suggestion. When the adverts were finally produced all consumption contexts were eliminated and attention was entirely on the product and its ability to pour. By this stage it was clear that branding , and not elusive sense of mood or character, was the sole focus.

The concept behind this campaign had passed from telling a story to specifying a consumption context to total decontextualization. This in turn produced another problem, described succinctly at one meeting as 'pouring too boring.' But this was rejected by the AM of the agency. The point she made was, that given the right creative input and appropriate technological capacity, the action of pouring could be made to look exciting and, more importantly, enticing. A decision was made to go abroad for the production. Trinidadian advertising companies often have agreements with agencies abroad to assist them with the more sophisticated graphical devices for which facilities do not exist in Trinidad. Agencies have agreements in Florida or more often in nearby Caracas to use facilities there to create those parts of their adverts that require special skills.

The clients themselves were sceptical as to how far the focus on pouring could be taken. After hearing a briefing one said 'I have just seen a whole avalanche of pouring shots. All I see is a band of blue coming across the screen, something coming from nowhere and going nowhere, it doesn't impress me, just a band of blue.' The 'pour' was already constituted by the memory of past campaigns. So that people would say 'the pour should not be a regular (Brand A) pour, but must be something interesting so that you want to know how they executed it, something more like a (Brand B) pour.' Indeed, most aspects of advert production, from the models employed to the way a text appears on the screen, could be discussed in terms of recent examples of adverts shown on Trinidadian television.

The advert which was finally produced seems at first relatively bland and innocuous. It makes some reference to the ingredients the drink is made from, but the emphasis is on the pouring, the bubbliness and the new package. There is, however, a considerable irony here. By following structural tensions between the account manager and the creatives which led to ever increasing conservatism, the end result is probably about as risky as any advert for this particular product at this particular time could have been. The entire advert is focused around the concept of bubbliness and thickness which were exactly the features that all the marketing research had suggested were weaker in this product than in its main rival. It certainly 'addressed' the true main issue, but, as all the participants must have known, it therefore contained the disastrous potential for simply drawing the attention of consumers to why they should buy the rival's product.

Indeed what might be seen as the dishonesty of the campaign is highlighted further by the juxtaposition of the spoken section which refers to the product as 'true to you' with images that suggest particular bubbliness and thickness of texture. Bubbliness and thickness were, of course, exactly what would not be true as soon as the consumer purchased the drink. The advert was made by creating visuals based on quite different materials to produce an evocation of something which, even if the drink was nigh perfect, could not have been derived merely from the sensation of drinking. In this case, the hidden suggestion was a promise that the drink was bubblier and thicker than the rival which was manifestly untrue. When watching the campaign over several months, I could not help the feeling that the slogan 'true to you' arose almost subliminally, despite the many hours of discussion over each detail, as a symptom of the worries that both the company and the agency had about the commercial prospects for this drink, given the intense competition.

This may be generalized and stand as a conclusion to my observations of advertising production. The primary factor in determining the nature of the advert actually produced is commonly neither profitability per se nor a consideration of the consumer. Rather, it tends to be a reactive fear of the competition. In many cases this may act to hinder rather than promote consumer desire and actual profits.

Case Study Two – Supligen

For a considerable time I could not understand one of the most unexpected results of asking viewers to comment upon adverts. When I had watched the advert for Supligen it has seemed to me the clearest example of a product that was being sold on the theme of sex. The drink is a soya milk product made by Nestlé and sold in a tetrapack. The television advert consisted of a female in a leotard working out as though in a gym followed by a male with rippling muscles and a pneumatic drill between his legs. The female is shown throwing a carton of Supligen to the male and giving a clear wink to the viewer as they leave together through a door made from a Supligen pack. The slogan to the advert is 'the nourishment behind performance,' the off-screen voice notes 'it will help you perform longer.' The pack itself is based on the profile of what might be taken to be a comet but is clearly intended to be also taken as a penis in action. All of this would seem to make the advertiser's intentions pretty clear.

In order to confirm my interpretation I discussed the advert with the 'creative' who had produced the material for her agency. She confirmed everything I had thought and described the campaign as being based entirely upon sex. The theme was further clarified when as the merchandising associated with the sale of the product at supermarkets was based on offering free packets of peanuts or chickpeas. Both of these are traditionally foods which are supposed to help men sustain their sexual drive. An example is the oft quoted street-corner seller of peanuts cry of 'bullets for your gun.'

As was clear from the study of various other products, the viewers were not at all reticent about ascribing sexual innuendo to advertisements. Indeed my surprise had been the extent to which adverts, such as that for Carnation hot chocolate, which to me did not have such connotations, were read by viewers as being sold on sex. I could not therefore assume some prurience or reticence when viewers of the advert for Supligen simply refused to see it as associated with the topic of sex in any way. None of them saw the packet as related to the theme. All of them saw the message as based on the drink giving nourishment and help in strenuous work or leisure activities – but not sex. Typical responses were 'it's a sort of health drink, shows people working hard', or 'they just put someone there to show he is doing a good job after he drinks it. He is very energetic, he is doing something very hard. I don't see any other thing in it. The package – I think it's a light bulb.'

No such hesitation was shown with other advertisements. My experience was not, however, an aberration, since this consumption of advertising turned out to be a fair reflection of the consumption of the product. The manufacturers found that while the product sold reasonably well, marketing research showed that the product was mainly being used first by children for their lunch boxes, where it was regarded as more sustaining than the usual milk drinks, or as a meal substitute by those in a hurry. Both of these are traditional consumption categories.

Two questions arise. First: what led the manufacturers to choose this particular theme? Second: what led the consumers to reject it so emphatically? The producers may have followed this theme since they felt they were being boxed in by the complex internal competition amongst milk drinks. There was intense competition at this time between Nestlé and Cannings over the range of chocolate milk, egg-nog and peanut punch, which are the standard milk drinks. Supligen was situated as between these and 'build-up' drinks such as Nutrement. There was a further incentive for the advertising agency. The relevant 'creative' was looking for an opportunity to express her creativity without the constraints of the field of milk drinks as already constituted. She therefore chose sex as one of the several possible alternative strategies which were well established in the industry, being used for many other products but not at that time having an established niche within the field of milk drinks.

So how do we account for the rejection of this given meaning and the impos-ition of another by the consumer? In this case I assume that the consumers were faced with a new product, and they were given a potential image from the advert-isers which should have acted like a shoehorn. That is it should have eased the product into their lives through simple incorporation into a given category of products and their commoditization. The attributes presented could, however, be appropriated in other ways, and the advertisers certainly left open the route to other connotations such as those given by the idea of soya and by the ambiguity of terms such as 'performance.' The consumer in turn found particular niches in which this particular commodity appeared to be an improvement upon previously available alternatives. Parents were concerned that their children should have a drink at school which would sustain them. Parents are often battling against their own children who would prefer sweet drinks. Chocolate milk is seen as more a woman's drink than a child's drink and the only real competitor in this niche would be Milo which is sold as good for sports. A product that has qualities which are supposed to sustain one in strenuous exercise has an obvious affinity with the needs of highly energetic school children. What Supligen added with its soya content was the idea that it was also rich in protein, which is often viewed as part of a general category along with vitamins as helping sustain mental activity in addition to physical strength. I assume that some parents came to this conclusion for themselves, but other parents took it up through copying the innovators until it became a reasonably widespread practice.

In as much as this was becoming the consumer niche for the product, the sexual connotations of the campaign were rendered inappropriate. About the last thing parents want to do for their school-aged children is enhance their sexuality or sexual drive. This then establishes a contradiction making the advertising campaign inappropriate. I believe that, as a result, viewers simply could not see the advert's sexual aspects. The result is rather like those popular visual illusions where you can either see two candles in black, or the figure in between in white. Consumers had constructed a consensual appropriation of the commodity which led it in one direction rather than another. Obviously this will not apply to all consumers. There are no doubt many Trinidadians who drink Supligen to enhance their sexual drive. Judging from the variety of readings of most adverts a number of other routes to the appropriation or rejection of the drink must have developed. Nevertheless the evidence is for a generalizable cultural norm which has developed through the collectivity of consumers as an appropriating body. If I am correct in my interpretation (and I fully acknowledge that there are other possible explanations), then it reflects upon the formation of cultural normativity. I still find it extraordinary that, without anything being said or made explicit, this level of implicit agreement amongst a population about what a drink should be used for and what within an advert should not be seen can arise. My case study shows this process of normativity in rapid motion, occurring as it were in front of my eyes.

As an epilogue to this campaign, the next stage taken by the producers was to attempt an entirely new strategy with regard to the adult consumption of Supligen which was to market it mainly as a mixer for rum. In this case the strategy merely followed upon developments in Jamaica where Supligen had rapidly become established as a rum mixer. There was no evidence that this had become a common practice in Trinidad, and in effect local developments were being ignored.

Case Study Three – Coca-Cola

I will only briefly summarize this third study since the case has been published in several places.[10] I called in the paper which described the case in detail 'Coca-Cola: A black sweet drink from Trinidad' since I wanted to counter our assumption that the only really important thing about Coca-Cola is its use as a symbol of globalization and cultural and economic homogenization. Through ethnography I wanted to show that what was remarkable about Coca-Cola was the capacity of each place to turn it into something essentially local and different. I have a sense that this assertion is less problematic when made with regard to consumption than with production. It is not hard to recognize that where Coke is linked to rum and coke as a nationalistic drink this might make a difference. I also showed that there is an important history to the meaning of soft drinks in the island that centres upon the development of two main categories – the red sweet drink and the black sweet drink. Locally these drinks are loosely related to the make-up of the population, which is composed of two main groups, those descended from slaves and those descended from South Asian indentured labourers, with the red sweet drink particularly linked to the latter. It follows that understanding Coca-Cola as the most prestigious example of the black sweet drink means that the way the drink is perceived and the significance of its consumption is saturated with local connotations and implications that can only be understood in relation to this specific history and social make-up of Trinidad. Still more complex is the link between sweet drinks and confectionary, and in the paper I make a more radical argument that I feel the advertising industry has failed to fully appreciate, which is that in some respects if I was to compare Trinidad and the UK there are grounds for seeing the massive sweet drink industry in Trinidad (including their milk-based drinks) as more the equivalent of the massive UK confectionary industry than of the UK's drinks industry. So much of the consumption of chocolate and peanuts, for example, is through drinks.

These points are generally acceptable since we still tend to think of consumption as somehow more cultural and production as more economic. I want to finish this paper therefore with the argument that began it. The term 'cultural economy' that describes advertising as an institution that demonstrates how economic activity is a form of, and not opposed to, cultural activity applies equally to production and consumption. We find it relatively easy to see diversity in consumption but we constantly use words such as 'capitalism' to describe production and fail to see the way this masks an increasing diversity of commercial practice. This is why the book these three cases are taken from is called *Capitalism: An Ethnographic Approach*. I am not denying that there are constant moves towards homogenization in areas of production and finance as indeed there are in consumption. But at the same time institutions that have become global often start to grow local roots that begin to break down their original homogeneity and turn them into something varied. Coca-Cola is a good example of this because it is sold through a franchise system in which actual production is given over to the local bottler. In a small country such as Trinidad everyone knows the few firms that exist for any given area of production. They have a sense of their history, their ethnicity, their status and so forth. So Coca-Cola cannot escape the local significance of its bottling company. Indeed, that the sugar comes from an industry central to the history of the island, that the gas is a by-product of chemical plants which

symbolize the island's modernity and that Trinidad is expanding in glass production to the extent of exporting to the US, all have a bearing. Indeed once one
confronts the historical evidence that the government for some time protected
drinks such as Coca-Cola as local products, placing high duties on foreign imports,
it is evident that things are not what one might have predicted before undertaking
this kind of study. The government and not just the anthropologist was capable of
seeing Coca-Cola as more importantly local than global. I will leave the interested
reader to follow the details as published elsewhere.

Conclusion

My personal interest remains more in why anthropologists should take advertising
seriously than in why advertising should take anthropology seriously. There is
still a long way to go in persuading people that it is often the most familiar and
ubiquitous aspects of our own society that we least understand partly because we
are so much more assertive about our assumption that we do understand them. In
former times the role of anthropology seemed obvious because cultural diversity
as a prior condition of the world seemed obvious. My stance is that at a time when
we constantly talk about globalization and homogenization, anthropology is more
important than it ever used to be since the new cultural diversity that develops from
the breaking down of global institutions is not nearly so evident, and will be
denied, if anthropologists fail to confront the assumptions behind general terms
such as 'capitalism' (but equally 'education' or 'bureaucracy'). Within this I
suspect almost every time we see a factor as obviously more 'cultural' or more
'economic' we get it wrong.

Let me end with one more example of this. I had assumed that advertising
agencies would themselves be agents for increasing globalization. I then discovered that, from the point of view of those agencies, to merely show global
adverts meant they were only paid to find media space and as such they would
never be of much size and significance. If, however, they could persuade companies to allow them to make their own television adverts this expensive and
complex process enormously increased their size and the scale of their operations.
In the event the Trinidadian companies were very successful at persuading large
conglomerates of the special nature of the local market and most adverts shown on
television were locally made. But to make this argument they had to emphasize
local particularity and therefore the adverts they produced had to be stuffed full of
local references in order to justify their being made in the first place. As a result it
was global advertising companies such as McCann Erickson that were amongst
the most assiduous in producing assertive images of how Trinidad was different
and local. In turn this meant having a large local office at the expense of the

profitability of the company when seen in global terms, when having a small office placing globally made ads could have saved a lot of money. Which of this is cultural and which is economic? You tell me.

Notes

1. Miller (1997).
2. Latour (1993, 1999).
3. Callon (1998).
4. Miller (2002).
5. Ray and Sayer (1999).
6. Slater (2002).
7. Miller (2002).
8. McFall (2002).
9. Schudson (1993: 209–33).
10. Miller (1997, 1998).

References

Callon, M. (ed.) 1998 *The Laws of the Markets*, Oxford: Blackwell.

Du Gay, P. and M. Pryke (eds) 2002 *Cultural Economy*, London: Sage.

Latour, B. 1993 *We Have Never Been Modern*, Hemel Hempstead: Harvester Wheatsheaf.

—— 1999 *Pandora's Hope*, Cambridge, MA: Harvard University Press.

McFall, L. 2002 'Advertising, persuasion and the culture/economy dualism,' in P. Du Gay and M. Pryke (eds) *Cultural Economy*, London: Sage.

Miller, D. 1997 *Capitalism: An Ethnographic Approach*, Oxford: Berg.

—— 1998 'Coca-Cola: a black sweet drink from Trinidad,' in D. Miller (ed.) *Material Cultures*, Chicago: University of Chicago Press.

—— 2002 'Turning Callon the right way up,' *Economy and Society*, 31: 218–33.

Moeran, B. 1993 'A tournament of value: Strategies of presentation in Japanese advertising,' *Ethos*, 58: 73–94.

Ray, L. and A. Sayer (eds) 1999 *Culture and Economy After the Cultural Turn*, London: Sage.

Schudson, M. 1993 *Advertising, the Uneasy Persuasion*, New York: Basic Books.

Slater, D. 2002 'Capturing markets from the economists,' in P. Du Gay and M. Pryke (eds) *Cultural Economy*, London: Sage.

–4–

Imagining and Imaging the Other: Japanese Advertising International
Brian Moeran

This chapter examines the build-up to a competitive presentation for the international division of the audio-visual manufacturer Frontier[1] by a Japanese advertising agency, which was asked to prepare a single coherent campaign for both Germany and the United States. It traces some of the problems involved in Japanese 'imagining the West,' looks at the agency's solutions to these problems, and describes the role played by myself, as an anthropologist, in some of the campaign ideas that, eventually, met with success when Frontier awarded the agency its international audio-visual account. As such, the chapter is designed to build on pioneering anthropological work that has focused on the *production*, rather than *reception*, of advertising images.[2] In particular, it is concerned with the social relations constituting the client–agency partnership and their direct effect on creative ideas and, by depicting one company's imaginings of the other, shows how an imagined world or community underpins business relations in the advertising industry.[3]

Orientation

Advertising industries everywhere are structured around accounts – the sums of money put aside by advertisers and allocated to agencies for the purpose of selling a particular brand or product group, sometimes through a selected medium. It is an advertising agency's job to persuade an advertiser that it (rather than its competitors) is best suited to take on a particular account. This it does by actively soliciting a prospective client, with the aim of being asked to participate in a competitive presentation or 'pitch' in which, together with other agencies, it will put forward marketing and creative strategies based on the advertiser's initial orientation of its needs.[4]

Whenever an advertising agency is asked to make a presentation to a (would-be) client, it finds itself having to learn – often extremely rapidly – as much as it can about that client's business. This learning process includes all there is to know (or all that the client chooses to let the agency concerned know) about its products, sales, targeted consumers, and so on. But the agency is not limited to the market in which the client operates (or to the 'field' in which it is located along with its several competitors). As Timothy Malefyt shows in his chapter in this book, it also tries to find out about how the client company is itself organized – in particular, the power structure that determines who are, and who are not, decision makers in its managerial hierarchy. It is mastery of this combination of market, field and organizational factors that enables an agency to win accounts and grow in size.

In the case discussed in this chapter, the agency was asked to present several sets of advertising ideas. It had, first, to find ideas that would meet and satisfy prevailing, but rather different, market conditions in Germany and the United States; and second, to include common language and visuals that would appeal to two national groups of consumers whose cultural backgrounds and expectations were very different. This meant that the agency had to construct an image for the foreign other.

But the agency also needed to know *who* in Frontier's Tokyo headquarters was going to make the final decision about whether its pitch was appropriate. This meant, third, that it needed to construct an image for a Japanese 'other,' since it had to take account of one or more particular Japanese managers' personal likes and dislikes, and their ideas of what might be the best way to appeal to Germans and Americans. This rather more abstract nature of the agency's work was complicated by the fact that – just as Europeans and Americans tend not to distinguish between the Japanese, Koreans, Taiwanese, mainland Chinese (themselves divided into different groups), and so on, but to see them all as 'Asians' – the Japanese tend to lump together all those living outside Asia and Africa as 'Westerners.' At the same time, moreover, their images of themselves as Japanese have very often been subject to 'Western' depictions of the other. In short, the agency found itself in a complex situation where the objective realities of the market tended to be confused with the subjective tastes and preferences of individual personalities, and, as we shall see in the final commentary, occidentalism was at times indistinguishable from orientalism. The problem facing advertisers here is that of all those actively involved in the making of myths. They are 'unable to imagine the Other . . . How can one assimilate the Negro, the Russian? There is here a figure for emergencies: exoticism. The Other becomes a pure object, a spectacle, a clown.'[5]

It is these confusions that this chapter sets out to address as it follows the agency's attempt to appeal to two rather different 'Western' audiences, as well as construct a Japaneseness about Frontier that would 'work' in the West.[6] At the same time, however, it seeks to link the twin professions of advertising and anthropology in two complementary ways. First, it describes how, as an anthropologist doing fieldwork in what has since become a rather large Japanese advertising agency, I was able to make a contribution to that agency's pitch to its prospective client and so came to be seen as an 'advertising man,' rather than just a 'professor.' Second, it suggests that those working in the Agency might themselves be seen as applied anthropologists. This is not just because they make a living by convincing their clients that they understand how 'the natives' think,[7] but because they also have to analyze and deconstruct the social organization and power hierarchy of those whom they are trying to convince of their abilities. The other is at home as well as abroad.

Entering the Field

In the spring of 1989, the international division of Frontier's headquarters in Tokyo asked its contracted agency, J&M, to prepare an advertising campaign that would elevate its brand image in both the United States and Germany. At the same time, because the agency in which I was conducting my research was already success-fully handling one of Frontier's domestic accounts, and because it had learned that certain people in the client company were not entirely satisfied with the work currently being done by J&M, it managed to persuade Frontier's international division to invite it to participate in a competitive presentation.

In its own orientation to the agency, Frontier made it clear that it had decided to manage its overall marketing strategy through three broad geographical areas: America, Europe and Asia. Its sales covered a broad range of products from laser disc software to car navigation systems, by way of computer CD Roms, CD players, multi-cassette players, projection TV sets, and so on. Some of these (e.g. laser disc players) were better established in the United States than in Europe.

Three problem areas had to be dealt with by the agency.

1. *Brand image*: Frontier was not seen to be as technologically advanced as Sony, in spite of the fact that it was the originator of laser technology, and was thus in danger of being relegated to the position of a 'mini Sony' in consumers' estimations.
2. *The market situation*: Frontier's targeted consumers were generally seen to be limited because there was an overall impression that they were older than Sony's customers. However, the reunification of Germany and the forthcoming unification of Europe (EU) provided the company with an opportunity to rejuvenate its overall brand image in Europe at least, even though the amount of advertising hitherto done in Germany did not measure up to that put out by Sony. Market potential was also seen to exist in the distribution of the company's software through the expanding rental markets in both the US and Germany.
3. *Products*: Most consumers saw no fundamental differences in the qualities of the products put out by Frontier and its competitors.

Following this orientation, the agency calculated that it was necessary to take account of a number of related points.

1. *Corporate image*: The client should emphasize its brand name – its strength as a 'Frontier' in audio-visual technology. It should also highlight its actual leadership in laser technology (it was the first company to produce laser discs, compatible LDs, and multi-CD players).
2. *Brand prestige*: It should emphasize its role as a technological innovator both in the past and in the future, as well as the reliability and high quality of its products (already established in the audio field), and the superiority of its laser technology in terms of density of information, durability, access, digitalization, 're-writability,' and so on.
3. *Aspirational value*: It should develop a broad corporate concept that pursued an emphasis on personal freedom and the idea of entertainment as a means towards enriching consumers' lives. Ideally, this concept should be a unified 'one brand, one voice' that would function globally and be reinforced by a set of coherent creative ideas (that hitherto had been absent from its advertising campaigns abroad).

To achieve all these aims, Frontier had to address two main target audiences.

1. An *outer audience group*, consisting of twenty- and thirty-year-old men and women in Germany and the US, who were in an upper-middle socio-economic bracket. This group also included those who already owned entertainment-oriented VTR players, and were influential in the development of information technology, as well as steady, rather than just trend-conscious, consumers.
2. An *inner audience group*, consisting of those employed in Frontier itself, at its headquarters in Tokyo, as well as at sales outlets and in branch offices abroad in Germany and the US. This group also included those working on Frontier accounts in American and German advertising agencies.

The campaign's immediate external purpose, then, was to improve Frontier's corporate image, brand prestige and aspirational value. Its mid- to long-term aim was to create a unified global umbrella brand image ('one brand, one voice') that would cover particular product advertising campaigns in individual countries around the world. Its internal purpose was to boost morale within the client company and ensure that employees appreciated the initiative being taken by headquarters management in creating Frontier's new image strategy.

This kind of information given by an advertiser to its selected agencies (and their response thereto) is crucial to the practice, and thus to the academic discussion, of advertising, since it acts as a ground plan on which competing agencies base their market analyses and creative work. In this respect, knowledge of a client's marketing strategy, problems and aims is akin to that gained by an anthropologist from reading around a particular subject prior to entering 'the field.' Such marketing and intellectual orientation permit both advertisers and ethnographers to formulate hypotheses that can then be tested prior to the presentation of material to the client and academic community respectively as part of the final 'pitch.'

Brand Concept and Pre-presentation

Having arrived at this analysis of the market and Frontier's position therein, the agency needed to come up with a basic brand concept, corporate slogan and communication strategy that included one or more sets of print advertisements illustrating the approach it was proposing that Frontier adopt. It was here that as an anthropologist I entered the game.

As part of my fieldwork in the agency, I was placed in different divisions – print media buying, television advertising, marketing, merchandising, and so on – for a month at a time in order to learn how employees went about their jobs. In due course, I found myself in the accounts services office, a particularly opaque part of the agency because of the extremely intimate relations developed by account executives[8] with their opposite numbers (product managers, advertising managers, directors, and so on) in client companies. I had heard about the existence of 'presentations,' but had little idea of when or where or how often they took place; of who attended them, or of what they consisted of in substance. It seemed likely that this part of the agency's business would be extremely difficult to observe because of the recurrent problem of 'client confidentiality.'

One evening, however, the head of the account services office called me at home and asked whether I would be free to help with the agency's preparations for its presentation to Frontier. The following morning, a Friday, I found myself in one of the agency's small, windowless meeting rooms, surrounded by half a dozen men – all smoking – and gazing at several large placards on the tables in front of us. Boards with ads by rival companies were placed on a thin shelf along one wall of the room in front of me. I was given the briefest of orientations (as described in more detail above) and was asked to give my opinion on six series of ads that the agency had prepared for a 'pre-presentation' to one of the Frontier managers that same afternoon. The real pitch would take place the following Tuesday.

I was then shown several series of pictures, all with headlines, dummy copy,[9] the client's name and slogan. These were named as follows:

1. *Perspiration* – because of the series' visuals consisting of stark black and white photographs of perspiring musicians (a flamenco dancer, jazz drummer and classical violinist).

2. *Nature* – consisting of slightly greenish-grey tinted photographs of what was almost certainly an American desert.
3. *Home Entertainment* – depicting various combinations of laser and compact disc outlines with photographs of different entertainers performing.
4. *Musicians* – consisting of photos of three men with musical instruments.
5. *Young Women* – featuring attractive young models asking which company made the first laser disc player and other Frontier products.
6. *Creativity Quotient* – taking its title from one of the series' headlines, had yet to arrive from the agency's international subsidiary down the road.

I did my best to say something about each and made various (perhaps ill-considered) comments. The Perspiration series might do better in Germany than in the US since it seemed to be aimed more at 'intellectual' than ordinary music lovers. Also, 'Performance (or Dance) is my soul's voice' might be a better headline than 'Music is my soul's voice' for the flamenco dancer, if only to avoid repetition of the word 'music' that was being used for the picture of the classical musician. The Young Women ads seemed fairly sexist (one model was standing by a doorway with a come-on look that reminded me of London prostitutes back in the 1960s) and might therefore cause offence in America and/or Germany. Both the Nature and Musicians series had some 'orientalist' headlines that were styled as if they were *haiku* poems ('Nature speaks / loudest / when silent' and 'A month of filming / five minutes / on the screen'). These would probably appeal to Japanese – in particular, the Nature ads – but I was not convinced that they would persuade the targeted American and German consumers of Frontier's merits. The Creativity Quotient series, when it arrived, I found hard to grasp. Ad mock-ups showed Jimmy Hendrix with his guitar, Walt Disney with a drawing of Mickey Mouse, and Orson Welles gazing down at Citizen Kane on stage (described in the body copy as the 'Kane Mutiny'!). What was the connection? Each picture, came the answer, showed Frontier's pioneering spirit. Was it a spirit, then, that existed only in the past?

The Frontier tag line, too, caught my attention: 'The pulse of entertainment.' I asked how this idea in particular had been arrived at, but was told that Frontier itself had given the agency this phrase to work with at its orientation two weeks previously. A second choice had been 'The art of entertainment' which seemed to be only marginally – if at all – better. A third alternative, much liked by a senior Frontier director, was 'The light of joy and creativity.' None of these tag lines seemed entirely right for the client's needs and aims.

By this time, it was well after midday and someone brought in some *bentō* packed lunches. I was being pressed to say which series I liked best. I went for the Perspiration series, mainly because of the immediate effect of the stark, black and white visuals of the flamenco dancers, jazz drummer and classical violinist, but I knew that this was a choice based on a combination of personal cosmopolitan eclecticism and (upper-?) middle-class taste. The Home Entertainment series seemed to be direct and to the point – something that both Americans and Germans might appreciate. The Creativity Quotient series was interesting, but not immediately understandable in the context of Frontier's future-oriented marketing strategy.

The pre-presentation took place early that afternoon. Those present included three members of Frontier's international division, and, from the agency: the account team; a creative team from its international subsidiary (including an American copywriter); the head of the account services office; the head of the international division; the agency's executive director and vice-president; and myself. During the best part of the following two hours, three different account executives explained the agency's marketing and communications strategies. There were some sharp questions from Tanaka, the chief Frontier executive present, who asked the agency to explain, for example, why it was using red rather than standard blue for his company's logo; and why it had not made use of the 'light' (*hikari*) tag line, even though it had been emphasized by the managing director of Frontier at the agency's orientation two weeks previously. He asked more detailed questions about the agency's media plan and budgeting, before wondering how the six series of ads presented were to be taken. Was the agency going to recommend a particular approach? Or was it going to leave Frontier to fumble around on its own (to Tanaka's mind, a fatal strategy)?

The senior account executive was clearly at a loss. Hesitating a few long seconds, he finally suggested that the Perspiration series would be the agency's recommendation – followed by the Creativity Quotient series with Jimmi Hendrix and his guitar. Tanaka did not seem that impressed. So far as he could judge, the Home Entertainment series would benefit sales, while the Nature ads would probably help Frontier's corporate image. Perhaps the agency should check consumer reactions to these series by Tuesday? Moreover the agency had made no attempt to distinguish between American and German cultural differences. This was a problem for Frontier's head office since it had to persuade its people in Germany that what it was doing was right; it needed back-up reasoning for its choice.

Symbolic Interaction

It was late afternoon by the time Tanaka and his colleagues took their leave. Once they had been seen off at the elevators, everyone reassembled in the same room for a post mortem. This kind of meeting – almost always held after visits from clients to the Agency – was extremely important because, first, it allowed all those present to give their own personal interpretations and assessments of what may have gone on in the meeting with the client; second, it then allowed them to form a strategy for further action; and, third, it gave them the opportunity to discuss and analyze the organizational structure of their client's company.

In these respects, advertisers can be likened to practitioners of symbolic inter-action theory. Both are concerned with the meanings that things take on for human beings – meanings that involve an interpretive process, on the one hand, and that derive from, or arise out of, social interaction, on the other. Like symbolic inter-actionists, advertising people adopt a down-to-earth approach to the understanding of group behavior and human conduct. During the preparations for, and execution of, a client's advertising campaign, they are obliged to fit their own actions into the organized activities of other people (in the client company, media organizations, and within the agency itself). It is the ways in which such people define, interpret and meet different situations at various points in the advertising process that advertisers seek to explain. For them, as for symbolic interactionists, 'large-scale organization has to be seen, studied, and explained in terms of the process of interpretation engaged in by the acting participants as they handle the situations at their respective positions in the organization.'[10]

In this particular post mortem meeting, the head of the international division suggested that, if the presentation proper was to go smoothly, the agency had to have no more than one presenter. This would ensure continuity in the analysis. As a result, a senior account executive, Ueno, was immediately singled out for this job. Next, the head of the account services office argued that the competing agency, J&M, would almost certainly take along at least one foreigner to its presentation. The agency had to do the same, to show its international orientation. But the American copywriter had to be in Chicago the following Tuesday on another job, so I was then asked to act as the agency's foreign 'spokesman' at the presentation. My participation as an observer was moving quicker than anticipated.

The next question that arose concerned the client's organization. Who was the agency's target man in Frontier? The head of the account services office needed to know who was going to have the greatest say in whether the agency was, or was not, chosen to represent Frontier in Germany and the United States. The senior account executive quickly mentioned a name, Oba, and added that it was he who was keen on the idea of 'light' as an overall concept. The head of account services then said that he would talk to fellow members of the agency's board of directors and try to find a way to talk informally to Oba in the hope that he might then select the agency to handle the Frontier account.[11]

The head of the international division took over. The pre-presentation had made it abundantly clear that the agency had to decide which ads Oba was likely to approve or disapprove of and to make its selection accordingly. The account team had better be quite clear, too, about why it had decided not to go for Oba's tag line, 'The light of joy and creativity.'

There followed a long, practical discussion about each of the series presented. Was there a problem of permissions with the Perspiration series? No, the agency had already got permission from the photographer concerned, but there might be a problem with the performers themselves or rather with their managers. Although the performers didn't have to do anything for the series since the photos had already been taken, and would probably be content with a flat fee of, say, ¥10 million (at the time US$100,000), their managers would want twice that amount and would probably demand backing from Frontier for their protégés' concerts, once they realized that the ads were for Frontier's overall brand image. Still, there were more than 100 photos available so the agency could always move to a new artist if one got difficult.

What about the Nature series? This aroused some controversy. Many of those (Japanese) present liked it, but the two (Western) foreigners in the room continued to wrinkle their noses at it for one reason or another – particularly because of the headlines. After some further discussion, the Musicians series was put aside, as was the Young Women series to which Tanaka had reacted in a manner rather similar to myself since he had been overheard muttering 'prostitution' to one of his colleagues. This left us with the Creativity Quotient and Home Entertainment series. The latter seemed more promising, given Tanaka's parting words and its obvious product sales approach. Could its design be altered somehow to fit in with the Perspiration series and so enable the agency to propose 'Phase 1' and 'Phase 2' stages in its presentation the following Tuesday? With a bit of playing around (first, by peeling off some letters down one side of one series), we found that design-wise they could be made to resemble each other. But Ueno, the account executive who was to make the presentation, did not feel very happy about the idea of 'phases,' even though it was clearly important for Frontier. He would have to come up with a rationale for them – starting with a broad theme, perhaps, before narrowing down to particulars – in order to justify why the agency had selected these two particular series of ads.

At this point, there was a long telephone call taken by the account executive in charge of Frontier's domestic account, already handled by the agency. It seemed that someone somewhere in the agency had already been in touch with Tanaka who had been more than pleased with the Perspiration and Nature series. Still, J&M were due to make their presentation the following Monday, so maybe we should postpone our final decision until we had heard what had gone on there.[12]

In the meantime, there were things to be done. The tag line, 'The pulse of entertainment,' had to be checked in the US by the American copywriter once he got there. He should also try to get feedback from the US on 'The light of joy and creativity,' since this was so close to Oba's heart, and it might be wise if he were to include tag lines used by competitors – like Sony's 'The one and only' – when gauging American reactions. I was to ask my foreign friends in Tokyo what they thought of these tag lines and told to try to get an overall ranking of each of the series, as well as survey visuals, headlines, body copy (where used), tag line, design and total impact. Did the separate elements in each of the series inter-connect? Did people actually shift from visual to headline to body copy to tag line? If so, why? And what did they think of Frontier as a result? In the meantime, someone had discovered half a dozen forty-year-old American men with artificial suntans sitting in the corridor waiting to audition for a television commercial. They were brought in and asked for their – as it turned out inconclusive – opinions of the ads propped up against the walls of our meeting room.

Structuring Theory

That evening I met up with friends in a pub, and showed them some of the ad series that I had been given. Not one of them liked the tag line. One – in a passable imitation of Laurence Olivier as Henry V at Agincourt – suggested 'To the Front-iers.' Another – who worked in the fashion industry – said that the trouble with Frontier was that it was too frightened of being forthright. 'Like its name says,' she said, 'It's a cutting edge company.' This helped me latch onto the tag lines, 'Like the name says' and 'It's (all) in the name.' While I sipped my beer, I also scrawled down another phrase that leapt to mind: 'Entertaining ideas for the future.'

Advertising often advances by means of a process of *post*-rationalization. I needed to justify 'It's (all) in the name' and found myself going back to principles of structural linguistics read many years previously. The marketing of products and the meanings they took on, I reasoned, seemed no different in principle from Ferdinand de Saussure's discussion of how 'the value of any given word is deter-mined by what other words there are in that particular area of the vocabulary.'[13] Thus every product (walkman or discman, video or tape recorder, laser or compact disc, and so on) took on meaning in association with those other products with which it was marketed. Moreover, a parallel could be drawn between products and their manufacturers, on the one hand, and syntagmatic and associative relations in language, on the other.[14] Products might be made by the same or different manufacturers, in series that were related to one another diachronically (different versions of a VTR player put out over time by Frontier) or synchronically across space (simultaneously competing VTR players manufactured by Frontier, on the one hand, and by Sony, Hitachi, National, GE, Phillips, and so on, on the other). Together, like components of a language, they formed a system.

I had my post-rationalized theory. The following morning I found myself explaining to Ueno over the phone how Frontier needed to set itself apart from its competitors by ensuring that its tag line did not have any associations with those of rival companies. 'The art of entertainment' ran into trouble with Aiwa's 'The art of Aiwa,' while any allusion to the 'future' would run foul of JVC's 'Founders of the future,' and a focus on technology would clash with Sanyo's 'The new wave in Japanese technology.' By focussing on 'entertainment,' I reasoned, Frontier would merely be falling in line with a set of associations (art, technology, future) that did not really differentiate one company from another, in the way that Sony had been able to do with its 'The one and only.' Frontier needed to be incomparable. It had to adopt a tag line that was distinctive and timeless, not subject to fashion. By going for something like 'It's (all) in the name,' 'The name says it (all)' or 'Like the name says,' Frontier would be able to re-enforce its image and turn back on itself in a never-ending cycle. Frontier produced cutting edge products at the 'frontier' – a descriptive noun that was also the company's name, and so on ad infinitum. In short, 'Frontier = Frontier.'

Ueno listened politely, but did not sound particularly enthusiastic. I had the distinct impression that he had a sound grasp of both the theory and practice of structural linguistics and had already done this kind of reasoning for himself. Nevertheless, he asked me to write it all down for a Monday morning meeting. In the meantime, I tried to get friends' reactions to the ad series dreamed up by the creative team, and added my own tag line for comment among the others given to the agency by Frontier. Although there was no clear-cut favorite so far as the series were concerned (the Perspiration and Creativity Quotient ads were generally preferred to the Nature and Home Entertainment series), a resounding majority of the two dozen or so people I asked picked out 'Like the name says' and/or 'It's in the name' as their preferred tag line (provided I drop the 'all').

On Monday morning I presented my findings to Ueno who was by then more preoccupied with other, seemingly more urgent, matters. So little time, so much still to do. The creative people had been working through the weekend and all the previous night, trying to get everything right. The media planner had been faxing back and forth between Tokyo and the agency's offices in Los Angeles and Frankfurt, trying to get the necessary information on costs, reach, frequency, gross impression and the other imponderables of audience reception. These would enable Ueno to answer any nasty questions about the proposed campaign budget when the agency's presentation was made the following afternoon. There did not seem to be much that I could do, apart from pointing out one or two spelling mistakes and misprints, so I went off and did other things about the agency. Maybe I had been a bit over optimistic about my own potential usefulness as both foreigner and academic in the creation of the Frontier campaign.

Tournament of Value

Or had I? The next afternoon we took a train down to Frontier's headquarters in Meguro, heavily loaded with slide and overhead projectors, a couple of dozen bound copies of the presentation proposal, ad story boards, and so on. We were sent up to the twelfth floor and prepared ourselves for the ritual event that was about to take place.

As I have had occasion to point out elsewhere, competitive presentations have been likened to what Arjun Appadurai, in a different context, has called 'tournaments of value.' These he describes as 'complex periodic events that are removed in some culturally well-defined way from the routines of economic life.'[15] It is by means of competitive presentations that the central tokens of value in the advertising industry – accounts – are usually distributed. Like all ritual events, presentations are marked by special kinds of space, performance and language – in particular by 'the pitch' that is made by an agency's designated speaker.

Frontier had assigned a room on the top floor of its office normally used only by the company's board of directors, with an anteroom for the actors to prepare in and retire to. The performance, which went through a number of carefully staged phases, brought together sponsor and supplicant in a rite of persuasion.[16] The agency fielded ten people all told (three of them senior executive directors who had not been involved in preparations for the presentation), while Frontier brought in almost two dozen – ranging from senior executives to middle- and low-ranking managers. We sat along one side of a long oval table, they along the other and at the end of the boardroom. Proceedings began with the usual greetings on each side, and the reason for our being there together was made clear before Ueno was invited to give his 'pitch.'

He started off on points made in Frontier's orientation to the agency, moved to a market analysis and then embarked upon the agency's proposed communication strategy. Making use of slides, he outlined the 'inner' and 'outer' target audiences, the campaign aims and basic brand concept, 'Towards new frontiers in entertainment,' before shifting to a discussion of the tag line. After outlining reasons for adopting 'The pulse of entertainment,' he suddenly flashed on the screen as an alternative, 'Entertaining ideas for the future.' My tag line, he said (without attributing authorship), had been very favorably received in the United States because it attracted one's attention,[17] gave off an impression of creative products, resonated well, was future-oriented and suitable for entertainment-related products.

To my astonishment, Ueno then introduced a new slide proposing a second series of tag lines – 'Like the name says,' 'The name says it all' and 'It's in the name' – under the umbrella concept of 'Frontier = Frontier.' He then proceeded to justify the agency's reasoning along precisely the Saussurean lines that I had used over the phone to him the previous Saturday morning.

The creative recommendations that followed were divided into 'depth' ('Frontier = Frontier') and 'scope' ('Entertaining ideas for the future') approaches. The Perspiration series was recommended for the depth approach (with 'Performance is my soul's voice' as the headline for the visual of the flamenco dancer), and the Nature series as back up. For its scope approach, the agency recommended the Home Entertainment and Creativity Quotient series in that order. Noticing my surprise, the head of the international division, who was sitting beside me, leant over and whispered in my ear: 'Very good ideas, Professor!'

But would they be good enough to persuade Frontier to choose the agency over its rival, J&M? We found out soon enough. The very next afternoon, Tanaka arrived (by appointment) to inform us officially that Frontier had decided to award the agency its international account. Apparently, those present at the two present-ations the previous afternoon had been involved in fairly lengthy discussions over the de/merits of each of the agencies' proposals. Two things had had to be decided: the brand concept and tag line, on the one hand; and the communication strategy and ad campaigns to be used, on the other.

While younger members of Frontier had felt more inclined to support J&M's vision of 'Power Technology,' older members had felt that the agency's Persp-iration and Home Entertainment series were closer to Frontier's vision. However, all agreed that the agency had *potential* and it was this potential – exhibited in its ability to come up with new tag lines in particular – which decided Frontier to award the agency its account. The 'pitch,' too, had been a contributing factor and Tanaka commented favorably on the way in which Ueno had clearly given every-thing to the presentation – so much so that he had more or less collapsed at the end.

Apparently *every*one present had initially agreed that the tag line to go for was 'It's in the name.' This, they felt, expressed exactly what Frontier was all about. But those at the top – and, remember, Oba was still keen on his 'light' idea – had felt that it was perhaps a little too ahead of its time (twenty to thirty years ahead in fact) and that it was a mite too close in concept to Sony's 'The one and only.' And the last thing Frontier wanted was to be seen as a 'mini' Sony. So, reluctantly, they had decided to shelve 'It's in the name,' even though the tag line remained consciously in their minds. Instead, it was agreed that they should go for 'The art of enter-tainment,' turn down all communication strategy ideas and ask the Agency to come up with new ad campaign ideas.

Imagining and Imaging the Other

What does this brief account of the agency's preparations – and my own role therein – for its presentation to Frontier for an advertising campaign aimed at American and German markets have to tell us? First, following on from what has just been said, we should realize that presentations serve to define, maintain and reaffirm organizational roles in the advertising community as a whole. Con-sequently, as a number of contributions to this book point out, it is usually *people* rather than *agencies* who are selected to handle clients' accounts[18] – a point made clear by Tanaka in his comment on Ueno's 'all or nothing' performance at the presentation. Accounts themselves then legitimate an agency (and the person or persons singled out therein by the client). Every time an account changes agencies, it is given a new identity (because of the 'personality' given to the product or corporation which is the focus of the account) and builds up a history or proven- ance which includes such details as the account's monetary value, the names of agencies associated with it (and for how long), successful (and failed) campaigns, and so on. This provenance accompanies an account during its circulation which, as shown by the very existence of the provenance, is not fortuitous. Rather, like the products that advertisers market, accounts operate within a system of distinction that includes products *and* advertisers *and* advertising agencies, in the process *re*producing markets, player positions and collective wisdom.[19]

The reproduction of collective wisdom comes to the fore here in the agency's imagining of a Western, as well as a Japanese client, 'other.' The former concerns Japanese understandings of those who are not Japanese, the latter business relations in the Japanese advertising industry. It is to these two related general issues that I will devote the rest of this discussion.

Generally speaking, the Japanese distinguish between themselves and other Asians (extending as far as India and the South Asian continent); between them- selves and Africans; and between themselves and 'the West' (*seiyō*). They also make less general classificatory distinctions between the 'Middle East' (*chūkintō*), 'Europe' (*yōroppa*), the United States (*beikoku*), South America (*nanbei*), and so on, but the (predominantly white) people who live there – with the exception of indigenous populations such as American Indians and the Inuit – are categorized as 'Westerners' (*seiyōjin*). In this respect, they promote the same sort of difference between 'us' (the familiar) and 'them' (the strange) that Edward Said has noted of Westerners (or orientalists) writing about the East. They also indulge in the same kind of essentialism and absolutism, since the Japanese – like those writing about Japan – define what is notable about the other by resorting to features such as non/individuality, non/hierarchy, dis/harmony and ir/rationality. In general, we may say that, as a result of their economic success in the second half of the twentieth century, the Japanese have been able to recharge images applied to them by 'Western' orientalists and now successfully propagate a form of 'counter- orientalism' as a new hegemonic discourse.[20]

An important point to note about the continued efficacy of orientalist and counter-orientalist images is that it is the *media* which are most active in their dissemination to *mass* audiences that have immediate access and reaction to such images throughout the world. In this respect, media have, perhaps, far greater influence than ever was exerted by the scholars and administrators discussed by Said in his exposition of orientalist practices in earlier times. Part of the reason for the media's adoption of these grossly contorted views of 'the other' is to be found in the constraints of time and/or space under which they operate. They can only offer mouthfuls of exotica to be consumed by means of rapidly masticating media bites.

Clearly, advertising also suffers from such constraints. It needs to get across a particular set of images that reflect a marketing need and appeal to a particular group or groups of people in a single printed page or television commercial that, in Japan, usually lasts no longer than fifteen seconds. To this end, advertising is obliged to make use of existing classifications that are readily understood by its targeted audiences, while ensuring that these classifications set advertised products *apart* from other similar products. It is thus likely to avail itself of existing orientalist or occidentalist images in order to achieve its aims, since it does not have the space or time for complicated, or for complicating, issues. In this respect, we may say that at one level the relentless dichotomy of orientalist and occidentalist images found in advertising indicates *stylistic* differences – which are compatible and comparable, rather than opposite and irreconcilable.[21] At a second level, as can be seen in the chapters by Kemper, Mazzarella and Miller, these common differences are not suppressed but *promoted* and *structured* by an advertising system that is now becoming global in its forms.[22]

In preparing for the Frontier presentation, the agency adopted as stylistic differences the general structural principles by which the Japanese classify foreigners. Americans and Germans were both 'Westerners' (in other words, not 'Japanese') and therefore more or less the same. If pressed, those concerned could fall back on secondary clichés. Americans were only interested in a 'hard sell' (hence the account team's preference for the Entertainment series, which was backed up in discussion by Tanaka when he visited the agency to award it the Frontier account). Germans worked hard and had a tradition of 'musical culture' (hence its choice of the Perspiration series, featuring flamenco, jazz and classical musicians).[23]

That these differences were also reflected in *my* comments as a European on the agency's creative work shows how much we all rely on this structure of common differences. After all, I pointed out that Germans probably valued their musical tradition more than Americans (in spite of the fact that one of the ads in the Perspiration series featured a black jazz drummer). I had no difficulty in accepting my Japanese colleagues' expectations that Germans would link the Perspiration series with their own (essentialized?) self-image as a hard-working people (making them akin to the Japanese themselves). And I could readily see how the straight-to-the-point Home Entertainment series would probably appeal slightly more to an American audience.

There is support here, therefore, for James Carrier's argument that there are two kinds of occidentalism: one existing within academic anthropology; the other used by people being studied by anthropologists. Just as anthropologists' constructions of the West are often shaped by their study of the non-West, so do Japan's advert-ising people construct stylised images of the West that are based on their own image of themselves as Japanese. And this image, of course, has been formed in the light of what – among others – anthropologists have written about them in the spirit of orientalism.[24]

At the same time, the example given here shows just how these orientalisms and occidentalisms (of both the agency and its client) tend to be shaped by political contingencies. Here we are concerned with that other 'other' – the agency's Japanese client. Throughout its preparations for the presentation, the agency did its best *not* to make a selection from its six main campaign series (until ordered to do so by Tanaka). In a way the account team wanted to *avoid* making a distinction between two audiences – one in Germany and the other in the United States – which were, in the normal course of things, not clearly distinguished, but lumped together as 'Western.' At the same time, though, because it was trying to win its client's account, the agency needed to find out precisely how those in Frontier themselves defined 'the West,' and what images they would use to differentiate between Americans and Germans. More specifically, members of the account team had to find out who in particular was responsible for the decision to award, or not to award, the agency the Frontier account. The final images – the final orientalisms and occidentalisms – used by the agency in its presentation, therefore, depended in large part on the *individual* interpretations of what constituted 'German' and 'American' by two members of Frontier's senior management (Tanaka and Oba).[25]

As a result of these contingencies, the agency eventually put forward four main ideas.[26] By then it had a pretty good idea that its two main choices – the Perspiration (musicians) and Home Entertainment (entertainers outlined against laser and compact discs) series – were approved of by Tanaka, if not Oba. But each of these series also reflected other aspects of the Japanese discourse of the Western other. The Perspiration series was proposed for 'depth' in the agency's com-munication strategy because Europe is seen by the Japanese as a repository of 'high culture,' and thus of cultural 'depth.' Similarly, the sheer geographical expanse of the United States was reflected in the agency's choice of the Home Entertainment series for 'scope' (*hirogari*), which was also epitomised by the supporting Nature series that made use of visuals of vast expanses of uninhabited American desert.

At the same time, having discarded the Frontier managing director's idea of 'light' (*hikari*) in both its choice of tag line and campaign ideas, the agency's account team *had* to find something that it knew would appeal to the client's decision makers. Thus, against the advice of its resident European anthropologist and American copywriter, the Nature series was included because the agency knew that it would appeal to both major decision-makers in Frontier (Oba and Tanaka). Why the appeal? Because it invoked an essential Japanese orientalism of 'naturalness' that not only posits a trinity of nature, harmony and race, but sets these against 'the West' in numerous different ways, often relating Nature to technological superiority.[27]

In other words, in trying to isolate and express corporate and commodity differences, the agency tried to narrow its client's gaze to *particular kinds* of difference. Rather like beauty pageants in Belize, therefore, advertising campaigns can be said to:

> Organise and focus debate, and in the process of foregrounding particular kinds of difference, they submerge and obscure others by pushing them into the background. They standardise a vocabulary for describing difference, and provide a syntax for its expression, to produce a common frame of organised distinction, in the process making wildly disparate groups of people intelligible to each other. They essentialise some kinds of differences as ethnic, physical and immutable, and portray them as measurable and scalable characteristics, washing them with the legitimacy of objectivity. And they use these distinctions to draw systemic connections between disparate parts of the world system.[28]

What this discussion shows us is just how difficult it is to separate the elements that go into our own and others' constructions of others (and ourselves). As Lise Skov and I have argued more generally elsewhere, the fact that Frontier and the agency were embarked upon a global campaign strategy merely complicated the way in which a proposed advertising strategy participated in cultural reproduction. Campaigns addressed at American and German target audiences had little choice but to adopt a *lingua franca* of consumerism which acted as a visual shorthand for specific places, dramas and meanings. In spite of the structure of common differences, therefore, orientalist and occidentalist images become focal points in a *global stylistic continuity* and tend thus to be the same, whether they are produced in Japan, Europe, or the United States.[29] They both integrate the other and are integrated in the other.

Finally, as a coda to this discussion of imagining the 'other,' I want to turn to the issue of global advertising. There was a splendid irony in Frontier's decision to go for a single advertising campaign in both Germany and the United States, in spite of the clear economies of scale involved. I say 'irony' because Japanese corporations have during the latter half of the twentieth century promulgated a philosophy of distinctively 'Japanese' managerial practices that have made out successful firms like Frontier to be substantially 'different' from their rivals in Europe and the United States.[30] At the same time, the Japanese advertising industry, in conjunction with its clients, has – like many other local advertising industries around the world (see chapters by Kemper, Mazzarella and Miller) – long argued that the Japanese market is distinctive, unique even, because of the cultural proclivities of its consumers who cannot, or will not, readily accommodate global advertising campaigns and their images. An impenetrable aura has been drawn around both the culture of production and the culture of consumption in Japan.

In his discussion of the global and the local in Trinidad, Danny Miller has argued that both local advertising agency and local transnational office collude against the global firm by arguing for the distinctiveness of their local market and for the production of local advertising campaigns to sell global products. This enables them to grow at the expense of head offices and to establish a viable local advertising industry.[31] Although the Japanese economy is, of course, on a somewhat different scale from that of the Caribbean island discussed by Miller, we should note that the (extremely successful) branding of the Japanese market has enabled domestic advertising agencies to eclipse the influence of foreign mega-agencies like JWT, Saatchi & Saatchi, and so on.

What is interesting is that when a 'uniquely Japanese' firm like Frontier wanted to market abroad, it made use of a local advertising agency that had – in part, at least – built its success upon orchestrating unique selling propositions in a 'uniquely Japanese' market. Thus, we find a globalizing Japanese manufacturer and globalizing Japanese advertising agency trying to create and market a global advertising campaign that specifically *ignored* the cultural differences that exist between Germany and the US, on the one hand, and between Japan and each of these two countries, on the other! This suggests that business strategy and profitability are stamped on both sides of the global–local coin. On the one hand, they help the Japanese strengthen their economy at home and protect it from foreign incursion (at least, until the 1990s). On the other, they contribute to preventing other domestic local economies from becoming stronger (which they would do, by Miller's analysis, if local advertising campaigns were conducted by local agencies and local branches of local firms). In both cases, the 'local identity' of employees is at stake. In this sense, therefore, globalization is not a matter of internationalism, transnationalism or multinationalism, but rather of plain old-fashioned nationalism.

In another sense, however, globalization does not seem to be about any of these four types of nationalism. What the evidence suggests is that there is little, if any, systematic difference in an advertising agency's approaches to global and local advertising campaigns. That is to say, the agency set about a 'global' advertising campaign for a Japanese client in more or less the same way as it did for local campaigns for a European client's imported product (Moeran 1993) and a Japanese client's Japanese product (Moeran 1996a). In all three cases, it was the agency's estimation of what particular individuals within the client companies might think of particular images that counted. The account team's decision as to whether to go for 'global' or 'local' images in the advertisements presented depended on the perceived personality of the client's decision-maker, and not on any 'intrinsic' product or consumer value in the ads themselves. This indicates that, in the advertising industry at least, globalization is as much – if not more – about the interpersonal relations between individuals representing different corporations, as about the strategic development of those corporations themselves.

Acknowledgement

I would like to thank Timothy Malefyt, Barbara Olsen and John McCreery for critical comments on an earlier draft of this chapter.

Notes

1. All names of people and organizations mentioned in this paper have been changed from their original forms. The advertising agency concerned was Asahi Tsushinsha, or Asatsu, now ADK, Japan's third largest advertising agency.
2. See, for example, Moeran (1993, 1996a, 2001), Lien (1997), Miller (1997), Kemper (2001), McCreery (2001), and Mazzarella (2001, forthcoming).
3. Anderson (1983) and Appadurai (1990).
4. See Moeran (1993, 1996a: 71–98).
5. Barthes (1972: 151–2). Of course, I refer here not to the actual West (whatever that may be), but to those aspects of the West (real and imagined) that the Japanese incorporate into their version of occidentalism (cf. Tobin 1992: 4).
6. I will sometimes use the phrase 'the West' as shorthand for Germany and the United States because Frontier's aim was ultimately to create a global advertising campaign that would be carried in other parts of Europe and the Americas.
7. Kemper (2001: 4).
8. Or account planners. In Japanese, they are called by the rather more down-to-earth title of 'salesmen.'
9. 'Dummy' copy is often used in presentations since a competing agency is not usually given all the information required for it to write the body copy of an advertisement. In other words, what is usually presented by an agency to its client at a competitive pitch is one or more series of visuals, headlines and slogans.

10. Blumer (1986: 58). In his account of preparations for the re-launch of a Trinidadian drink (also discussed in his chapter in this book), Miller (1997: 182–7) comments on how an experienced advertising executive knew exactly how to read between the lines spoken by her client's marketing director and product manager at an orientation. But, while she ignored the substance of their discussion, the creative team preferred to make use of what was said to back their approach to the campaign in question.

11. As Miller (1997: 96) points out – and I myself have noted in my discussion of a Japanese advertising agency (Moeran 1996a) – it is these 'small worlds' of business contacts that continuously interfere with the logic of profitability.

12. It was abundantly clear that the agency had an extremely good communication channel, or 'pipe,' to someone in Frontier (cf. Moeran 1996a: 87–8).

13. Saussure (1983: 114).

14. Saussure (1983: 121–5).

15. Appadurai (1986: 21); cf. also Moeran (1993) and Lien (1997: 267–73).

16. And note that in advertising, as is shown in this book by Barbara Olsen and Timothy Malefyt, the real persuasion takes place between agency and client, and not between advertiser and consumer.

17. I later learned that he actually had had the tag line checked in the US.

18. Lien (1997: 271). See also Moeran (1993: 83) and Miller (1997: 189).

19. Moeran (1993: 84).

20. See Said (1978) for the definitive outline of orientalism, its history, practices and consequences. On Japan's counter-orientalism, see Moeran (1996b).

21. Moeran and Skov (1997: 182). Such 'stylistic reference points' have also been discussed more generally by Marilyn Ivy (1989).

22. See Wilk (1995: 118).

23. O'Barr (1994: 198) also looks briefly at Japanese fantasy constructions of America and points out how Japanese dreams of the United States parallel American dreams of Japan. Lien (1997: 174) gives a nice example of how a Norwegian food manufacturer resorted to such visual clichés as the stars and stripes flag, the Statue of Liberty, a cowboy on bucking bronco, jazz musicians and so on, in order to promote its Pan Pizza as 'American.'

24. See Carrier (1995: 8–14) and Moeran (1996b).

25. They also had to cater to decision-makers' self-image of what Frontier was as a company. The Home Entertainment and Creativity Quotient series openly stressed and implied, respectively, the historical role Frontier had played in the development of new audio-visual technologies.

26. Carrier (1995: 8). These contingencies also included the agency's own need to adapt creative ideas to its market analysis of Frontier's situation and an Anglo-Irish anthropologist's views on what made sense to himself as a European (after living a dozen years in Japan and having to struggle with orientalism during most of his academic life).

27. See Moeran and Skov (1997: 182–5). In fact, by openly advocating Frontier's technological superiority in the Home Entertainment series, the agency was in danger of playing into the hands of 'techno-orientalists' who use the association between technology and Japaneseness 'to reinforce the image of a culture that is cold, impersonal and machine-like, an authoritarian culture lacking emotional connection the rest of the world' (Morley and Robins 1995: 169).
28. Wilk (1995: 130).
29. Moeran and Skov (1997: 191–4). On occidentalism in Japanese advertising, see O'Barr (1994) and Creighton (1995).
30. In Europe (and also in Brazil) there was a consolidation of national advertising markets in the 1970s that helped establish local cultural identities *vis-à-vis* US advertising networks by successfully competing through 'creativity' (Mattelart 1991: 34–6, 41–3).
31. See Miller (1997: Chapter 3).

References

Anderson, Benedict 1983 *Imagined Communities*, London: Verso.

Appadurai, Arjun (ed.) 1986 *The Social Life of Things*, Cambridge, Cambridge University Press.

Appadurai, Arjun 1990 'Disjuncture and difference in the global economy,' *Public Culture*, 2 (2): 1–24.

Barthes, Roland 1972 *Mythologies*. London: Jonathan Cape.

Blumer, Herbert 1986 [1969] *Symbolic Interactionism: Perspective and Method*, Berkeley: University of California Press.

Carrier, James (ed.) 1995 *Occidentalism: Images of the West*, Oxford: Berg.

Creighton, Millie 1995 'Imaging the other in Japanese advertising,' in J. Carrier (ed.) *Occidentalism: Images of the West*, pp.135–60, Oxford: Berg.

Ivy, Marilyn 1989 'Critical texts, mass artifacts: The consumption of knowledge in postmodern Japan,' in M. Miyoshi and H.D. Harootunian (eds) *Postmodernism and Japan*, pp. 21–46, Durham: Duke University Press.

Kemper, Steven 2001 *Buying and Believing: Sri Lankan Advertising and Consumers in a Transnational World*, Chicago: University of Chicago Press.

Lien, Marianne 1997 *Marketing and Modernity*, Oxford: Berg.

Mattelart, Armand 1991 *Advertising International: The Privatisation of Public Space*, London: Routledge.

Mazzarella, William 2001 'Citizens have sex, consumers make love: marketing KamaSutra condoms in Bombay,' in B. Moeran (ed.) *Asian Media Productions*, pp. 168–96, London: Curzon.

—— (in press) *Shoveling Smoke: Advertising and Globalization in Contemporary India*, Durham: Duke University Press.

McCreery, John 2001 'Creating advertising in Japan: A sketch in search of a principle,' in B. Moeran (ed.) *Asian Media Productions*, pp. 151–67, London: Curzon.

Miller, Daniel 1997 *Capitalism: An Ethnographic Approach*, Oxford: Berg.

Moeran, Brian 1993 'A tournament of value: Strategies of presentation in Japanese advertising, *Ethnos*, 58: 73–94.

—— 1996a *A Japanese Advertising Agency: An Anthropology of Media and Markets*, London: Curzon.

—— 1996b 'The Orient strikes back: Advertising and imagining Japan,' *Theory, Culture and Society*, 13 (3): 77–112.

—— (ed.) 2001 'Promoting culture: The work of a Japanese advertising agency,' in B. Moeran (ed.) *Asian Media Productions*, pp. 270–91, London: Curzon.

—— and Lise Skov 1997 'Mount Fuji and the cherry blossoms: A view from afar,' in P. Asquith and A. Kalland (eds) *Japanese Images of Nature: Cultural Perspectives*, pp. 181–205, London: Curzon.

Morley, David and Kevin Robins 1995 *Spaces of Identity: Global Media, Electronic Landscapes and Cultural Boundaries*, London: Routledge.

O'Barr, William 1994 *Culture and the Ad: Exploring Otherness in the World of Advertising*, Boulder, CO: Westview.

Said, Edward 1978 *Orientalism*, New York: Vintage.

Saussure, Ferdinand de 1983 *Course in General Linguistics*, translated and annotated by Roy Harris, London: Duckworth.

Tobin, Joseph 1992 'Introduction: Domesticating the West,' in J. Tobin (ed.) *Re-Made in Japan: Everyday Life and Consumer Taste in a Changing Society*, pp. 1–41, New Haven: Yale University Press.

Wilk, Richard 1995 'Learning to be local in Belize: Global systems of common difference,' in D. Miller (ed.) *Worlds Apart: Modernity through the Prism of the Local*, pp. 110–33, London: Routledge.

–5–

The Revolution in Marketing Intimate Apparel: A Narrative Ethnography
Barbara Olsen

Marketers are change agents whose product development and innovations make our lives more comfortable and efficient, and in the process also contribute to the transformation of culture and history. This chapter is about my immersion into the world of advertising. I recount how the first agency I worked with, W&F, solved a serious marketing problem for a brassiere client, Warner's.[1] Ultimately it was our self-service concept for Warner's that revolutionized distribution for the entire industry.

The campaign reflects how understanding sales from a customer's perspective oriented brand strategy. It also demonstrates how advertising is shaped by executives' attitudes at particular moments in time. Particularly sensitive was the migration of gender, status, and class values that framed marketing rationale. As an anthropologist working in advertising, the thrill of the creative process was often complicated by conscientious objection to values surfacing in ads that were beyond my control.

I begin with the agency setting on Madison Avenue in the late 1960s. The narrative unfolds by illustrating how an original sales promotion client evolved into an advertising account for W&F. The campaign transformed Warner's from a little known company into an innovator in branding and distribution and, in the process, changed the way in which women purchase their bras.

Immersion on Madison Avenue

A decade before Twitchell coined the term 'Adcult,' Sherry noted that advertising was 'A cultural system [that] acts as both a model *of* and *for* reality': 'More than merely communicative in itself, advertising provides the revenue underwriting our mass communication media and the incentive for much of our word-of-mouth communication . . . and has been used as a vehicle for understanding the structures of reality within a culture.'[2] Reading old ads through the lens of history connects us to our social evolution. As texts they hint at who we were and who we have become especially in terms of gender, class and status.[3] In this chapter I use a reflexive narrative ethnography to recollect one campaign and describe how I was captivated by the imagination of marketing with its vision to solve real-life consumer problems and, in the process, to influence social mores.

During graduate school at Hunter College in 1968 I began working in New York City as a freelance artist in one advertising agency's Bull Pen (art department) doing paste-ups, mechanicals and illustrations. I was deciding between a career in social work, advertising, or anthropology. My anthropology mentor and master's thesis advisor, Anna Marie de Waal Malefyt, introduced me to the Caribbean through her work in Aruba and writing on religion. The Caribbean would ultimately frame much of my anthropological research.[4] Between fieldwork trips to Jamaica for the next few years, I worked at W&F, a creative boutique, where the owner creative director trained me as an account executive. The agency gave me the time I needed to accommodate my studies until I joined full-time. I liked the business and ascended into account management eventually becoming a principal in the firm's affiliated agencies.

W&F was located on 54th Street and Madison Avenue in the penthouse suite. The elevator opened to a windowed waiting room with palm tree in the corner and four beige leather and chrome chairs situated around a square white cube table. Most of the time this area was overflowing with impatient people waiting for appointments. Down a wide hallway sat two secretaries opposite offices of the owner/creative director and the bookkeeper/controller. Further along were account executive offices and a large rectangular conference room dominated by a giant black table where meetings and client presentations took place. At the back of the agency was the art department called the Bull Pen. This is where I first worked making our ads with the tools of my trade, T-square, triangle and glue pot, pasting type and artwork on oaktag boards that were called mechanicals. The agency was capable of full service from packaging and sales promotion to advertising and media placement, but the key staff consisted of a handful of us who did a little of everything, often pulling our weight wherever it was needed.

The creative director had Ivy League degrees in art, law and accounting. Typical of an owner/creative director, he oversaw and approved everything we wrote and designed, which put those of us with strong opinions often at odds with his decisions. A brilliant though difficult man to work for, his ability to take our suggestions often stimulated insightful collaboration that mitigated the consternation shared by most of the staff. I will digress to describe him because it was his energy and vision that drove the agency to win many awards. He was typical of a Madison Avenue 'Big Man' at the time and looked more like a banker or financier. He always wore a three-piece suit with a pocket watch whose chain dangled to the vest pouch. Short and stocky he was never without a huge Hoya de Monterey cigar. His temper was infamous and we all feared his wrath. Most of us who stayed on through the years respected his intellect and truly benefited from learning from a master despite his conflicted personality.

More problematic were the tensions that emerged between client aspirations for an account and his interpretation of a solution. Before sophisticated tools like Malefyt's agency's consumer-brand architecture and mutually intelligible vocabularies like their agency–client warfare argot (see his chapter in this volume) became customary, we relied on intuition and intimidation. I was present during many client–agency meetings in client offices or during lunches, dinners or other social occasions, and frequently observed altercations in the client–creative director dialogue. The creative director claimed that clients, most often, did not know what they needed. Our job was to tell them, even if they were offended. Hence, W&F's slogan, 'We're looking for trouble,' held mixed interpretations.

While it was in the creative arena that I found greatest fulfillment, it was in account management that I learned how advertising influenced contemporary capitalism. I came to appreciate why every cultural anthropology student should take an introduction to marketing course and every business student should take economic anthropology to understand how hunting and gathering evolved from the walkabout to the supermarket. Although we dealt with clients' marketing mix, manipulating the four Ps of product, place (distribution), price and promotion, to accomplish marketing plans, I wouldn't appreciate this handy dictum as marketing science until much later when I taught marketing to business students.

Narrative Ethnography

'For the woman who would rather be in *Cosmopolitan* than in *National Geographic*.
She reads *Vogue, Saturday Review* and *Life*.
She's into The League of Women's Voters and The P.T.A.
She even dabbles in women's lib.
She's our customer and yours too.
She's in your Foundation Department.
POIRETTE [the bra] For Real Women'

Women's Wear Daily, Poirette trade advert to store buyers

Advertising defines social contexts and hierarchies. It is part of the popular culture it parodies – along with movies, literature, drama, and music – while it combines with and is transported by media that carry such entertainment: radio, TV, the Internet, magazines, and newspapers. Advertising entertains as it informs and this is what implicates its power on society. The extent to which it impresses and persuades depends on the ideas that are being transmitted, to whom, for what purpose, and, perhaps most importantly, the values contained within the ads. One cannot be part of this process without appreciating its social influence. A narrative ethnography involves the observation of one's own participation. It is contrasted with the more autobiographical ethnographic memoir by comprising one's experiences plus, 'ethnographic data, epistemological reflections on field-work participation, and cultural analysis.'[5] Coincidentally, this mode of reflexivity gained currency in anthropology during the 1970s. While my actual anthropological research site was thousands of miles away, I was working in one of the richest culture-producing industries in the world, but, unfortunately, did not fully appreciate it at the time.

Advertising competed with my affection for anthropology. For nearly two decades I kept my feet in both camps, juggling work and classes at the School of Visual Arts on alternate evenings with graduate courses in anthropology at the New School for Social Research. The faculty at the New School looked askance at my day job on Madison Avenue and my colleagues in the agency resented and denigrated my anthropology. Both domains competed for 100 per cent of my attention. The pressure was intense. Although this narrative describes events from the beginning of my tenure in advertising, my diaries from the mid-1980s, during ownership years, hint that the stress never let up. Most of the time I yearned to be an anthropologist living far away with another tribe in some exotic location.

25 October 1983 – The Marines, Bahamians and Britons invaded Granada because Maurice Bishop was assassinated. Yesterday I went to B . . . Press in W. Orange, NJ where I had a shouting match with the printer. At lunch his daughter told me she works the hardest but because she's a woman the business will be left to her brothers. I'm here at work (and it's a school night) at 8.00 p.m. in SF's office with a rush ad for *Name that Tune*. We frantically worked on it all day, and now with one hour until the engraver's deadline, S is still on a conference call by phone to get last minute input. It's a riot just on the edge of panic and anxiety for me. Call *Broadcasting* and get an extension for time.

28 October – So after all that, SF cancelled one ad for *Name that Tune* and went with new copy on *Brides*. Fortunately, the engraver also sets type. I got home at 11.30 p.m. on the 25th.

6 November – My God! The rush never ends and just gets worse. Twentieth Century Fox (for an ad for *The Fall Guy*) went for the headline, 'A smash like this is no accident' with a truck hitting a Ferrari, but no one got the double entendre. For the last ten days it's been 11 o'clock nights. Insanity! I've missed Symbolic Anthropology for two weeks now but make Type class at SVA.

The transition from account executive to owner meant increasing responsibility to keep clients happy and have enough money in the bank to meet overhead costs. Often enough the thrill of landing a big account or doing a superior campaign, like Warner's, kept me excited about the business. Anthropologists fortunate enough to work as 'action researchers' in advertising, often participate in 'the role of change agents of the processes and events they are simultaneously studying.' Or having 'lived through important and often dramatic events with unique access . . . reflect on what they had been through.'[6] Thus, this narrative ethnography is about working on a campaign at a particular juncture in time when the confluence of social history and trends in marketing represented a rare opportunity to participate in a revolutionary industry initiative.

Warner's Bra Campaign

The first women's movement at the turn of the nineteenth century had the potential to liberate women from old cultural roles, releasing them into full educational and occupational equality with men. However, as Barthel notes, males defended the challenge to their authority calling it 'unnatural' and women reacted:

> In their place, a New Woman emerged. Her achievement lay not in liberating herself from the confinement of her separate sphere in service of the world of education, work, and social action, but rather in liberating herself from female sexual innocence, real or feigned. Under this definition, the New Woman of the 1920s was no longer, as previously, a threat to man. Instead, she was his accomplice in modernity. No longer a challenge, she became a playmate.[7]

Over the centuries, women's advancement in social and political history finds parallels in undergarment innovation.[8] The Warner Brothers Company was founded by two doctor brothers in Bridgeport, Connecticut in 1874 who promoted their corsets to prevent the health problems they believed were caused by an untrussed body. During the First World War many American women went to work in jobs left vacant by men who had gone to fight. As a result of this, and of the suffragette movement which was gaining influence at the time, women's corsets were increasingly discarded in favor of girdles and brassieres. During the more athletic 1920s sports and dance designs appeared. Beginning in the 1930s elasticized fabrics yielded better fitting designs. The Warner's Company also changed with the times by designing lighter foundations, but it continued to appeal to its original full-figured customer. The second women's liberation movement during the late 1960s and 1970s brought with it a serious challenge for Warner's.

By the late 1960s and during protests against the Vietnam War, women burned their bras in sympathy with male counterparts burning their draft cards. Similar to the suffragette era when condoms first became available, the second liberation movement coincided with a sexual revolution predicated on scientific advancements in birth control. Social change was again expressed in fashion, with women wearing looser fitting undergarments, and abandoning girdles and bras. However, in the 1960s the birth control pill was a catalyst that enhanced breast size. Before 1972 the average bust size of American women was 34B. However, department store buyers began noticing a demand for bigger sizes and fuller cups. While part of this trend could be attributed to a taller population born after the Second World War, many attributed bigger breasts to the pill, which simulated the effects of pregnancy. The irony for bra design in the late 1960s was that, even with bigger breasts, younger women preferred less confinement.

The older generation who desired firmer undergarments was disappearing. As one buyer said, 'Every time a hearse goes by, we lose another control girdle customer.'[9] A younger generation was displacing the old and the transition in bra sales affected all brassiere manufacturers. Many redesigned according to demand for a no-bra look and feel. One trade publication at the time reported, 'How a category as incongruous as minimal little nothing bras grew to be 20% of upstairs department store bra business is in itself somewhat of an enigma.'[10] Others floundered wondering where their market had gone.

Maidenform was every bra manufacturer's greatest competition because of the visibility of its consumer ads. Since 1949 its campaign focused on 'The Maidenform Woman' with its dream theme ads. Playtex, however, had been the leader in materials development since its inception in 1932. Competition for customers intensified by the late 1960s and Playtex was a market leader with innovative consumer packaging for both bras and girdles, and in 1969 with a design called the Cross Your Heart bra.

Upstairs Stores and Highbrow Consumers

W&F was initially hired to do a sales promotion and trade ad campaign to help increase Warner's share of the brassiere market in upstairs (upper-class) department stores such as Macy's, Lord and Taylor, and Bergdorf Goodman. Thus, a significant factor in this campaign was recognizing social class distinctions between upper and lower-class consumers.

> The U.S. has its own cultural hierarchy, its own cultural *economy* which defines, circulates, and ranks categories such as 'high brow' and 'low brow' (high brow being, for example, a preference for classical art, opera, and museum, versus a low brow taste for things like popular music, street art, comic strips, etc.) . . . such cultural segregation is brought about when advertisers conceptualize people as consumers, and when they organize the 'market' into neatly distinct segments in accordance with class boundaries.[11]

Warner's competition in the upstairs department stores had successfully followed market trends by offering barely-there and no-bra alternatives, while Warner's stood by a dwindling older consumer selling fewer firmer foundations. I was requisitioned, along with the other two account executives in the agency, sisters in their thirties, to work on the problem of increasing sales to younger women while keeping existing older customers. Being young bra buyers, it was obvious to us that Warner's had to change its image if it was to make more sales as our marketing problem was complicated by the gender politics and fashion symbolism of the late 1960s: 'By the end of the 1960s, a new androgynous aesthetic had emerged. The feminist movement took on the bra as a symbol of patriarchal societal constraints . . . While fashion pursued a path that endorsed the linear ectomorphy of high fashion models, the erotic imagination continued to prize the large breasted woman.'[12]

This marketing problem seemed to provide a perfect opportunity for anthropological research and analysis. From my perspective as a student of anthropology, we could feasibly enter 'the world of purpose, meaning, and attitudes'[13] of customer and clerk by using Harris' fieldwork approach to analyze forces that were colliding across the aisles of commerce. During a client meeting I suggested we view bra buyers as the underwear clan of the fashion tribe and that conducting customer-focused research was akin to anthropology's participant observation in the field. We could apply anthropology's fieldwork methodology by going to stores, watching customers shop, and asking them what they wanted in a bra. The creative director later told me I should never have made an analogy between Warner's customers and 'primitives' (the kind, I suppose that were found in *National Geographic*). He said I should keep my anthropology to myself, especially when with our clients. My suggestions henceforth were contributed without an anthropological label. Now, thirty years later, anthropological methods are at last appreciated by advertisers.

The creative director did have an open mind for good suggestions and an intuitive appreciation for understanding customers as informants in the field. From my perspective, observing and interpreting socialized gender roles in the ritual of hunting for brands in a crowded marketplace were categorized as emic and etic. Learning the emic was discovering how the insider, the other, the customer or clerk, experiences an experience. The etic was the observer or agency's interpretation of their experience. The store became the ethnographic site and the clerks and shoppers were the informants. It was classic anthropology I learned from Dr Anna Marie de Waal Malefyt and from reading Marvin Harris! The things that resonate on reflection, from my perspective as a 'situated narrator, who is also present as a character in the story,[14] are some of the value judgments that framed the discussions with the creative director and with the client about how and why women would react to our marketing decisions.

W&F's creative director had a tenacious determination. He believed there was always a solution to any problem. If we worked hard enough, we would find an opportunity in spite of the prevailing no-bra look and Warner's diminishing full-figured market. The two female account executives and I turned our attention to promotional suggestions. Warner's did not have the budget to do much more than trade ads in *Women's Wear Daily* (*WWD*) specifically for Market Week. Their May 1970 trade ad solicits buyers to the showroom for Fall Market Week. Instead of showing an older and full-bodied woman, it portrays their customer as a thin young woman. Her right arm extends across her chest while her left hand is fingering her hair. The modest invitation is clearly sexually suggestive. However, from the fuzzy image it appears that Warner's are not completely sure who their target really is. The headline, copy and tag play against this shadowy figure and the whole acts like a teaser ad:

> We Believe All Women Want a Believable Body and We Design Accordingly. Come to our showroom during Market Week to see what we've done. We're very excited about it. Warner's designs the believable body.

By delivering honesty and offering the consumer a 'believable body' the ad allowed the company and customers to acquire a social credibility. As the campaign evolved, Warner's ads became more emotionally charged, reflecting new twists in popular values woven around improvements in materials and design.

Our brainstorming sessions concluded that using sales promotions to sell existing products to department store buyers would not move a product if its image appeared atrophied to customers. We thought Warner's needed a new brand to sell. Perhaps by giving a real name to a bra instead of a numerical product line, we could conduct a promotion around this new brand. At this time, Warner's adopted a textile innovation being used in the fashion industry called doubleknit for the construction of its softer bras. The client held several focus groups to determine what the customer wanted in a bra but these did not provide much insight.[15] Warner's consumer analysis found that most of their customers were still older, conservative, prudish, full-figured women whom the sexual revolution had bypassed and they bought better bras in what the trade called 'upstairs' department stores (see fn.11). Their initial decision was to keep attention on this original customer.

W&F also conducted its own focus groups but found that women lied, especially when one person was a prude and influenced others. Instead, with a very limited budget the two sisters and I found that using a small number of one-on-one interviews, woman-to-woman, was more productive in discovering what women really believed. The individual interviews suggested that women were not the prudes the client imagined. Our research concluded that most of the women we spoke to thought Warner's was old fashioned. We concurred that Warner's had to change, beginning with its image. As an art director previously at Y&R, the creative director had learned the value of selling the sexuality in cosmetics while working closely with Charles Revson on the Revlon account. So, considering the sexual revolution underway, the creative director suggested coining a new bra called Love Touch that would have a contemporary, emotional appeal. Warner's management agreed. Using new materials, Love Touch was made with a 'double-knit' process and lace for a sexier image.

The creative director coined the name Love Touch to convey sexual appeal as well as comfort. Initial sales using doubleknit for Love Touch were so successful that Warner's brought out two other designs which they called Body Crème and Comfort Curve. Our ad in WWD in May 1971 featuring these bras ran with the headline, 'Warner's does it again! Doubleknit bras: a sellout!' The ad was all copy describing the success of their new material. Trade ads are not for consumers, but are designed to attract store buyers to purchase advertised brands for the coming season. This ad had two columns of type hailing doubleknit as 'the biggest bra fabric breakthrough since tricot' with testimonials from two buyers. Further along, the copy hinted that Warner's was still unclear about who they were selling to, even though they were sure they now had a great product:

Doubleknit bras. Hold themselves to the body. Any body.
As though they were custom made. Doubleknit bras.
With seams so thin and flat, nary a seam can be seen under clothing.
Doubleknit bras. For the smooth gently rounded shape of fashion today.
Doubleknit bras. They feel and fit like no other bras have ever felt before.
Don't miss out on this great new bra breakthrough.
Come in and fondle them for yourself.
At the Warner's Showroom . . .
Warner's designs the believable body.

While the male copywriter and creative director believed they were stretching the image with a sensual appeal, my female colleagues and I all thought the word 'fondle' was poorly chosen, having salacious overtones which might not appeal to the buyers who were mostly women. Contrary to advertising bombast, Warner's softer doubleknit designs did not dramatically alter sales trends. The company's old-fashioned image still represented a problem.

Retail analysis showed that upstairs department stores such as B. Altman, Sacks Fifth Avenue, Bonwitt Teller, Bergdorf Goodman, R.H. Macy, Gimbals, Lord and Taylor, were in a crisis, being challenged by downstairs mass-market chain stores like K Mart, Caldor's and J.C. Penny selling Playtex in packages and Maidenform brands that were backed with massive advertising. The upstairs department stores had cut back on sales help, often with the lingerie sales woman serving several departments. It was time for more fieldwork to observe the customer in the market place to see what was actually happening. The creative director sent the sisters and me (as participant observers) into the stores to test the retail setting. We discovered what we already knew. We found uncaring sales women who were stressed out, overworked and rude. The significant factor was that in the upstairs stores bras were kept in drawers behind the counter and out of sight. For the creative director it was a critical observation. A customer had to ask the sales woman to bring the requested bra by size and color or brand out of the drawer. Agency logic correctly believed the solution was to convert the sales woman to the Warner's brand so she would bring a Love Touch bra from the drawer for each customer to evaluate.

Appeal to Three Target Markets Concurrently

The account staff at W&F sat in the conference room around the big black table for a week trying to figure out a new plan. Similarly to those working on Moeran's Japanese campaign for contact lenses,[16] we ultimately recognized the need to appeal to three target markets at the same time: the store buyer, the retail clerk and the consumer. Our three-tier approach included trade ads, product brochures to store buyers, promotions to sales clerks, consumer ads and a revolutionary innovation at point-of-purchase. The agency recognized that the most important customer was the sales clerk. She was perceived by us to be distraught, overworked, and sullen. We hoped to influence a positive attitude toward the Warner's brand, and to assist her interaction with the customer. For this unappreciated clerk, the agency conceived a seasonal promotion campaign for the five or six largest markets where Warner's was sold.

To our knowledge, W&F created the first sales promotion to the store sales clerk. At Christmas we offered a helpful recipe booklet called the 'Guide to holiday shortcuts for tired salesgirls.' (Note the clerk was not yet a woman at the time, and even trade articles described sales clerks and buyers as 'girls.')[17] The inside photograph showed a middle-aged woman slumped in an overstuffed Queen Anne chair with her legs outstretched in pigeon-toed exhaustion. Her face wore a scowl and neatly pinned to her left breast was a sign saying 'May I help you?' The living room area in which she sat was strewn with remnants of Christmas wrappings and tree decorations. Her two sons peered devilishly from a partially opened door behind her. Clearly, she was a worker whose second shift was no more fun than the first. The booklet is an example of early relationship marketing that tried to turn the store clerk into Warner's new friend. We promised to make her holidays more fun with recipes like 'North Pole Pudding Pie. The booklet concluded by saying, 'It's all from Love Touch™ the great new Doubleknit bra from Warner's. Happy Holidays.' For New Year's we created a series of horoscope charts with the idea that that year each lingerie clerk would receive a birthday present from Warner's. For Valentine's Day we created a palm reading kit for the clerk to assist in reading a customer's palm. The glossy red cover announced 'Love is right in the palm of your hand.' A pocket insert held a clear acetate outline of a palm with all significant lines drawn to scale and labeled so the clerk could interpret a customer's heartline and romance lines with advice for her future. It was hoped that with this incentive the clerk could also entice the customer to try on a Warner's Love Touch bra. For Easter Warner's sent the store clerks flowers.

To appeal to the desirable younger customer, the creative director wrote a point-of-purchase promotion booklet entitled 'Fifty ways to please your lover' that was free for the taking at the bra counter. He was specific about targeting the *Cosmopolitan* magazine reader. The '*Cosmo* Girl' would be receptive to tips on catering to her lover with innovative massage and lovemaking and would be positively induced to buy the sexy Love Touch bra. The booklet generated a great deal of controversy. The creative director, however, believed that any publicity was good publicity.

The marketing plan began by targeting the five or six largest markets for Warner's, where their bras were an established brand. It was in department stores in these markets that the promotions were engaged. The plan with the entire promotional campaign was to convince the stores that Warner's was supporting its marketing effort and to prove that the brand would sell. If successful, the stores would order more bras from Warner's. In a recent conversation with the creative director, he reminded me that the budget was decidedly small for the aspirations he had for this campaign. In many ways similar to those involved with Moeran's initial promotion campaign for Nisshoku, an instant noodle manufacturer in Japan, W&F hoped to build up from the sales promotion to a consumer ad campaign once the sales began warranting adding to the promotional budget.[18]

Ads that Pull

The advertising budget was increased to enable W&F to conduct a more aggressive consumer and trade campaign. Initially, two consumer print ads were produced that ran in national magazines and Sunday newspaper magazine supplements that we hoped would pull customers into stores for Warner's bras. Both ads maximized cost-efficiency, creating a two-page spread effect by buying one full page and a one third-page outside column on the facing page. The creative director wanted Irving Penn to do the photographs, but cost was prohibitive so his assistant, Neil Baar, also possessing an artist's touch for lighting, was hired to take all the photos.

The first consumer ad (see Figure 1) was a full-page four-color photo of the model Pam Southern whose smiling face was thrust to the side arching back over her right shoulder. Nose and chin were obscured by surrounding white feathers that caressed both sides of her torso, revealing only her lace covered bra. The dramatic lighting cast soft brown shadows directing one's glance down toward her cleavage.

Figure 1 Warner's consumer advertisement.

Centered at the top of the page, the only copy read 'Indulge yourself in Warner's. No matter what goes on outside, you feel like more of a woman with Warner's underneath.' The one third-page column ad on the facing page showed the model in three versions of the bra with copy that read:

Please yourself with Doubleknit softness that molds to a perfect fit . . . Pamper yourself in precious lace, delicate tricot, and purr-like-a-kitten contour comfort . . . Please yourself in contour, too . . . with a soft, natural profile that lets you look as nice as you feel.

The ad was positioning Warner's bra as an erotic, sensual addition to any real woman's wardrobe, as well as challenging Maidenform's advertising that featured what was happening on the outside.

The second consumer ad announced 'Love Touch feels as good as it sounds. The Doubleknit bra by Warner's,' above the model who sat on the end of a couch. She wore white trousers and held her long white satin blouse open to reveal the Love Touch bra beneath. Her forward gaze directly into the camera suggested a 'Here I am!' pose, but the lighting only illuminated half of her face, creating a serious mood with romantic appeal. The facing page with four poses, featured a new addition, 'Meet the perfect partner, Love Lace . . . It's practically sensuous the way Love Touch molds its Doubleknit softness to your body.' Both ads suggested that two years after the 1970 trade ad, Warner's customer was no longer the amorphous personality hiding her breasts. She now seemed narcissistic, more emotional and to be demanding sensuous creature comfort.

For the store lingerie buyers, the agency designed a pocket brochure. The brochure held product shots and descriptions that could be easily added to or changed. The main pitch to the buyers reminded them, 'When the summer is almost over . . . The place [customers] start a new wardrobe is underneath it all.'

Point-of-purchase Self-service Empowerment: Take it From Warner's!

The campaign so far was an apparent success, but sales took a dramatic turn with the development of our self-service concept. While on an excursion through Warner's showroom with a buyer, the creative director and I noticed that the brassieres were hung on hangers for all the store buyers to easily see and feel. Back in the office, the creative director drew a prototype hanger appropriate for self-service that could be hung on a rack in department stores. We, in the agency, all thought it was a great idea. None of us women had any qualms about buying a bra that several other women might have already tried on. At our next meeting with the client, Warner's vice-president thought the concept had potential as it was a challenge to Playtex's packaging concept. He presented it to the president. The male hierarchy at Warner's overwhelmingly hated the hanging bra. They said open merchandising for bras was too unsanitary and their upstairs customers would never accept the idea. Warner's management, all males, believed women would never buy an undergarment that had been touched or tried on by other women. We knew that one buyer in a local department store was an ally and she believed the idea would be a sensation. In the agency the creative director believed 'Women are pigs, they just want to take home a bra that fits.' He convinced Warner's management that women would not care about the cleanliness issue. They decided to give it a try and for the following year Warner's developed the concept in test markets. During this process, the creative director worked with management to refine the distribution angle. He said the trade display rack should be incorporated as a floor stand to hold the hangers. He named the display rack the Money Maker tree. The concept in test markets became a marketing phenomenon. The proof was in the sales and the concept became retail history.

The distribution solution clearly addressed the sales problem by interpreting the customers' needs. Our research had shown that the nature of department stores was changing. The customer wanted faster service and convenience. Most importantly, the customer wanted to be in control. With W&F's self-service concept Warner's had inspired an industry trend that needed to be shouted in a trade ad for the upcoming 1972 Market Week. A trade campaign would chronicle the achievement. Two black and white trade ads were produced. The first headline said, 'Take it from Warner's, everyone else is.' The second headline featured a phone number with 'Call us. We'll hang up.' Body copy for both ads told the story:

> People keep hanging us up. And we couldn't be happier.
>
> Since we introduced our revolutionary concept in open merchandising a year ago it's made lots of money for lots of our customers.
>
> Merchandise is hung on our exclusive clear plastic hangers on attractive Money Maker fixtures. It's easy for a shopper to see, touch, feel and select any bra she wants. So it's easy to see why the Money Maker lives up to its name.
>
> The competition has just borrowed our idea. We don't really mind. Imitation is the sincerest form of flattery. But if they just came up with last year's idea it should take them till next year to get where we are now. And we're still getting better.
>
> That's why we want you to see the real Money Maker (and real money making merchandise) during Market Week May 15 to May 26 at our show room on the 12th floor of 90 Park Avenue in New York City. If you already have a Money Maker in your store what can we say? Thank you. Warner's™

Along with these ads an eight-page, gatefold, product brochure of the bra line was sent to store buyers. It was elegantly produced using reverse (white) type on glossy black, printed on a heavy stock (paper weight) cover and was titled 'Inspiration by Warner's. She'd love to have some.' The same attention to photographic detail as the consumer campaign featured a central oval picture on the cover with a woman in a diaphanous robe sitting on a white rattan chair in a Victorian setting, strikingly back lit with sun streaming through the window. The mood of the photo seemed to connect the past with the future, using a sensual setting that suggested a playful availability. The last page showed the Money Maker display stand to be used for open merchandising with the self-service hangers holding the bras. Each hanger included this backlit photo in a center oval situated between the hanger's arms.

Although naming a bra Love Touch was a key to the image problem, the self-service, open merchandising concept transformed point-of-purchase bra distribution for the entire industry. Warner's was the first company to introduce this idea and the trade press acknowledged our accomplishment, noting the permanent changes it represented. During a time of cutbacks of retail sales staff, a store foundations manager said the hanger system allowed his store to 'stretch our sales help.' One store buyer said the 'innovative rack displays are a boon to bra sales' and another claimed, 'The items on the racks sell like crazy.'[19] The brassiere manufacturers overwhelmingly agreed the display rack was the way to make more sales. The trade press acknowledged Warner's innovation saying, 'One of the foremost proponents of the rack concept is Warner's with an estimated 1,700 and 1,800 supplied fixtures currently in foundation areas.' Bra competitors like Maidenform, Bali, Loveable, Rogers Formfit, Bestform, Exquisite Form and even Playtex copied the idea from Warner's within the year. Some companies simply sent their bras to stores on hangers to be placed on Warner's Money Maker racks. The trade report continued, 'Like the firms which deal with upstairs departments, these firms have had little difficulty with buyers using their fixtures for other manufacturers' goods.'[20] By 1974 other competitors were placing similar trade ads lording their 'new' hanger innovation. Flexnit's *Women's Wear Daily* ad in May 1974 is a case in point. Along with a photo of the hanger with cardboard promotional cover, the copy says,

> Judge for yourself how your customers will respond. This product and hanging display program involve a completely new tactile and spatial approach. See it and feel it in person during market week at our showroom.

Our ad's suggestion, 'Take it from Warner's, everyone else is,' turned out to be true, as well as a huge success for Warner's and for W&F.

Along with our accomplishment came increased bra sales and additions to the advertising budget. Eventually, the consumer ads were expanded to a national campaign and were featured, for instance, in *This Week* Sunday supplements and the *New York Times* Sunday magazine section. A TV commercial backed up the campaign. To bring more customers into the stores, a series of four different TV commercials was run in cities with the largest department stores, with models testifying how important Warner's bra was to their success in the business. The commercial with Jaclyn Smith, later a 'Charlie's Angel,' drew the most attention and got the most play in metropolitan markets where Warner's sold in upstairs department stores. The campaign was such a success that Warner's increased its share of the market to become number two behind Maidenform. As I climbed the corporate ladder at the agency and through its transformations, the Warner's campaign became a staple in my portfolio pitch for new clients.

Warner's – In Reflection

The creative director turned Warner's stodgy image into a brand for the young or young at heart by targeting the sensuous '*Cosmo* Girl.' During my 2002 interview with the creative director, he told me that the self-service idea had to work because 'All women are slobs.' He knew women would not mind trying on a bra other women had previously worn. He also said that the consumer booklet 'Fifty ways to please your lover' when resurrected in the mid-1970s was even more popular because the sexual revolution had relaxed prudish sentiments. It was a popular sample that neither of us had any longer, so I asked him to refresh my memory on what some of the suggestions were which had drawn initial negative comments from the feminist community. He said he helped write the copy for the booklet because he considered himself an authority on women. The booklet, he said, offered 'guidance on how not to act like a prude, how to get and keep a man, tips on flattering a man in front of his friends and how to tell him he was a good lover. It had tips on massage, and advice for pregnant women about how to satisfy husbands in bed.' Perhaps time and his age, now near seventy, had enlivened the copy, but I was embarrassed that there might have been good reason for the critique of tasteless content.

Advertising and promotion are about creating and changing attitudes, but the executive as participant in the process is not an immune bystander to value judgments bantered about for copy creation. I recoiled every time the creative director told the story that 'self-service worked because women were slobs.' Anthropologically, how observers of participation categorize experience is a matter of choice. As Tedlock says, 'our lives as ethnographers are embedded within field experience in such a way that all our interactions involve choices . . . what we see or fail to see, reporting a particular misunderstanding or embarrassment, or ignoring it, all involve choices.'[21]

I disliked *Cosmopolitan* magazine. The *Cosmo* Girl image that most brassiere ads seemed to want stereotyped their audience. Our campaign for Warner's targeted a hybrid female who was voluptuous and sexy, supposedly read *Cosmopolitan* and just might have believed she was a *Cosmo* Girl. She was similar to the Poirette audience mentioned earlier, except the new Warner's woman was not yet ready for the P.T.A. Warner's 'Girl' was closer to *Cosmopolitan*'s 'typical reader' as described in *WWD* ads to fashion manufacturers.

> I'm a strong, healthy girl . . . I work hard . . . I make a terrific salary – Since for the *moment* I don't have family responsibilities, most of what I make is spent on *me* . . . plus a few good friends and some worthy causes. What's to be gloomy about! I love life and a special magazine that tells me how to get it all together. I love the magazine, too. I guess you could say I'm that COSMOPOLITAN GIRL.[22]

Perutz suggests that *Cosmopolitan* supplied the 'script' for obtaining global travel, the party life and 'marrying a millionaire.' This 'girl' stands apart from the mediocre:

> Her stupid sister still reads the *Ladies' Home Journal* or *McCall's* or *Family Circle*, getting hints on how to prepare the meal and how to prepare herself for her husband, who should be her lover too. The *Cosmo* girl scorns this. Husbands appear in her magazine only after divorce or infidelity; children don't come near the pages. The sentimental stuff of women's magazines is not for her.[23]

Vestergaard and Schroder remind us that, 'In its visual and verbal representation of the sexes, advertising comes to function as an ideological apparatus for the reproduction of our gender identities.' In their analysis of the British *Cosmopolitan*'s beauty ads, the magazine's editorial content and a reader survey, they note the contradictions between the female as 'sex object' advertising, the 'take control of your life' editorial content, and the readers' self-defined liberated attitudes. Although Vestergaard and Schroder focused on the *Cosmopolitan UK* edition, their findings are applicable to *Cosmo*'s US beauty product ads and their female readers. In their review of the *Cosmopolitan UK* survey of 'typical' female readers, they found that the women were not 'entirely' influenced by the male definition of beauty and viewed themselves as liberated from sexual objectification. However, the ads in *Cosmopolitan* appear to negate this liberated definition. The beauty product ads focus on how women depend on the assistance of brands to attain the objectified feminine ideal while the editorial stream toward self-actualization and reader self-reports flow against the advertising tide. Vestergaard and Schroder come to the conclusion that 'advertising presents a feminine beauty ideal which doesn't recognize beauty as a property resulting from natural characteristics.' The ads hint that women seek beauty defined by a male gaze, using sexuality to be attractive to a man, and so reflect the patriarchal notion 'that a woman's principle task is to find a man.'[24]

W&F used this idealized *Cosmo* Girl image as a new target market. Sexual appeal to men was at the heart of the Love Touch campaign. But, it is also true that since the 1960s women had been discovering new and more sexually liberated selves. Brands like Love Touch provided an intimate appeal to further explore and express this new self. The Love Touch brand personality we created and nurtured in our sales promotions and in the ads was consistent with whom we thought the new liberated women wanted to be.

The legacy of this bra brand and of the sexual revolution it reflected is seen all around us today in the commercial exploitation of a breast culture whose designs inflate, pump and push up more flesh exposing cleavage. Nachman's scope of the field covers most of them.[25] She says Victoria's Secret does it with the Miracle Bra. Ultimo's bra called The Ultimate obtains this effect with gel lining the cup. Frederick's of Hollywood sells three brands. The H_2O Waterbra uplifts with cups containing oil and water, the Captivator has 'deep-plunge foam cups' and the Hollywood Kiss Bra uses 'wish-bone straps and all-around wiring' to contribute cleavage. Lilly of France has the X-Bra with seamless, padded cupping and a front clasp that can be tightened for greater cleavage.

Finally, in July 2000, Warner's introduced their antidote to the flat chest with Nothing But Curves whose tag line, 'Why torment yourself in their push-up bra when you could be torturing guys in ours?' leaves no doubt about who the bra is meant to impress. Thus, intimate apparel and its titillating advertising continue to evolve because, as Barthel suggests, 'Today, there's a new New Woman for advertisers, and her efforts at liberation similarly suggest new themes and cultural references.'[26]

Warner's Bra campaign strategies over the years began with a rational offer to obtain a 'believable body' to enhance social credibility with others. The initial campaign was 'other' directed. With the incorporation of 'Doubleknit softness' for 'purr-like-a-kitten contour comfort,' Warner's took an emotional turn. It offered 'inner' directed sensual satisfaction with the Love Touch brand that let the wearer 'feel like more of a woman.' With the recent Nothing But Curves campaign, the advertising pitch serves two purposes. It combines 'outer' directed allure with 'inner' directed comfort. The 'New Woman' now owns the moment by obtaining dual satisfactions. She can torture the male gazer in ultimate comfort.

Reflections on Gender and Class

Before teaching marketing, business theory existed for me only in a practical application to make good judgments that would help clients sell more product. Selling bras involves multiple factors – from having a convenient selection available, to finding a comfortable fit, to the more highly involved time-consuming task of finding the perfect erotic lure for mate entrapment. Along this sales path, marketers tread carefully around existing social boundaries. This has always been problematic because brand executives have vested interests and agendas of their own regarding their product line and the clients they serve. My career in advertising inspired me to try to understand how advertising helped situate class, status and gender in contemporary American culture.[27]

So much of the Warner's story is about class and gender attitudes. First, there is the distinction between upstairs and downstairs stores that divided the upper-class customer from the working-class customer looking for bargains in chain stores that marketed to the masses. The clerks were 'sales girls' and all were working class serving upmarket women in the upstairs stores. The downstairs stores changed the way bras were sold before the upstairs stores in order to facilitate more efficient customer evaluation and purchase of their brassieres, but this new distribution also appealed to the working and lower-middle classes who had less time for shopping. The retail landscape was changing, with discount department stores offering a greater variety of goods closer to people's homes. Most rural and suburban folk in the 1970s preferred shopping at such chain stores that were often within five miles of their homes.[28]

Upstairs department stores were in turmoil, reacting to recessionary times. Over the decade of the 1970s the retail staff situation became increasingly dismal, with full-time clerks being replaced by untrained part-timers who cared little about catering to customers' needs.[29] As the self-service concept crept upstairs, we might analyze the attitudes of Warner's male executives towards prudery as a way to defend their brand's status, safeguarding it for the upstairs ladies. These men may also have transferred their own disgust of trying on under garments onto upmarket women. Do men, after all, never try on underwear?[30] Further, male executives might have been trying to protect the class divide, defined architecturally on the store floor, by trying to preserve the fitting room and female sales assistant who fitted the garment to the customer. By clinging to this antiquated service idea that the new retail reality had obliterated, male executives were actually slower to evolve modern marketing philosophies than their ad agency or the female customers they served.

The lingerie clerk as fitting assistant was the last vestige of a bygone era. At the beginning of the twentieth century, 'corsetières' were clerks trained in corset schools to properly fit corsets on their customers. Warner's pioneered training these specialized clerks in the 1920s. Warner Brothers, for example, sent out pamphlets in 1921 to corset departments throughout the United States to explain their figure type classifications and the corsets designed for each type, with the expectation that having an illustrated guide on hand would direct saleswomen to sell Warner's corsets.[31] W&F's promotional campaign to the sales clerks was a postmodern version of this initiative to give incentives to sell the Warner's brand. Our seasonal promotion campaign, in retrospect, appears to degrade the clerk by using person-alized propaganda to entice her to suggest Warner's brand. The 1921 fitting guide, by contrast, conveyed a professional distinction that added to the clerk's status, as she became a necessary specialist in fitting the garment to the body.

Valdivia, in a study comparing the 'gendered class representations' of Frederick's of Hollywood and Victoria's Secret catalogs, notes that 'the study of advertising and gender cannot be discussed without considering issues of class'. She contrasts the Victoria's Secret catalog which is aimed at the middle class and in which the models use body language that is passive, demure and sexy with the Frederick's of Hollywood catalog which is aimed at a more working-class audience and in which the models represent a working-class, take control, are more active and thus a deviant female.[32] Warner's consumer Love Touch campaign reflects purposeful targeting of the upper- and middle-classes, using an erotic sensuality to capture attention. The photographer, Neil Baar, was joining a league with Avadon, Penn and Scavulo, the most expensive fashion photographers at the time. He did the campaign justice with a mix of Eros and his classic artistry. The photograph was sexier than most bra ads attempted at the time. The model's neck arched backwards and around, forcing her head passionately (or tortuously?) over her shoulder. She was surrounded by exquisite, rich, elegant white feathers. The visual was consistent with positioning Love Touch to demand a specifically male tactile response. The head thrown back and to the side with subtle sensual lighting conveyed this seductive invitation. This pose can be compared to Valdivia's description twenty-five years later of Victoria's Secret models' posturing with 'the head thrown back or turned sideways, one hand draped over the curve of the hip.'[33] Both Victoria's Secret and Warner's position their brands for an upper-middle-class audience by recasting the postmodern definition of lingerie as more than sensual: it is erotic.

Thus, an effort to increase share of the market for a stagnant brand produced a variety of promotional solutions. Each marketing application for Warner's had its own effect on the marketplace, on consumers, and possibly influenced how the public now perceives lingerie advertising.

Conclusion

The Warner's case, most significantly, demonstrates how an advertising campaign evolves. To adopt Hackley's[34] definition, advertising refers 'to any communications activity whatsoever that, at some level, has a marketing motive. This perspective allows advertising to be seen as a cultural totality.' Rather than following a linear path of predetermined construction, many campaigns begin with a client problem to be solved and, more often than not, morph in various directions. These potentially include combinations of trade and consumer ads, sales promotions, as well as a range of point-of-purchase and distribution alternatives and various merchandising and event marketing occasions, depending on research gathered during the campaign's evolution. Agency 'surveillance' that is consumer, client and culturally driven, as Hackley notes, casts a 'panoptic' lens that has 'panoptic' effects: 'Advertising creativity can be seen to hinge on the extent to which cultural meanings can be extracted from the consumer's milieu and re-formed in juxtaposition with marketed meanings . . . These might include interior or exterior settings for the advertisement, models, body postures, gestures, clothing and any other means of signification that features in the ad.'[35] An effective advert-ising campaign that incorporates meaningful communication therefore represents a cultural synthesis in marketing praxis, ostensibly to enhance consumer self-identity and lifestyle needs while servicing corporate ends.

The advertising 'panopticon,' to borrow Hackley's metaphor for the Warner's campaign, utilized both diachronic and synchronic research in order to understand and encapsulate the present, while appreciating the past in preparation for the future. In such a campaign, advertising research encompasses probing product category history, as well as the socio-cultural and economic forces that impact past and contemporary contexts. This knowledge base, most importantly, is then commingled with agency creative intuition that is inspired toward advertising solutions. According to O'Donohoe[36] and Scott,[37] advertising is 'the literature of consumption' and the consumer-interpreters of advertisements rely on the com-municative data, including images and words, to meaningfully make sense of advertising texts. This interpretive ability has been coined 'advertising literacy.'[38] To be effective, the communicative logic informing advertising literacy draws on the same historical and cultural reservoir shared by consumers and advertising creators.

Considering the Warner's campaign on a broader plane, what is the social effect of advertising and its communication events? How does a campaign affect culture? Can advertising challenge our attitudes or change our values? Ritson and Elliott[39] claim that academic research in advertising theory has 'tended to ignore the social dimension of advertising in favor of an emphasis on the solitary subject.' They maintain that the subject of advertising research has been and remains the sole individual whose psyche is probed for critical input on how one processes meaning inherent in an ad to establish how well an ad might work to sell a particular product. Consequently, 'advertising research has generally ignored the social uses that emerge from advertising reception.' Using participant observation and interviews with high school students in England, they found that these teens used ads as a common currency to learn what was up to date and useful 'to fit in.' Particularly revered ads served a 'phatic function' defining common themes that framed later social interactions between the students. This 'phatic function' has been operational in advertising throughout the twentieth century.

Ads turn our heads by first appealing to what we want to become and then help tell us what to buy and where to buy it. While many consumers strive for distinctions of class by shopping in upstairs stores to acquire high-status brands, it is not the excess of material acquisition that is problematic in this narrative, but the latent puritanical legacy that defines sex and eroticism as lower-class attractions. The Warner's campaign helped to remove the lower-class stigma attached to provocative erotic lingerie. Also, the self-service concept (when downstairs crept upstairs) that revolutionized bra marketing and consumer selection became part of retail's evolution in a transforming 'servicescape' that makes shopping a pleasurable experience which increasingly involves entertainment to engage us in the hunt for our products.[40] Holbrook's assessment of the democratization of the entertainment cultural hierarchy is appropriate to our once 'unsanitary' innovation for the upstairs bra market. At the time, self-service in the bra industry also represented:

> a breakdown in the once-prevalent cultural hierarchy; the effacement of the boundaries . . . [and] the blurring of the distinctions between high culture and popular culture; the widely observed promiscuous cross-fertilization in which highbrow art [or shopping style] has climbed into bed with lowbrow pursuits, in which the division between class and mass has disappeared, in which the once refined world of serious culture has embraced the dirty detritus of everyday life.[41]

Warner's open merchandising for intimate apparel is now so much a part of our shopping experience that we take it for granted. A generation of women has matured not knowing that buying bras was once an intimate affair. Brassieres were so provocative as not to be visible at the point of purchase and it was considered indecent to reveal bras through our clothing. Over time cultural values change and intimate apparel has now become public spectacle.

Notes

1. Identities of advertising agency and personnel and clients' personnel have been altered for anonymity.
2. Twitchell (1996), Sherry (1987: 447, 441).
3. See Barthel (1988), Gold (1987), Goldman (1992), Lears (1994), Marchand (1985), Scanlon (1995), Schudson (1984) for critiques of advertising's evolving nexus with gender, class and status in the US.
4. Olsen (1989, 1997).
5. Tedlock (1991: 77–8).
6. Gummesson (2001: 37).

7. Barthel (1988: 123).
8. Fields (2001), Fontnel (1997).
9. 'The American figure: Bigger, bustier,' *Women's Wear Daily*, National Survey, 2 November 1972, p. 23.
10. 'A firmer foundation for bra and girdle departments,' *Clothes*, 11: 45–6, 15 January 1977. The apparel industry distinguishes downstairs stores from upstairs department stores as the latter carry more expensive brands and cater to an upscale clientele.
11. Vermehren (1997: 198–9).
12. Koda (2001: 53).
13. Harris (1968: 571).
14. Tedlock (1991: 77–8).
15. While traditional anthropological research studies an exotic other, in this case the Other was the brassiere customer.
16. Moeran (1996: 142). Moeran's agency recognized three audiences for Ikon Breath O_2 breathable contact lenses, the manufacturer-client, the user-consumer, and the medical profession (doctors and ad regulators).
17. Brady (1971: 17).
18. Moeran (2001: 279–80). It is not unusual to begin with a portion of a client's account creating sales promotions with an eye on obtaining the more lucrative advertising business in the future.
19. Hertz (1972: 20).
20. Levine (1972: 17).
21. Tedlock (1991: 72).
22. *Women's Wear Daily*, *Cosmopolitan* magazine ad, 14 March 1974.
23. Perutz (1970: 18).
24. Vestergaard and Schroder (1985: 74, 88, 89). The article which they cite is by Jones (1982).
25. Nachman (2000).
26. Barthel (1988: 124).
27. Olsen (1995, 2000).
28. 'Discount stores reaching more people: MRI/DuPont study probes consumer attitudes and preferences,' *Hosiery and Underwear*, 56: 36–7, October 1973.
29. 'Sales help: May I Help You . . . Help You . . . Help You,' *Clothes*, 12: 22–8, 15 August 1977.
30. I am grateful to John McCreery for this insight.
31. Fields (2001: 127).
32. Valdivia (1997: 229, 239, 241).
33. Valdivia (1997: 239).
34. Hackley (2002: 212).
35. Hackley (2002: 215).

36. O'Donohoe (2000: 151).
37. Scott (1994).
38. O'Donohoe (2001) and Ritson and Elliott (1995).
39. Ritson and Elliott (1999: 260, 262, 266).
40. See Miller (1998), Rappaport (2000) and Sherry (1998).
41. Holbrook (2001: 156).

References

Barthel, D. 1988 *Putting on Appearances: Gender and Advertising*, Philadelphia, PA: Temple University Press.
Brady, K. 1971 'Foundations makers are waiting for orders,' *Women's Wear Daily*, 2 December, p. 17.
Fields, J. 2001 '"Fighting the corsetless evil": Shaping corsets and culture, 1900–1930,' in P. Scranton (ed.) *Beauty and Business: Commerce, Gender, and Culture in Modern America*, pp. 109–40, London: Routledge.
Fontanel, B. 1997 *Support and Seduction: The History of Corsets and Bras*, New York: Harry N. Abrams.
Gold, P. 1987 *Advertising, Politics, and American Culture: From Salesmanship to Therapy*, New York: Paragon House Publishers.
Goldman, R. 1992 *Reading Ads Socially*, London: Routledge.
Gummesson, E. 2001 'Are current research approaches in marketing leading us astray?,' *Marketing Theory*, 1 (1): 27–48.
Hackley, C. 2002 'The panoptic role of advertising agencies in the production of consumer culture,' *Consumption Markets and Culture*, 5 (3): 211–29.
Harris, M. 1968 *The Rise of Anthropological Theory*, New York: Thomas Y. Crowell.
Hertz, E. 1972 'The yes and no of manufacturers' display racks,' *Women's Wear Daily*, 20 July, p. 20.
Holbrook, M. 2001 'Time Square, Disneyphobia, HegeMickey, the Ricky Principle, and the downside of the entertainment economy: It's fun-dumb-mental,' *Marketing Theory*, 1 (2): 139–63.
Jhally, S. 1990 *The Codes of Advertising: Fetishism and the Political Economy of Meaning in the Consumer Society*, London: Routledge.
Jones, B. 1982 'How we grew along with you,' *Cosmopolitan*, March.
Koda, H. 2001 *Extreme Beauty: The Body Transformed*, New York: The Metropolitan Museum of Art.
Lears, J. 1994 *Fables of Abundance: A Cultural History of Advertising in America*, New York: Basic Books.
Levine, B. 1972 'Display essential, all agree, but how?,' *Women's Wear Daily*, 27 July, p. 17.

Marchand, R. 1985 *Advertising the American Dream: Making Way for Modernity, 1920–1940*, Berkeley: University of California Press.

Miller, D. 1998 *A Theory of Shopping*, Ithaca: Cornell University Press.

Moeran, B. 1996 *A Japanese Advertising Agency: An Anthropology of Media and Markets*, Honolulu: University of Hawaii Press.

—— 2001 'Promoting culture: The work of a Japanese advertising agency,' in B. Moeran (ed.) *Asian Media Productions*, pp. 270–91, London: Curzon.

Nachman, B. 2000 'Bras battle for attention,' http: //enquirer.com/editions/2000/05/17/loc_bras_battle_for.html

O' Donohoe, S. 2000 'Reading advertising texts, understanding advertising consumption,' in S.C. Beckmann and R.H. Elliott (eds) *Interpretive Consumer Research*, pp. 151–75, Copenhagen, DK: Copenhagen Business School Press.

—— 2001 'Living with ambivalence: attitudes to advertising in post-modern times,' *Marketing Theory*, 1 (1): 91–108.

Olsen, B. 1989 'The personal and social costs of development in Negril, Jamaica, West Indies, 1971–1988,' PhD thesis, New School for Social Research.

—— 1995 'Brand loyalty and consumption patterns: The lineage factor,' in J.F. Sherry Jr (ed.) *Contemporary Marketing and Consumer Behavior: An Anthropological Sourcebook*, pp. 245–81, London: Sage.

—— 1997 'Environmentally sustainable development and tourism: Lessons from Negril, Jamaica,' *Human Organization*, 56 (3): 285–94.

—— 2000 'Sourcing elitist attitudes in early advertising from the archives,' in *Advances in Consumer Research*, Provo, UT, 27: 295–300.

Perutz, K. 1970 *Beyond the Looking Glass: America's Beauty Culture*, New York: William Morrow.

Rappaport, E. 2000 *Shopping for Pleasure: Women in the Making of London's West End*, Princeton, NJ: Princeton University Press.

Ritson, M. and R. Elliott 1995 'A model of advertising literacy: The praxiology and co-creation of advertising meaning,' in M. Bergadaa (ed.) *Proceedings of the 24th Conference of the European Marketing Academy*, pp. 1035–54, Paris: ESSEC.

—— 1999 'The social uses of advertising: An ethnographic study of adolescent advertising audiences,' *Journal of Consumer Research*, 26 (3): 260–77.

Scanlon, J. 1995 *Inarticulate Longings: The 'Ladies' Home Journal,' Gender, and the Promises of Consumer Culture*, London: Routledge.

Schudson, M. 1984 *Advertising, the Uneasy Persuasion: Its Dubious Impact on American Society*, New York: Basic Books.

Scott, L. 1994 'The bridge from text to mind: adapting reader-response theory to consumer research,' *Journal of Consumer Research*, 21 (December): 461–80.

Sherry, J. Jr 1987 'Advertising as a cultural system,' in J. Umiker-Sebeok (ed.) *Marketing and Semiotics: New Directions in the Study of Signs for Sale*, pp. 441–61, New York: Mouton de Gruyter.

—— (ed.) 1998 *ServiceScapes: The Concept of Place in Contemporary Markets*, Chicago, IL: NTC Business Books.

Tedlock, B. 1991 'From participant observation to the observation of participation: The emergence of narrative ethnography,' *Journal of Anthropological Research*, 47 (1): 69–94.

Twitchell, J. 1996 *AdCult USA: The Triumph of Advertising in American Culture*, New York: Columbia University Press.

Valdivia, A.N. 1997 'The secret of my desire: Gender, class, and sexuality in lingerie catalogs,' in K.T. Frith (ed.) *Undressing the Ad: Reading Culture in Advertising*, pp. 225–47, New York: Peter Lang.

Vermehren, C. 1997 'Cultural capital: The cultural economy of U.S. advertising,' in K.T. Frith (ed.) *Undressing the Ad: Reading Culture in Advertising*, pp. 197–224, New York: Peter Lang.

Vestergaard, T. and K. Schroder 1985 *The Language of Advertising*, Oxford: Blackwell.

-6-

Models, Metaphors and Client Relations: The Negotiated Meanings of Advertising
Timothy D. Malefyt

The world of advertising, like much of human activity, is socially constructed. While some cast advertising as a cold calculated monolith that dictates consumer choice or coerces consumers with brand manipulation,[1] I will present advertising as a hot-blooded activity performed by a range of people. We eventually witness the ads that arrive on television, outdoor billboards, radio, in print magazines or on the Internet, but the way they get there is through carefully staged social interaction between an advertising agency and its corporate client. In the world of art production, Howard Becker[2] has shown how a network of people cooperates in various ways to produce art. In a similar fashion, my discussion continues along the lines of Brian Moeran[3] and Michael Schudson[4] who contend that the world of advertising must be treated as a social process, not a product. The process of ad production that I show is one directed by key members of an agency, not so much at the brand, consumer or even rival agencies, but towards the client. Because the marketing world in which advertising operates is so uncertain and unstable, the value placed on managing impressions and directing human relations is at an all time high. This becomes apparent as this paper examines the tenuous nature of relations between advertising agencies and their corporate clients and the ways in which agencies attempt to moderate the tension.

Advertising agencies face a number of uncertain elements, any one of which can potentially derail a campaign, or even an agency. At various stages of production ads are shaped by the collective efforts of teams, groups and key individuals who influence others. Agency account planners, account executives and client brand managers develop research ideas; agency teams write the advertising creative brief; copywriters and art directors sketch the ads; media teams then place the ads. This sequence of production, however, is anything but smooth and continuous. It is one that progresses in jumps and starts, from inspirational meetings to setbacks in acquiring music, talent, or the right media placement for a particular ad. Brilliant strategies are created only to be altered later to accommodate the wishes of contentious clients, rushed deadlines or legal restrictions. Not infrequently, strategies are dropped altogether in mid development and new ones taken up.

Exacerbating the situation, as Moeran and Daniel Miller point out, competition among agencies over client accounts is fierce, precisely at a time when client loyalty is at an all time low. In this light, the advertising process reveals more a state of precarious uncertainty than one of calculated precision.

To mitigate this situation, advertising executives attempt to direct and control as much of the interaction with their client as possible. Beyond the multiple daily interactions that service a client's account, key individuals from the agency join on certain occasions with the client to negotiate the aims, means and direction the advertising should take. Especially in the early stages of developing ad strategies, concepts about what a brand means, what appeals to consumers and the nature of the competitive marketplace are debated. These occasions are commonly called brainstorming sessions but are referred to in the following case study as strategic brand workshops.

Workshops are occasioned by a new relationship with a client, either after winning a pitch or after having been assigned a new business opportunity from an existing client. In both cases, new teams from the advertising agency and corporate client are brought together under, perhaps, the most stressful of expectations. These events are not only explicitly charged with an objective of finding a differentiating insight to drive the brand, target consumer and market position, but also implicitly contribute to assessing the interpersonal dynamics among the personalities assembled. Under such heightened conditions, the art of negotiation takes place.

This stressful condition arrives from the fact that the world of consumption in which agencies operate is never neutral; it is about power and position. Agencies must seek, in the words of sociologist Erving Goffman,[5] an advantage of position from which they can assess or define the situation and react accordingly. Along these lines, Mary Douglas and Baron Isherwood note that social life is a matter of alignments where goods have social purposes, 'they can be used as bridges or fences.'[6] In the world of advertising, information over goods, such as their meaning and use by consumers, becomes a particular form of power. Those who are able to control access to information seek a monopoly advantage in their position. Since the world of advertising revolves around relations with the client, power for an agency resides not in the actual production of goods, but in the shaping or 'producing' of information about those goods. It is therefore to an agency's advantage to manage information about the client's brand and consumer, or at least, manage an impression of the information, so as to present the best 'front' as possible to the client.

The brand workshop offers an ideal setting in which to analyze the ways an agency manages strategies in building relationships with its corporate client. An agency must manage information while it seeks to foster affinity so as not to put its client off. To accomplish this an agency faces a particular dilemma or double bind, a concept identified by anthropologist Gregory Bateson.[7] On the one hand the agency has to present itself as competent in a service or skill that is perceived by the client to 'add value.'[8] At the same time, an agency places a premium on human chemistry,[9] and so must demonstrate to the client that working together will be amicable, cooperative and mutually beneficial. This presents a challenge to negotiation since it requires one to stand apart as distinct, and yet blend in and show affinity with others. This paper analyzes and illustrates the specific ways in which an agency attempts to achieve both ends, using particular styles of impression management, symbolic representations and figurative language in the process.

To highlight the importance of negotiation, I situate my study in a small New York ad agency. Dynamics here are different from those of larger agencies, since members of high rank and different function have a greater opportunity to interact. With accounts that are typically smaller in size and with fewer people involved, the entire negotiation process happens more quickly. This study presents the occasion of a brainstorming workshop when an agency has been recently assigned the task of developing a brand position for a new liquor product called Smirkov (a pseudonym). In the analysis, I draw from my experience as an anthropologist employed in account planning over the past five years to show how the art of negotiation and managing impressions are central to the long-term success of an agency.

In looking at how negotiations can be directed by an agency, I take a symbolic and sociolinguistic view. In particular, I explore the way symbolic representations and conversational style can be used as tools to mediate interaction between and among people. The context of the workshop serves as a guide to show how agency people strategically direct much of the negotiation process to achieve certain ends, rather than leaving client negotiation open to chance. In so doing, this paper aims to show that any business meeting supports unspoken strategic implications for participants that transcend the apparent functional motives of information exchange. Meetings give the appearance that they are guided by practical aims and reason when they really facilitate relationship negotiations, struggle for positions, and commentary.[10] By this I mean that the agency's intentions are not realized in the rational exchange of information about brands and consumers. Rather, they become apparent in the subtle interpersonal dynamics that occur between people when they are carrying out specific tasks. In other words, the workshop offers a view into the type of interaction and devices used by the agency to build client rapport. Goffman[11] termed this type of interaction 'impression management,' a concept and practice examined throughout this study. I hope to illustrate how impression management is more important to building relations with clients than are the stated goals of developing brand strategies and consumer targets.

From an objective viewpoint, the workshop appears to offer an ideal way for an agency and client to collectively identify a position in a highly competitive marketplace. It is also an ideal place for an agency to demonstrate its expertise and knowledge of the client's brand and consumer. The agency typically does this by bringing out its proprietary tools to position the client's brand. Models of the client's target consumer are constructed, and colorful aggressive language typically circulates in heated discussions about the competition. But while the stated purpose of the workshop is for the agency to gain a closer understanding of the client's consumer, brand and competition, I claim the true purpose is to convince the client of the value of entering into a union of collaboration and to build relations of affinity. In fact, the proprietary tools demonstrated by the agency and the metaphoric language used to deride the competition, are devices intended to structure relationships and cement loyalties between the agency and client, rather than provide the client strategic direction or enhance their market position.

In this regard, we might consider advertising as a two-stage process of persuasion. First, an agency has to persuade a prospective client to embark on a relation of affinity through its images (creative sketches/marketing models) and rhetorical language (metaphors). Second, the client and agency have to persuade consumers about products and brands with advertised images and persuasive language. This study examines the former stage, where the brand or product is the agency and its capital (its people, ideas, reputation). This paper intends to show how communicative styles – based on proprietary models and figurative language – are powerful tools an agency uses to demonstrate its competence and win support from a client.

The Uncertain World of Advertising Today

The marketing world in which advertising agencies contend is as uncertain and unstable as ever. Increased competition among agencies over new and existing accounts has led to what some have termed a battle to capture the consumer's 'share of mind.'[12] Concerned about losing market share to rival companies, agencies may increase spending on consumer advertising even in declining markets. But they do so for reasons that often have more to do with 'defensive strategies' than gains in consumer margins.[13] The marketing climate breeds an environment of such intense competition that agencies and marketers may lose focus on the consumer and fixate on rival firms.[14]

Competition among rival agencies is not the only reason for uncertainty today. Client loyalty is not what it used to be. The average length of any given contract commitment between an agency and client has dropped precipitously in recent years. What once was an average commitment of eleven years in the US has now dipped to around two and a half years.[15] The disastrous events of 11 September 2001 have only exacerbated conditions. Overall advertising spending among corporations in the US has declined by 7 per cent, the worst decline in forty years. As a consequence, the top 200 US agencies in 2001 eliminated 21,750 jobs.

Agencies are therefore desperate to maintain current relationships with clients as they continue to seek new ones.

To cope with increased competition and rising marketplace instability advertising agencies have figured out ways to attract new accounts while retaining existing clients. An agency cannot simply rely on its reputation. It has to position itself as offering the client something of added value, such as its proprietary marketing approach that differentiates it from rivals. For instance, D'Arcy Masius Benton & Bowles boasts its 'Brand Leadership' model, while Saatchi and Saatchi claims it is the 'Idea' agency. Advertising agencies in effect resemble their advertised brands in how they market their competitive advantage to attract and retain their first customer – the client. To appropriate a cliché made famous by Leo Burnett, it's no longer the sizzle of the steak that sells; now what sells is the sizzle of an agency.

Account Planning Sizzle

Making an agency sizzle, especially in the early stages of building client relations, is increasingly a function of the account planning department. Account planning helps generate new business by demonstrating an agency's strategic competency through its proprietary marketing approaches and brand and consumer models. As corporations increasingly turn their attention to research that plumbs the depths of consumers' relationships to products and brands, account planning becomes central to bringing the client's brand and consumer to life.

The planner's role in adding value to the agency has become important because consumer focus has taken center stage in the marketing world. Exploring consumer relations to products began in the 1950s, when research shifted from focusing on more mundane functional statistics of marketing to understanding consumers' desires and in relation to products. Probing the inner world of consumer thought reveals the more imaginative properties of the brand than demographic numbers, and provides marketers with a richer source for inspiring creative and effective advertising.[16] Current marketing literature is replete with consumer-focused books that offer how-to guides on targeting the inner world of consumers.[17] The planner's task in all of this is to unlock the rich inner world and discover consumers' hidden emotional connections to products and brands.

Account planning came to the US from Britain in the 1970s – first to a handful of shops before its epidemic spread. Contrary to earlier advertising research practices, which took consumer feedback more as a last minute check on creative work, account planning incorporates consumer input into every stage of the advertising process, from initial idea to finished execution. In this way account planners are said to bolster advertising's emotional connection to consumers by acting as 'partners' with them.[18] By hiring psychologists, anthropologists or even hypnotists, whose techniques include psychoanalysis, in-home ethnography, hypnotism and metaphor analysis, planners probe the emotional depths of consumers for insights.

Nevertheless, even with the help of the latest technique, discovering the 'right' consumer insight can be a daunting task. Planners must creatively interpret consumers per the research in ways that make it meaningful and relevant to the client's brand. The account planning director of DDB in England exclaims, '[planners] can't just discover a brand's heart and replay that in the advertising – we have to create a whole new truth or future for the brand, inventing a fresh relationship between [the brand] and the consumer.'[19] Thus planners must not only make the consumer come alive from research, but conjure up creative ways to make research insights relevant to the brand. If the planner cannot discover a compelling insight or brand truth, he or she may just resort to inventing one.

The planner's role as 'insight' expert brings us back to the purpose of the workshop. It is during workshop meetings that planners best demonstrate their persuasive skills, creatively positioning the agency's strategic thinking and proprietary research tools in ways that add value for the client. Planners demonstrate their value not only in the insightful analysis they yield to the client, but also in the particular language they use with the client. Since most clients tend to be marketers themselves and are more comfortable dealing with the language of strategy than of advertising, they often identify more easily with an agency's planner than with its account or creative person.[20] Indeed, it is the way in which insights are communicated and presented to the client that is vital for creating connections, rather than marketing facts about the client's consumer, brand or competition. By presenting proprietary models that engage social interaction and by expressing ideas in a language that evokes shared emotion, the agency hopes to draw the client deeper into long-term relations of affinity.

The Workshop

A number of elements are involved in the workshop that allow the agency to present an impression of itself to the client. As Goffman notes, when an individual or group enters the presence of another in the framework of a social establishment, many sources of information become accessible as 'sign-vehicles' to carry an impression.[21] The particular bounded space of the off-site setting itself, the careful agenda the agency sets before the client, the planned activities of model-building and brand charting, and the figurative language used in discussion. All these elements combine to set the stage for a performance that will ensure the right impression of competency while creating a closer affinity between the agency and client.

Workshop Setting

Brand workshops are frequently held 'off site, for instance at a nearby full-service hotel or resort. The remote setting removes daily distractions of phone, personal interruptions and meetings and provides an open environment where participants can think freely and speak casually. As the agency invitation states: 'members will share a common goal in a casual setting, so that cooperation and teamwork will build towards the larger good of the corporation.' New creative ideas are expected to flourish in a neutral territory or 'liminal zone.'[22] The meeting thus appears to promise an ideal setting in which the agency can liaise with the client. Nevertheless, while the agenda calls for a casual roll-up-the-sleeves, let's-all-work-together type of affair, it is anything but carefree and relaxed. As Huizinga[23] reminds us, even the apparent carefree nature of play involves rules of engagement that underlie intentions to win.

In a less obvious and more deliberate sense, the remote locale offers an ideal 'stage' from which the agency can best perform its routine before a captive client audience. To the fullest extent possible, the agency seeks to control the setting thereby maximizing the effectiveness of its impression on others. Weeks prior to the workshop date, strategic goals are predetermined, a tight agenda is scheduled, and documents are prepared for brand, consumer and competitive analysis.

The Workshop Agenda

Agency planners have arrived a day earlier to set up their stage. A series of task stations are carefully arranged around the periphery of the room. The center of the room is made comfortable to accommodate the collective group. Couches and lounge chairs open to the front where a large blank positioning map is posted on the wall. The space is thus divided in such a way as to allow individuals to move around the room in small teams and members to regroup in a center region for open discussion.

The workshop begins promptly at 8.00 a.m. and will last the full day. Eight executives from the ad agency are invited, including the account group director, two senior account managers, two creatives (an art director and copywriter), the director of account planning, and two senior planners (including myself). From the client side, eight attendees include two senior brand managers, a vice-president and key people from logistics, sales and distribution. This range of top management is ostensibly selected to add differing views and raise the likelihood of divergent 'new' thinking. But, from the agency's view, key people are brought together who can make a clear impact on fostering agency–client relations. Part of the agency's attempt to control the situation involves minimizing interaction that might contradict, discredit or disrupt the flow of engagement. As much as possible, the eight people from the agency are intentionally matched in symmetry of position, skill and personal interest to the eight client members in attempt to build a harmonious 'working consensus.'[24]

After an informal breakfast, the agency's director of account planning, John, takes center stage and invites everyone to gather in the center of the room to listen to the day's agenda. It is clear that he will act as moderator, and will guide the multiple tasks that people will be engaged in throughout the day. The three work sections include 'knowing our consumer,' 'rebranding Smirkov,' and 'mapping a strategic position.' For each section a specific task will be assigned that requires the corroborative work of client and agency in teams. As moderator, John will float through the team assignments to answer questions on specific tasks, but also to joke, liaise and make everyone feel comfortable.

John explains that there will be a briefing to refresh the teams on key points prior to each breakout section and before they engage in the task at hand. For the first two tasks, the teams are assigned to take the information provided by the briefings and create models of the consumer and brand. Each team will make its models, and then present its findings to the entire group, after which the best model will be voted for and selected. The third task will be a collective effort, whereby the entire group will map a strategic position for the Smirkov brand.

The first section, 'knowing our consumer,' begins with an overview of the Smirkov target. The agency has invited a practicing psychologist to give a psychological profile of the typical consumer. He begins by discussing the 'needs' of a typical male youth, aged 21–25, from an emotional, life-stage point of view. He explains that the youth is in transition, moving from a state of youthful play and rebellion into an adult role of responsibility. The psychologist reports that the youth is in need of transitional objects to help form attachments as he makes the move. He implicates Smirkov as an ideal source of attachment for the searching youth. While the client is aware that the agency has hired a psychologist to present a need-state description, they may not be aware that the agency is briefed on the psychologist's 'findings' before the meeting begins. This detail importantly provides the agency a chance to plan how information will be used in the workshop.

The group then breaks out into assigned teams and each team moves to a different task station around the room. The first task is to apply the psychologist's learning and create a consumer model that will encompass the needs, values and benefits of the typical Smirkov consumer. Visually, the consumer model is shaped like a pyramid (see *Figure 2*). Filling in the pyramid is an effort that requires each team to jointly rank consumer benefits from general attributes to specific core values.

The uncomplicated design of the model makes it widely used by other agencies, and stems from the fact that marketers share a common belief about human

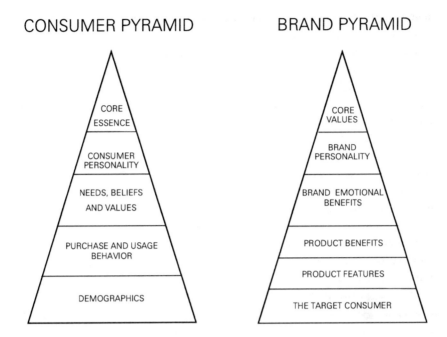

Figure 2 Consumer models.

motivations for products. Psychology is the favored analytical framework that permeates marketers' perceptions of consumer motivation (see Sunderland and Denny, this volume). Consumer selection of a product or brand is thought to be driven by certain psychological needs. In popular marketing belief, consumers are thought to act upon the world of consumption fulfilling certain individual drives intrinsic to them.[25] Maslow's hierarchy of needs (*Figure 3*) is popular because this simple ranking allows marketers to match human needs to a particular brand benefit. The effect of ranking consumer needs is to lend an air of scientific credibility to the task, while allowing marketers to break down complex consumer behavior into simple units of analysis. The matching of models to human need-state descriptions has another benefit: the activity facilitates social interaction and teamwork that builds consensus in the process.[26] So while the making of models may reduce and overly simplify otherwise complex human behavior, their construction facilitates cooperation and a sense of affinity between an agency and client.

After completion of the task about an hour later, the teams reconvene in the center of the room to discuss the models they have created. Each team has appointed a leader to present his or her consumer model to the entire group. The teams, comprised of agency and client members, compete over who has created the

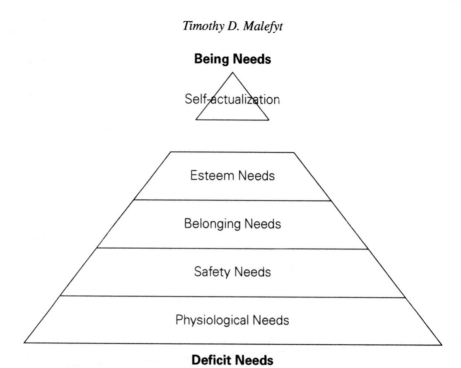

Figure 3 Maslow's Hierarchy of Needs.

best model of a consumer. Team members rally in support of each other and for their leader against other teams, and so strategic personal alliances are made between agency and client members in front of others. It is hoped these brief alliances will carry over into normal working relations.

The group as a whole then votes on which model best represents its target consumer. While others debate the appropriate consumer need, the decision is actually determined by the client vice-president who highlights 'social confidence' as the appropriate human need for Smirkov. In other words, in an environment that is intended to feel cooperative and free, group consensus ultimately yields to top management decisions. The director of account planning supports the VP's claim, so that the client stands out for his 'insight' in front of all present. The stage has been set to direct compliments to those deemed most important. The agency has not only directed the flow of information, but has also directed the flow of recognition that will hopefully pay off in renewed client loyalty and support.

Deconstructing the Brand

After a short break, participants are called to the center of the room to listen to a briefing on the brand. This topic of discussion is led by the brand manager of

Smirkov rather than by an outside expert. He reviews the liquor brand, summarizing statistics of market position, volume sold, primary distribution channels, brand image, and so forth. After the briefing, each team is assigned the task of creating a brand pyramid in an exercise similar to the one previously completed. Charged with a new assignment, the teams head for their respective stations and begin to discuss the brand in detail.

Teams start by ranking the brand according to attributes, benefits and values that match the target consumer's need-states identified in the previous exercise. In building the brand model, team discussions center on matching a particular brand benefit or attribute with the consumer need it satisfies. The consumer is the point of reference by which brand components are matched. The brand model is thus constructed out of corresponding consumer wants and needs, so that, in effect, one model becomes a composite mirror of the other.

After an hour of building brand models, the teams reconvene in the center to present their findings to the entire group. An agency account executive describes the brand's role as that of a social lubricant, fulfilling the target's emotional need for 'fitting in' socially. Other members concur and the group arrives at an agreement on the brand's role as social connector. In the discussion, though, it is again the client who finally decides on the brand's image. The vice-president agrees that the brand image of Smirkov should be that of a social connector. Up to this point an impression of cooperation has been reached. The collective activities have served to enhance the overall relations between the agency and client, and so the performance of the workshop, so far, has proceeded successfully.

Mapping and Owning a Human Need

The third and probably the most important task of the day is the collective mapping of a brand position for Smirkov. Having identified Smirkov's core essence as social connector and as fulfilling a consumer need for social confidence, the agency and client must now agree upon a strategic position for the brand that distinguishes it from rival brands. The mapping exercise is the final task of the day, and the one that causes the most debate among the participants assembled. For the agency, this is the real opportunity to demonstrate its marketing savvy while bringing about affinity. The agency's director of account planning must at once invite participation in leading the discussion, as well as guide the conversation in a way that is fruitful for the client's brand.

John begins this process by asserting his authority and market knowledge. He assumes dramatic and directive dominance by presenting another model that will integrate the information from the previous exercises. By introducing the Consumer Needs Map as a new strategic device to incorporate all the previous learning

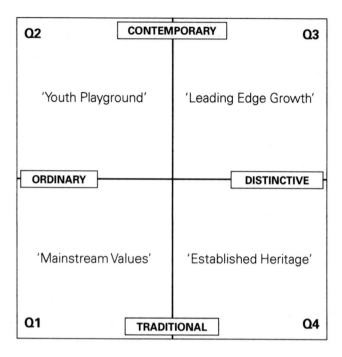

Q2 CONTEMPORARY	Q3
'Youth Playground'	'Leading Edge Growth'
ORDINARY	DISTINCTIVE
'Mainstream Values'	'Established Heritage'
Q1 TRADITIONAL	Q4

Figure 4 Consumer Needs Map.

(see *Figure 4*), John intends to control and channel the information that has been circulating, while fostering an impression of cooperation and team building by requiring the input from others.

The consumer needs map that John presents is specific to the US alcoholic beverage market, and is one of the agency's own design. The map segments the market by drinking occasions on the basis of two consumer variables: ordinary versus distinctive needs, and traditional versus contemporary needs. The division of the map into four quadrants provides a landscape on which spirit categories and the competitive brands are plotted according to the social and personal needs they fulfill for consumers. Each quadrant of the map represents a defined territory of consumer values from which marketers collectively select an ideal position for their brand. As Brian Moeran notes, marketers typically use binary types of classification to explain the numerous forms and, apparently arbitrary nature, of consumer behavior.[27] The map, in other words, offers marketers a total 'view' of the consumers' emotional territories they want to 'own' as well as the consumer 'territories' occupied by rival brands.

John once again leads the discussion. He claims quadrant one represents 'Mainstream Values,' where domestic beer and bargain gin, scotch and Canadian blends provide liquor consumers with the most alcohol for the least amount of money.

This territory is described as fulfilling the basic consumer need for social acceptance and ease of drink. John then discusses quadrant two as a 'Youth Playground,' where consumers' social need for excitement, experimentation and rebellion are fulfilled by the consumption of drinks such as tequila, shooters, cordials and flavored rums. He then describes the third quadrant as the realm of deluxe brands, such as single malt scotches, quality vodkas and gins. These spirits ostensibly satisfy the consumer's need for discrimination, individuality and achievement. John then details the fourth quadrant as a domain for brands of classic status. He states that only the most premium brands of scotch, cognacs and champagnes belong here.

The mapping exercise is new to the client and John's description of the consumer territories causes great consternation over where best to situate the Smirkov brand. Quadrant one is agreed to be too basic and low-end for Smirkov. The fourth quadrant is also dismissed since it has been associated with classic brands long established, and so would not be appropriate for a new spirit that appeals to a youth market. Dismissing this quadrant also eliminates the threat from more classic brands of spirits, since Smirkov does not want to own 'classic' consumer values.

From John's description, quadrant two appears ideal for situating the Smirkov brand since this area appeals to an upscale youthful image. But the third quadrant is also pointed out as offering an ideal territory for situating a premium brand. John and the vice-president of marketing decide on a point midway between quadrants two and three as the ideal position for Smirkov. John points out that this area is currently unoccupied by rivals and so best provides an opportunity to satisfy the target's aspiration for social connection. Other members concur on this new position for the brand, one they claim is distinct from rivals'. Since no other brand can offer the consumer the same social benefits of 'fitting in,' the agency and client feel they have reached a unique and ownable brand position for Smirkov.

Following this day of intense work, with heated discussions over building models and mapping a brand, the agency and client celebrate by having dinner out together. Dinner is the final episode and serves to tie up loose ends. The agency can feel confident of having conveyed the right impression of itself to the client while having strengthened ties of affinity. The agency has not only demonstrated its competence, but also corroborated with the client in discovering a unique and ownable position for the Smirkov brand.

Discussion

The dynamic that underlies any strategic meeting between an advertising agency and its client is one in which we can view the subtleties of directed communication in play. Within the framework of a brand workshop, a team of performers (the agency) cooperates to present to its audience (the client) a given 'definition of a situation.' We can examine how the making of maps and models and the use of linguistic styles can facilitate personal connections from a symbolic and pragmatic perspective. Each mode of communication reveals how the agency, intentionally and unintentionally, manages impressions to build affinity and demonstrate its competence. What appears as friendly cooperation and lively discussion aimed at carving out a brand identity is more likely social communication that is symbolically and pragmatically directed to achieve certain ends.

Maps and Models of Equivalence[28]

Along symbolic lines, the mapping of strategic positions and the making of consumer and brand models illustrate the way marketers collectively imagine their consumer domain. Mapping, in this sense, becomes a powerful strategic tool for creating affinity. Benedict Anderson notes the historical importance of mapping to the colonial British rule of India. Maps and charts provided the empire with a totalizing classificatory grid; one that could be applied to anything and anyone under the state's control, including people, religions, languages, products and so forth. The effect was to create a bounded, determinate domain of 'total survey-ability,' at least in the imagination of its officials.[29] In a similar fashion, the human needs map on which marketers plot their brand creates an objective landscape of perfect visibility. It is a landscape on which marketers discuss, debate and imagine their brand and other brands relative to consumer 'facts' they have jointly created.

This activity plays a key role in building affinity. Transforming human motivations into objective marketing facts on the map is a way of ordering, containing and homogenizing them. Once turned into facts, they can be scrutinized, maneuvered and redefined to suit particular ends. Removed are the highs, the lows, and other idiosyncratic characteristics that distinguish actual human beings from the reconfigured abstract versions of the marketer's own design. Along the lines that Said laid out as the orientalists' project of the Middle East, numbers and objects become increasingly important to sustain the illusion or even create a reality in which countable abstractions of people's ideas, beliefs and behaviors become a controllable reality on paper.[30] The type of classification that maps and grids lay out helps marketers create a totalizing view, which not only scales back the uncontrollable variables of consumption but further reduces and simplifies the range of consumer behavior into 'manageable collections.'[31] Mapping thus allows the agency and client a means of collective imagining over a human subject, which in reality is unpredictable, uncontrollable and full of its own source of resisting, adapting or making irony of consumption.[32]

If maps work to help marketers jointly imagine, homogenize and contain their domain, the pyramid models of consumer and brand work another way. They pave a way for the agency to transform the consumer and brand into entities of comparable equalities. On a pragmatic level, constructing brand and consumer models collectively is a way for the agency to generate affinity with the client. On a more symbolic level, the intent of making models structurally equivalent and relationally dependent implies a degree of mutual complementarity between the agency and client, when none may naturally exist. The consumer and brand pyramids are constructed to be not only mirror images of one another but deliberately set off as structurally interdependent, so that the qualities of one enhance the qualities of the other. The structural equivalencies of the models provide marketers with a way of transposing the emotional characteristics of consumers onto the attributes and benefits of the brand. When human needs are ranked and ordered through a binary type of representation, they become structurally complementary to brand benefits that are correspondingly ranked and ordered.

This process operates from the principle that meaning is not intrinsic to a structure, but comes from comparative differences across structures. In the world of advertising, the values of consumer and brand gain relevance from their relationship to each other.[33] They take part in a system that Douglas and Isherwood call a 'world of goods.' Complementarity thus used by the agency as a tool to generate relevant relationships between brands and consumers tends to tacitly highlight a mutual association between the client and agency.[34] We can now understand why the agency not only creates models *for*, but *with* the client. The very act of making the brand and consumer into parallel and equal constructs suggests, in itself, a working relationship of mutual corroboration and dependency between client and agency.

On still another level, building models as equivalent is a way for the agency to gain control over the client. Douglas and Isherwood remind us that in the world of consumption, exchange is seldom transacted without interest or intent. Power resides in possessing information or control over access to information.[35] In our case, it is not the raw information about consumers and brands that wields power for the agency, but the way in which the meaning of that information is presented, understood and interpreted for the client. Goffman informs us that in order for any individual or group to direct the activity of another, power must be 'clothed in effective means of displaying it,' for it may have different effects depending on how it is dramatized.[36] For the agency to interpret the client's consumer and brand and 'clothe' the information in the agency's proprietary models is to seek an advantage over the client's own currency. The simplest way of infusing a brand with more excitement – especially if little is left to say about a client's brand – is by transforming it into a living mirror of the consumer.[37] To paraphrase McCreery's assertion, advertising can work like magic: if a totemic image can magically confer power to a 'primitive' clan, a pair of symmetrically constructed models can magically enliven a client's brand, if not the client itself.

Beyond viewing symbolic equivalencies as a way of building client relations, we can also examine the language of workshops as a pragmatic means of managing impressions and directing relationships with the client. As such, the style of language exchanged during group discussions affects the quality and depth of personal and professional relationships the agency will have with its client.

Metaphors of War

Linguists inform us that in any conversation, the intentions of speakers are communicated through stylistic features of language that have less to do with what is being said, and more to do with how it is being said. To understand a speaker's message, we need to know how the words spoken are meant to be taken, that is, seriously, in jest or in some other way.[38] Figurative imagery and metaphor are just two stylistic features of a language's poetic function that help facilitate understanding and connection between people in conversation.[39] When, for example, a speaker utters the figurative phrase, 'once upon a time,' or starts a conversation with the familiar, 'did you hear the one about,' the listener typically prepares for a story to begin or for a joke be told, without knowing the particular content. In his analysis of art production, Becker refers to these as conventions, which provide the implicit rules of meaning and the basis on which participants can act together.[40] These rules, nonetheless, can be intentionally and unintentionally directed to achieve certain ends. The degree to which people communicate using stylistic features of speech is germane to our understanding of how agencies use metaphoric language to calibrate and maximize interaction with their clients.

Metaphors are intended to compel the feelings of an audience to move in certain directions. They are also purposefully ambiguous so that people become involved in making sense of them. So, for example, when expressed in battle hymns such as 'Onward Christian Soldiers,' metaphors rally participants to express militance in fighting against iniquity and are often put forth into action with accompanying ritual.[41] In our case, metaphors used in group discussions and team building exercises do not help clarify brand objectives or market positions, but, instead, rally feelings of affinity among all present. Exchanged in business meetings, metaphors are ideal devices for fostering emotional bonds when there may be little affinity to begin with.

Nevertheless, the figurative language with which the agency and client describe their domain is one that is not value free. It is hinged on a narrative metaphor that is meant to evoke strong sentiments among all present. Oddly enough, the type of metaphor spoken most freely in the workshop and the one most likely to muster feelings of affinity between agency and client is one about warfare.

Using the war metaphor, the director of account planning rallies participants by describing long-range marketing objectives in terms of 'targeting' the consumer and increasing market 'penetration.' He claims that taking a 'harder' look at the consumer data will 'strike the brand message home.' He offers a plan to 'increase market penetration' by 'aggressively growing the category in the summer' and 'stealing share defense in the winter.' He then stresses the need to 'take a stronger position against the competition' in an effort to 'shore up Smirkov's position and leverage the brand's equity.' The goal, he continues, is to achieve 'campaign objectives' by 'carving out' a unique 'brand territory' against the competition. After his speech, the participants respond with great enthusiasm.

Needless to say, the language of warfare does not terminate with the planning director's talk. During mapping exercises Smirkov's competition is wholly described as 'the enemy.' This view is further articulated in phrases such as 'getting wind' of the competition's marketing plan through 'field intelligence,' 'taking the high ground,' and 'leaving the enemy in the dust.' A team leader suggests using 'guerrilla' marketing to minimize the efforts of rivals. Guerrilla marketing involves implementing a marketing plan to counter the competition's efforts, such as saturating a local radio station with ads timed precisely during the airtime-run of a competitor, thereby diminishing or confusing the impact of the rival's message. Another suggestion is to launch a media 'blitz' event. The idea of blitzing is to provide a focused level of media spending, rather than spending over a broad time frame or in multiple markets. During idea generation exercises, the director of marketing instructs others to 'capture ideas' for those members 'MIA' (missing in action). One member suggests that the agency should conduct a SWOT analysis of the brand. Similar to SWAT which identifies a special operations police unit, SWOT is an acronym used in marketing to describe an exercise in which a brand's Strengths, Weaknesses, Opportunities and Threats are evaluated. The term itself describes a war-like attitude and a way of thinking about the brand and consumer that is aggressive, belligerent and competitive. We then move from 'strategic' to 'tactical' issues in discussing our campaign objectives, terms that also denote a warrior-like stance towards the consumer and competition. When a sales representative joins the discussion, he expresses the need for Smirkov to 'lock up' in-store shelf space 'against other players' to make our trade dollars 'work harder' for us.

Launching campaigns, striking the enemy and targeting the consumer are all military terms of conquest that an agency and client use to describe a war-like orientation towards the consumer and competition. But while aggressive talk is shared freely during meetings, it terminates abruptly when meetings pause or conclude altogether. During lunch or refreshment breaks when members chat more casually, no one describes his or her personal life in terms of launches, targets or blitzes. Indeed, while the exchange of metaphors may join the agency and client in feelings of affinity, it also separates and frames a certain 'us versus them' orientation towards the consumer. This flies in the face of marketing efforts that attempt to build trust, confidence and brand loyalty with the consumer. After years of this type of marketing, it comes as no surprise that consumers are wary and critical of marketers, since built into the very structure of marketing discourse is an implicit antagonism towards them.

While using metaphors of war in business meetings may seem counterproductive to connecting with consumers, they are ideal for creating affinity between the agency and client in three ways. The first has to do with the general familiarity of war to participants. War is a well-known domain for expressing a type of us-versus-them relation that is easily understandable to all involved. The rhetoric of war gives a semblance of mutual understanding, even when the specifics are vague. For example, most Americans support the US government's 'war on drugs' without knowing any of the specific steps taken. President Bush has evoked the war metaphor against the Taliban in terms of a battle of 'good versus evil.'

A second reason the war metaphor is so effective in building affinity comes from its use as a call to action. All participants in the group express affinity through a common vocabulary that summons them to concretize the 'enemy' brand or target consumer as whole entities. By expressing objectives through war metaphors, the agency does not have to specify the idiosyncratic differences of its brands, consumers or competition, but need only refer to a generalized essence of what they stand for. Without specific content that might be challenged or disputed, the consumer and competition become reduced to abstract constructs. Calls for 'clobbering the competition,' 'leaving the enemy in the dust' or 'targeting the consumer' thus become fuel for a collective imagination and the very subject of relationship building between the agency and client.

The third and perhaps most important reason for evoking the war metaphor is that it allows for corresponding metaphors of possession and containment. As a call to action for marketers, metaphors of war and pursuit are made complete by complementary metaphors of containment and capture. The idea that the consumer's mind is a receptacle in which meaning can be pursued and retrieved follows from the notion that meaning is a tangible entity that resides within humans. Our Western cultural assumptions often conceptualize the self as a vessel with the mind as a container. We commonly say, 'the lights are on,' or that one is 'out of his mind' to express either intelligence or lack thereof.[42] In branding lingo, marketers gather consumer 'insights' assuming they can access the mind as if it were a container in which to delve and retrieve 'facts.' The following offers one such description of the consumer as container for General Motor's automotive service brand, Mr. Goodwrench:

> A brand such as Mr. Goodwrench is much like a 'box' in someone's head. As information about GM service programs is received, a person will file it away in the box labeled Mr. Goodwrench. After time passes, little in the box might be retrievable. The person knows,

however, if it is heavy or light. He or she also knows in which room it is stored – the room with the positive boxes (that is, objects that have earned positive feelings and attitudes) or the one with the negative boxes.[43]

Understanding human experience in terms of tangible objects and quantifiable substances allows marketers to pick out parts of consumer behavior and treat them as discrete entities of a uniform kind. Once they can identify experiences and emotions as concrete entities, they can refer back to them, categorize them, group them and quantify them, and, by these means, reason about them.[44] So when consumer experiences are organized and labeled as human 'needs' and rendered into corresponding maps and models as brand 'insights,' they provide the agency and client with a way to collectively rank, order and manipulate behavior that otherwise is intangible, vague and largely unpredictable. The consumer and brand are thus not only discussed as subjects of pursuit, but become reified as objects of desire to be captured and contained. Indeed, this explains how the marketer's challenge to 'own' a particular product benefit or a consumer insight ahead of its rival becomes a marketing 'fact,' when the benefit or insight is made real from a discourse of the marketer's own design. Figurative expressions of war and capture are not mere expressions of an agency's concern over rival agencies.[45] Rather, they have a true purpose in making the consumer and competition living realities, which ultimately provide the agency and client with a powerful means for collective action.

Conclusion

From the foregoing discussion, we note how the agency's attempt to direct relations with the client has communicative purposes that can be studied along several dimensions. We've seen how affinity can be generated through practical efforts of directing individuals and groups in collective practices. Modes of communication can build bonds of unity by fostering symbolic relationships in models and maps, and by encouraging emotional bonds through the exchange of metaphors. In fact, as I have claimed, models of consumers and brands are not primarily intended to achieve a closer understanding of the consumer; nor is figurative language intended to vent an agency's anxiety over rival agencies, but rather, both show themselves to be ideal devices by which an agency can convince a client to enter a union of collaboration and build feelings of affinity. As Leach (1976) reminds us, in the use of pragmatic and symbolic modes of communication, one can indeed be the transformation of the other.

On a broader level relating to the theme of this book, the use of models and metaphors by agencies reveals much about the way symbolic representations of consumers and brands, as well as stylistic features of language, function as a system of knowledge. The borrowing of ethnography as a tool in this effort adds to the creative process by which agencies construct those representations and circulate their metaphors. And this subject is as germane to the field of marketing as it is to anthropology.

In any field of cultural inquiry that addresses the making of cultural representations, whether it be anthropology or advertising, we must recognize that knowledge is not 'found' in culture or 'discovered' in consumer behavior, but rather is 'made' by its observers. One of the primary intents of knowledge-making is to construct edifices of order and categorization, thereby preserving and maintaining the knowledge in a format that is pseudo-scientific and legitimate.[46] Anthropology once claimed to be the 'science of man,' and many 'scientific' projects under the clause of humanistic endeavors sought to bring the puzzlement of cultural forms and human variation into a system of knowledge for classification. Yet, in undertaking such endeavors, anthropological projects also revealed the aspirational motives of their inquirers, as well as the ways in which the anthropological subjects of those projects were constructed by the inquirers themselves.[47] Versions of knowledge made by anthropologists were shown to be filtered through various individual and group agendas that later became part of the system of investigation itself.

The performed nature of social relations between advertising agencies and their clients informs us of their system of knowledge; one of which the consumer and brand are very much a part. In this system, we can understand the value of consumer and brand representations as 'managed' goods. The intent of managing impressions and directing communication in advertising indicates the high value placed on the production and circulation of brand and consumer images. Their value, however, is not realized through the accuracy of representing the consumer or brand in any 'real' way, but rather, through the act of presenting and managing those representations toward some 'real' end with the client. Ethnography in this sense becomes a purposeful tool with which advertising executives attempt to build relations with their capricious clients.

This assertion has powerful implications for the relevance of ethnography and other forms of consumer-focused research approaches that agencies use to make consumers come alive for clients. For whenever a consumer insight is 'found,' a brand truth 'discovered,' or a market position 'claimed,' it must eventually be abandoned and replaced with another brilliant insight, brand truth and market position, since it is not the 'fact' of the insight itself that maintains the relationship with the client. Rather, it is the interactive process of 'discovery' with the client that matters. In other words, it is the dynamic of finding and shaping information *with* the client that is essential to relationship building, rather than the actual content of *what* is being discovered. The agency's *raison d'être* is evidenced in the dynamics of client interaction, and so the agency is tacitly charged with maintaining a level of excitement and discovery in the interaction. This makes the *making* of maps and models and the *use* of emotionally charged discourse an ongoing component of the relationship itself.

Indeed, the entire workshop enterprise – of making models and metaphors, and of finding facts and figures – reveals more of a process of 'invention'[48] than one of any actual representation of consumer culture. The inventive process, none-theless, importantly contextualizes the interplay of group dynamics, idea formation and presentational skills, so that personal, corporate and marketing agendas effectively collude with the task of knowledge making and securing relationships. This invites the workshop to be a site for the invention and idealization of consumer culture, rather than one for undoing any biases held about consumers. The process by which the consumer's experience is represented in models, made into metaphor, and transformed into material 'facts' becomes the very subject of group dynamics and personal relations between the agency and client. Workshops importantly allow the agency to reinvent the client's consumer and brand in an image that concomitantly supports the reinventing and strengthening of the relationship between the agency and client.

This conclusion is not intended to imply that the performative nature of social interaction between an agency and its client is somehow disingenuous or even spurious. Nothing could be further from the truth. Rather, it highlights the emergent quality of meaning in social interaction. The social dynamics of an advertising agency are most meaningful in the interplay between and among people. This affirms Lash and Urry's assertion that, in an age of modernity, sign images have become the new 'goods of production' increasingly valued over the material products they represent.[49] Indeed, abstract models and rhetorical styles of language about consumers and brands have become the true 'goods of advertising,' increasingly valued over the actual people and products those signs intend to represent. Ethnography will continue to be of value to agencies. Yet, it will be esteemed not for its 'true' representation of consumers, but for the way in which it allows an agency to add value in the presentation of itself to others.

Acknowledgments

I am indebted to William O. Beeman for his suggestions on language and meta-phor, and to Brian Moeran, John McCreery and Barbara Olsen for their critical commentaries.

Notes

1. Phillips (1997: 28) and Klein (2000).
2. Becker (1982).
3. Moeran (1996).
4. Schudson (1984).
5. Goffman (1959: 1).
6. Douglas and Isherwood (1996: xv).
7. Deborah Tannen (1984: 2) brings to light Gregory Bateson's (1972) theory of the double bind in conversation, such as when people express the need to assert their independence against their need to connect with others.
8. Davidson (1992: 23–30).
9. Moeran (1996: 52).
10. Schwartzman (1989: 42).
11. Goffman (1959: 208–37).
12. There are numerous marketing references to battles and wars over consumers. See Ries and Trout (1997), Davidson (1992: 27).
13. Schudson (1984: 24–5).
14. Miller (1997: 4).
15. O'Connell (2001).
16. Davidson (1992: 51).
17. e.g., Fortini-Cambell (1992), Gobe and Zyman (2001).
18. Steel (1998: xv).
19. *Campaign*, 24 January 1997, p. 33.
20. See E. Hall (1997). Planners' skills in communicating research language makes them crucial in advertising pitches as reported by executive vice-president, Cheryl Greene, of Deutch advertising.
21. Goffman (1959: 1).
22. Turner (1969).
23. Huizinga (1950: 50–2).
24. Not coincidentally, the agency learned of a client's personal relations to Spain. Since I was the agency's resident 'Hispanophile,' I was strategically paired up with him to liaise and build a personal relationship.
25. Campbell (1987: 43–5).
26. See Moeran (1996: 278–80).
27. Moeran (1996: 126).
28. I realize the somewhat arbitrary distinction I make between models and maps, since maps are indeed models. I do so, however, following the practical distinction made in brand marketing. Stephen Gudeman and Mischa Penn give an account to the wide use of models in anthropology, based on the Western Galilean-Cartesian tradition of scientific explanation. The authors hold that

models are popular not only for the intent of pursuing an objective 'recon-stuction' of the data, but for undercutting the 'reflexivity inherent in other modes of inquiry' (1982: 98).

29. Anderson (1983: 166).
30. Said (1978: 32).
31. Stewart (1993).
32. Appadurai (1996: 7).
33. Moeran (1996) and Davidson (1992).
34. See Moeran (1996: 278–80).
35. Douglas and Isherwood (1996 [1979]: 62–3).
36. Goffman (1959: 241).
37. Davidson (1992: 56).
38. Tannen (1984: 2).
39. Jakobson (1960).
40. Becker (1982: 47).
41. Fernandez (1986: 20–1).
42. Lakoff and Johnson (1999).
43. Aaker (1996: 10).
44. Lakoff and Johnson (1980).
45. Miller (1997).
46. Bendix (1997: 220).
47. Stocking (1989: 3).
48. Wagner (1975).
49. Lash and Urry (1994: 2–4).

References

Aaker, D. 1996 *Building Strong Brands*, New York: The Free Press.

Anderson, B. 1983 *Imagined Communities: Reflections on the Origin and Spread of Nationalism*, London: Verso.

Appadurai, A. 1996 *Modernity at Large*, Minneapolis: University of Minnesota Press.

Bateson, G. 1972 *Steps to an Ecology of Mind,* New York: Ballantine Books.

Becker, H. 1982 *Art Worlds,* Berkeley: University of California Press.

Bendix, R. 1997 *In Search of Authenticity: The Formation of Folklore Studies,* Madison, WI: University of Wisconsin Press.

Campbell, C. 1987 *The Romantic Ethic and the Spirit of Modern Consumerism,* Oxford: Blackwell.

Cook, S. 1995 'The evolving role of planning: The creative interface,' *Marketing Review*, 17 (May): 6–17.

Davidson, M. 1992 *The Consumerist Manifesto: Advertising in Postmodern Times*, London: Routledge.

Douglas, M. and B. Isherwood 1996 [1979] *The World of Goods: Towards an Anthropology of Consumption*, London: Routledge.

Fernandez, J. 1986 *Persuasions and Performances: The Play of Tropes in Culture*, Bloomington: Indiana University Press.

Fortini-Cambell, L. 1992 *Hitting the Sweet Spot, the Consumer Insight Workbook: How Consumer Insights Can Inspire Better Marketing and Advertising*, Chicago: The Copy Workshop.

Gobe, M. and S. Zyman 2001 *Emotional Branding: The New Paradigm for Connecting Brands to People*, New York: Allworth Press.

Goffman, E. 1959 *The Presentation of Self in Everyday Life*, Garden City, NY: Doubleday Anchor Books.

Gudeman, S. and M. Penn 1982 'Models, meanings and reflexivity,' in D. Parkin (ed.) *Semantic Anthropology*, pp. 89–106, London: Academic Press.

Hall, E. 1997 'Does planning have a future?; Planners in advertising agencies: United Kingdom,' in *Campaign*, (January): 32, United Kingdom: Haymarket Publications.

Huizinga, J. 1950 *Homo Ludens: A Study of the Play Element in Culture*, Boston: Beacon Press.

Jackobson, R. 1960 'Concluding statement: Linguistics and poetics,' in T. Sebeok (ed.) *Style in Language*, pp. 350–73, Cambridge, MA: MIT Press.

Klein, N. 2000 *No logo: Taking Aim at the Brand Bullies*, New York: Picador.

Lakoff, G. and M. Johnson 1980 *Metaphors We Live By*, Chicago: University of Chicago Press.

—— 1999 *Philosophy in the Flesh: The Embodied Mind and its Challenge to Western Thought*, New York: Basic Books.

Lash, S. and J. Urry 1994 *Economies of Signs and Space*, London: Sage.

Leach, E. 1976 *Culture and Communication: The Logic by which Symbols Are Connected*, Cambridge: Cambridge University Press.

McCreery, J. 1995 'Malinowski, magic, and advertising: On choosing metaphors', in J. Sherry (ed.) *Contemporary Marketing and Consumer Behavior*, pp. 309–29, London: Sage.

Miller, D. 1997 *Capitalism: An Ethnographic Approach*, Oxford: Berg.

Moeran, B. 1996 *A Japanese Advertising Agency: An Anthropology of Media and Markets*, Honolulu: University of Hawaii Press.

Phillips, M.J. 1997 *Ethics and Manipulation in Advertising: Answering a Flawed Indictment*, Westport, CT: Quorum.

Ries A. and J. Trout 1997 *Marketing Warfare*, New York: McGraw-Hill Professional.

Said, E. 1978 *Orientalism*, New York: Vintage.

Schudson, M. 1984 *Advertising: The Uneasy Persuasion*, New York: Basic Books.

Schwartzman, H.B. 1989 *The Meeting: Gatherings in Organizations and Communities*, New York: Plenum.

Steel, J. 1998 *Truth, Lies, and Advertising: The Art of Account Planning*, New York: John Wiley & Sons.

Stewart, S. 1993 *On Longing: Narratives of the Miniature, the Gigantic, the Souvenir, the Collection*, Durham: Duke University Press.

Stocking, G. W., Jr 1989 'Romantic motives and the history of anthropology,' in *Romantic Motives: Essays on Anthropological Sensibility, History of Anthropology*, Vol. 6, Madison, WI: University of Wisconsin Press.

Tannen, D. 1984 *Conversational Style: Analyzing Talk Among Friends*, Norwood, NJ: Ablex.

Turner, V. 1969 *The Ritual Process: Structure and Anti-Structure*, Chicago: Aldine.

Vranica, S. and V. O'Connell 2001 '2001: Year of the hard sell,' in *The Wall Street Journal*, 20 December 2001, p. B1.

Wagner, R. 1975 *The Invention of Culture*, Englewood Cliffs, NJ: Prentice-Hall.

–7–

Fame and the Ordinary: 'Authentic' Constructions of Convenience Foods

Marianne Elisabeth Lien

From the perspective of an advertising agency, it may appear that *uncertainty* is a characteristic trait of the advertising profession (Malefyt, this volume). While advertising agencies compete fiercely for corporate accounts of clients whose loyalty can no longer be taken for granted, their clients may appear to enjoy a more stable situation. Particularly, if clients supply basic products such as food – stable material goods that consumers cannot do without – one might expect their marketing departments to construct their products and their marketing strategies on the basis of some sense of certainty. However, from the perspective of a marketing department, it is not that way at all. They, too, struggle to understand the needs of their consumers, their competitors, and a market that is seen as highly unstable. In addition, they worry whether the money spent on advertising services and market research is really worth it. Because really, how do you know?

The Problem of Affluence

This chapter explores the challenges of modern food manufacturing from the perspective of a product manager in the marketing department of a Norwegian food company. In Norway, as in most of Western Europe and North America, food is abundant, consumers affluent and few go hungry. In such a country, an increase in the overall consumption of food is difficult to achieve. Unless we all become bulimic or obese,[1] it is not very likely that we are all going to eat a lot more. Consequently, the only way for manufacturers to grow is either by conquering market share from competitors, or alternatively by constructing products that will make consumers pay more for the same amount of food; in other words, to construct new products that are value-added in ways that justify a higher price. While the first strategy is a zero-sum game, the second implies that a greater amount of money is spent on food, and represents a more promising strategy, particularly for manufacturers who already dominate the market.

The transfer of labor from the domestic to the industrial sphere represents one of the main reasons for the construction of value-added products in industrialized societies. This explains, in part, the significant growth in the area of so-called convenience foods in most industrialized countries. However, as we shall see, domestic cooking methods cannot always be immediately applied to the requirements of industrial mass production. Furthermore, consumers' willingness to spend some extra money on a ready-made alternative is contingent upon factors beyond the control of experts in product development. The efforts to construct new products through processes of value adding have carved a prominent position for marketing professionals in an area of decision-making which was previously dominated by food technicians in white laboratory coats. In order to succeed in what is perceived as an increasingly competitive food market, product development in the laboratories must be guided by cutting-edge knowledge of consumer trends. Consequently, the marketing profession has gradually gained an upper hand in decisions that involve product development and, boundaries that were previously established between product development and marketing are now increasingly blurred. But how does a product manager, with professional training in marketing, reach his decisions about the texture and flavor of a new product? Why is it that almost all Norwegian convenience foods end up as varieties of Italian pasta? And why do celebrities in Norwegian food testimonials have to appear as ordinary as your next-door neighbor?

The following discussion draws upon an ethnographic study involving eight months of fieldwork in the marketing department of a major food manufacturer located outside of Oslo, Norway.[2] With a background in social anthropology and no experience in marketing or advertising, I entered the field as an outsider. In hindsight, I believe that it is precisely this ignorance that allowed me to ask the questions that eventually turned out to be most interesting, from a theoretical point of view. Questions such as 'what is a market?' and 'how do you know that *Deutsche Knödeln* will never succeed?' triggered discussions and revealed uncertainties that were crucial for further analysis.[3] With a broad knowledge of anthropology, I had a strong basis from which to question what was taken for granted within a field, which is, after all, a variety of what is often referred to as 'anthropology at home.' It is this ability to unsettle what appears to others as self-evident which is, I suggest, the virtue of anthropology and the ethnographic method. As Clifford Geertz notes: 'We have, with no little success, sought to keep the world off balance; pulling out rugs, upsetting tea tables, setting off firecrackers. It has been the office of others to reassure, ours to unsettle.'[4]

Convenience Foods in Norway: Fertile Ground for Growth

In the early 1990s, food manufacturers in Norway observed a paradox. On the one hand, research on demography, family structure and eating habits indicated a significant demand for convenience foods among Norwegian consumers. On the other hand, the actual consumption of convenience foods was very low, compared with countries in the EU and with the US. For Viking Foods,[5] this was good news. For some time, they had searched for ways to increase the so-called 'added value' of their product range. Convenience foods appeared as a promising area in which they might achieve this aim.

The term 'convenience food' (*ferdigmat* in Norwegian) usually refers to an industrial product, which combines elements that have previously been put together in the home. For instance, a package of dry spaghetti is usually not referred to as a convenience food, as the possibility of making spaghetti from raw materials is generally not considered. Once the pasta is purchased in a mixture with a pre-prepared sauce, however, the product is more likely to be referred to as convenience food, as the preparation of pasta sauce in the home is fairly common. Convenience food may thus be conceived of as a relative rather than an absolute term. Its meaning derives not only from industrial processing, but also from the absence of culinary elaboration in the household. An increase in the consumption of convenience foods thus indicates a transfer of certain household activities from the private sphere to the industrial domain.

The case that is about to unfold took place in the early 1990s in the marketing department of Viking Foods, one of the largest private food manufacturers in Norway, and the market leader in the field of frozen convenience foods. For several decades, Viking Foods had operated within a highly regulated national food market in which a major political aim had been to ensure the viability of Norwegian agricultural production.[6] In the early 1990s, however, these protective regulations were challenged. First, Norwegian membership of the EU was once again on the political agenda as a national referendum on this issue was to take place in autumn 1992. A positive outcome would – it was assumed – imply a radical shift towards a less protective agricultural policy and trigger a much more competitive and internationalized (domestic) food market. Second, the trade regulations being developed through the GATT agreement (subsequently the WTO) were expected to require significant long-term adjustments of Norway's protective food and agricultural policy. Hence, preparing for foreign competition was a high priority strategy among domestic food companies, and was also, as we shall see, reflected in marketing decisions.

The Bon Appétit Project

'*Bon Appétit*' is the name of a range of frozen dinner products, launched by Viking Foods in March 1991. I first entered the project half a year later, in October 1991, when I joined Henrik, a product manager in charge of Bon Appétit on his visit to *ANUGA*, a biannual international food fair in Cologne. Henrik was in his early thirties. With a degree in marketing, and several years of experience in Viking Foods' marketing department, he clearly represented the marketing profession. The main purpose of his visit to ANUGA was to see other products, which might give him some ideas to take home, and to get a general update of what was going on in the international market. As we stopped at a stand with German convenience foods, Henrik spent a long time looking at the varieties of ethnic convenience foods offered, many of which I had never encountered in Norwegian food stores. I noticed that while some dishes caught his interest, others were immediately discarded. It seemed to me that these judgments were made intuitively, and when I asked him about what he was actually doing, he replied:

> *Henrik*: I just pick up some ideas. A lot of these are not relevant for the Norwegian market. It is simply too strange. Like for instance *Deutsche Knödeln*.[7] This is food for the Germans. But then there are other things that are interesting.
>
> *Marianne*: Like what?
>
> *Henrik*: Lots of things. Italian dishes, obviously. And spring rolls as well. I think spring rolls have now reached a point which is suitable in terms of a launch.
>
> *Marianne*: How do you know?
>
> *Henrik*: I guess it relates to an overall knowledge of the Norwegian market.

At this time, Bon Appétit had been on the market for about six months, and the product range included lasagne, tagliatelle, spaghetti bolognese, tortellini, chop suey, oriental stew and a popular Norwegian dish called '*lapskaus*.' However, as the Bon Appétit product range was a flexible concept, with single products being added or eliminated over time, product development remained an issue that Henrik constantly had to consider.

According to the Brand Strategy, the Bon Appétit product range consisted of 'complete meals' characterized by 'high quality and good taste at a reasonable price' that could 'be heated in the package either in an oven, a microwave oven or in hot water.' The primary target group was defined as 'modern, busy urban people with a high income, eating conveniently during weekdays' and 'not particularly gourmet oriented. This group had been labeled 'live for the present' by consumer segmentation surveys, and was described in the Brand Strategy as being 'engaged and active' and 'with an individual, unstructured meal pattern.' The secondary target group was referred to as the gourmet segment. However, as it turned out, this target group was difficult to please. In relation to this segment, convenience food was described as having 'a credibility problem in appearing as natural products precisely because (they are) pre-prepared at the factory.'[8] Thus the ability to come up with new products that were palatable and appealing to critical consumers was a key challenge.

Getting Things Right; Technology and Taste

When Bon Appétit was launched in March 1991, several problems remained with regard to material features of the products. Consequently, during the following months, a continuous process of product development took place. The difficulties in product development were mostly related to specific problems regarding comb-inations of ingredients, flavor, or packaging that Henrik insisted on getting solved, and were elaborated in written messages that were sent from him to product development staff. For instance, in a letter to Arne, the head of product development, Henrik identified a number of problems. Referring to a pasta dish, he wrote:

> The presented product is not satisfactory. The sauce is too thick. There is too much cayenne – very strong aftertaste. Must be added more taste that is experienced immed-iately. Drop the broccoli. Make two varieties, one with green onions, the other with vegetable stock.

Regarding a Salmon Hollandaise, not yet on the market:

> Arne undertakes production trials with rice and the vegetable dish (broccoli) in order to find out how much we can put into the form without getting problems in welding the tinfoil.

Regarding a fish casserole, which was still in an experimental phase:

> Out of the four different toppings presented, we will continue development of a combin-ation of cheese and sliced carrots.

Such statements illustrate how Henrik established a dialogue with product devel-opment staff regarding fairly detailed matters. Moreover, the documents reveal that to a great degree it was Henrik who defined the further choice of direction, specifying to the product development experts what to do, and in what order of priority. These negotiations involved a level of detail, which was quite far removed from the abstract product concept defined in the Brand Strategy. Decisions about the right amounts of cheese and carrots, and the correct viscosity of a particular sauce could hardly be made by referring, for example, to the degree of modernity of the target group. Henrik's task may thus be perceived as the work of translation between the abstract level of general consumer characteristics, and the very concrete level of material composition (and vice versa). Clearly, the Brand Strategy provided no manual of how to go about this. And the target group analysis, which explored in detail the characteristics of the most relevant consumers, hardly provided any clues with regard to the taste and flavor of the actual product. How then, did Henrik manage these translations? How did he know that the pasta sauce was too thick, and on what basis did he select the combination of cheese and carrots?

Faced with such questions, Henrik used the expertise that was most readily available: himself, his family and a few colleagues in the marketing department. In the middle of the marketing department office area, there was a tiny kitchen, which allowed for certain experiments. Sometimes the smell of hot food spread into the office area, whereupon Henrik, mostly without any advance warning, gathered whoever was present to try something out. Other times, during discussions, he jokingly referred to recent test results from '*Edvard Griegs vei 54*,' his home address, and to informal trials that he had undertaken together with his wife. Thus, while the written documents mostly reflected professional market research, informal, ad hoc testing was part of decision-making as well, although it was not always referred to as such.

Frank Cochoy (1998) has described marketing as a distinct body of knowledge located halfway between supply and demand, but also between science and practice. Henrik's pragmatic combination of formal and informal marketing strategies illustrates this. He consulted consumer surveys and applied market research when it was available or appeared to be a practical solution. But formal market research can never provide answers to every single issue that needs to be solved on a day-to-day basis, particularly when the issues relate to product development. Consequently, Henrik did what was expected with regard to formal market research, but beyond that he relied on his own 'gut feeling' and common sense.

In February 1992, almost a year after the Bon Appétit concept was first launched, three new products were included, all varieties of common Norwegian dinner recipes: Salmon Hollandaise, and two varieties of 'fish au gratin.'[9] In the meantime, tagliatelle had been taken temporarily out of production due to technical difficulties (see below), while three other products (tortellini, lapskaus, and oriental stew) had been omitted from the product range. None of the new products had formally been subject to consumer testing.[10] Henrik commented: 'It is risky, but then, there are also many fiascos that *have* been tested.' He added that the development process had largely taken place at the product development side, and that the three new products would be included in the product range without any extra advertising effort.

Why Pasta? The Foreign and the Familiar

As we have seen, Bon Appétit was a flexible concept for which the actual product range was continuously in the making. The fact that a single unsuccessful product could be quietly removed without seriously altering the Brand Strategy allowed for some trial and error. Each new launch could therefore be interpreted as an act of negotiation in which 'real' consumers were confronted with 'real' products that they might or might not choose to buy.

Henrik's interpretation of these negotiations was based on sales results. Sales figures collected during autumn 1991, half a year after the launch, indicated that lasagne was the true 'winner,' accounting for as much as 45 per cent of the total volume of Bon Appétit products sold. Other pasta dishes constituted another 22 per cent of the total, making Italian pasta dishes by far the most important product group within the Bon Appétit concept. Chop suey and oriental stew constituted no more than 15 per cent of the total volume, while the only dish based on a typically Norwegian culinary concept, *lapskaus*, accounted for only 4 per cent of the total volume sold. Partly for this reason, it was later omitted from the product range. In addition, there was beef Stroganoff, a popular meat stew that accounted for approximately 15 per cent of the total volume sold.

The strong emphasis on dishes of foreign origin, and particularly on Italian pasta dishes, reflected a general tendency during the 1990s associating convenience foods with foods of foreign origin.[11] But how can this connection be explained? And why did Italian cuisine gain such a strong position? During a period when Henrik planned to launch another two pasta dishes in the product range, I had the chance to discuss this with him. He explained that a recent consumer survey on Norwegian eating habits had indicated that among all ethnic foods, Italian food was rated number one.[12] He continued: 'In addition, pasta is the kind of dish which tastes good even when there is not a lot of meat in it. In other words, we avoid some of the problems related to high costs of production.'

At the same time, Henrik also tried to establish more typically Norwegian products. This was reflected both in the three new fish dishes mentioned and in several product development trials. One of the most promising products was *finnebiff*, a common and fairly popular Norwegian dish based on thinly sliced reindeer meat. For Henrik, this was part of a deliberate strategy, and when I asked about the rationale behind it he replied:

Henrik: Part of our product strategy goes kind of like this: in order to protect ourselves against foreign competitors, our only possibility is to develop typically Norwegian dishes out of Norwegian raw materials. Here we have a competitive advantage compared to the foreign competitors, while with international dishes, we are more equal. I don't mean to push Norwegian food down people's throats. But the idea is that *if* we can develop such Norwegian dishes, which sell fairly well, then that's a good thing. In addition, there are signals from the sales corps. They often ask why there aren't any

> more Norwegian products in the product range. Especially from peripheral areas of Norway, we tend to get such signals.
>
> *Marianne:* I would assume that it is precisely in peripheral areas that you find consumers who'd rather cook such traditional dishes themselves, and are less ready to accept convenience foods?
>
> *Henrik:* We've thought about that. That's why we deliberately do not launch *fårikål* (a meat and cabbage stew) and *kjøttkaker* (meatballs). Instead, we try to make other things, like for instance *finnebiff.* I believe in that. And *rensdyrkaker* (reindeer meatballs). I don't know if that will work, whether people will want it. But if it works, it is something we might compete on. Norwegian casserole is another attempt: something which is Norwegian, but which is not prepared exactly like this in the households.

As Henrik strived to achieve a balance between foreign and domestic culinary traditions, several voices of interest could be identified. First of all there were the consumers, whose attitudes and interests were voiced directly through aggregate purchase behavior, through the success of competitors or indirectly through market research interpretations. When Henrik decided to introduce two new pasta varieties, he referred explicitly to consumers' preferences for Italian foods, as reflected in external market research surveys. In addition, his decision was in accordance with current sales figures.

Further, the popularity of Italian dishes could be explained in terms of the material advantages involved. Norwegian consumers generally perceived convenience foods to be expensive. In the marketing department, controlling the cost of production was therefore of key importance, and dishes made with inexpensive raw materials were at a definite advantage. Pasta, which is filling and inexpensive compared with meat, fulfills this requirement. As an additional quality, pasta is a culinary concept which may be varied endlessly, thus giving rise to a wide variety of different products (tortellini, spaghetti, lasagne and so on). These features may partly explain the dominant emphasis of 'Italianness' in the Bon Appétit product range, and in convenience foods in general. This exemplifies how certain material characteristics of product components contribute to shaping the symbolic connotations of a product range.

Imagined Cuisines

But the popularity of pasta and other foreign food items may also be related to the way they mediate between the realms of culinary knowledge, food experience and imagination. In creating a new product, a product manager seeks to achieve a certain coherence between the material product (in terms of taste, texture, etc.) and the anticipations evoked by the product through name, appearance and visual design. Put more simply, there is an expectation among the consumers that the product should be what it claims to be. Such judgments of coherence are based upon knowledge and previous experience on the part of the consumer, and imply a shared cultural repertoire between producer and consumer. Almost intuitively, Henrik knew that *fårikål* was not going to work: *fårikål* is a dish which most Norwegian consumers are accustomed to preparing at home, and for which judgments of coherence are likely to be very precise. Norwegians 'know' what *fårikål* should taste like. Hence, any deviation from the homemade variety (due to requirements of industrial production) is likely to be detected immediately and judged negatively. When it comes to foreign culinary concepts, however, knowledge among consumers is generally far more limited, their expectations are less precise, and they themselves are much less likely to be critical. Consequently, when creating new products based on foreign culinary concepts such as Chinese chop suey, the producer is, to a far greater extent, free to define the product in a way that suits the specific requirements and conditions of industrial mass production.

Many authors have argued that food provides a particularly suitable medium for representing 'the other,' making ethnic cuisine an excellent paradigm, or metaphor, for ethnicity itself.[13] However, such representations of the other are also locally constructed, as they tend to be influenced not so much by the 'others' they claim to represent as by cultural configurations of 'otherness' among the consumers they address. This is particularly salient in industrial food manufacturing and marketing.[14] Foreign ethnic cuisines, as they are expressed in modern manufacture, are therefore largely based upon local imagery of the other, and may be conceived as *imagined cuisines*.[15]

As we have seen, certain culinary formats such as pasta are particularly suitable for the requirements of low-cost mass production. In addition, a foreign cuisine which few consumers have first-hand knowledge of will easily lend itself to the technical requirements of mass manufacture. I suggest, therefore, that it is precisely the 'imagined-ness' of foreign cuisines which makes them suitable for industrial production. This applies especially to convenience foods, for which scepticism with regard to product quality is perhaps most enhanced.

Each time a locally defined image of the exotic is disseminated through a commercial food product on the Norwegian market, it will also contribute to a process of routinization. Through processes of routinization, elements that were previously exotic will eventually become familiar to consumers. This, in turn, may force product managers to search for other, still unspoiled, imagined cuisines in order to present their products as exotic, thus contributing to a constant acceleration of new culinary concepts offered to Norwegian consumers. These mechanisms, I contend, may account for the constant attempts in food marketing and manufacture at appropriating and launching foreign novelties, and contribute to what we may refer to as a *routinization of the exotic*.

Appropriation of exotic elements must, however, be balanced with some level of *familiarity* and of *significance*. Even though the appropriation of food from, for instance, New Guinea would imply an extreme degree of freedom on the part of the manufacturer to define the cuisine in a suitable – and potentially profitable – manner, this strategy was rarely pursued. The reason for this, I suggest, is that a place like New Guinea still fails to constitute the careful balance between foreign-ness and familiarity that is required for marketing purposes. Most importantly, New Guinea cannot be said to represent a significant 'other' for Norwegian consumers, in the way that, for instance, 'America' or 'Italy' does. Although all nations are 'foreign' in the strict sense of the term, only the latter two nations are familiar enough to be elaborated in the construction of imagined cuisines.

The extent to which a manufacturer's definition of a certain product influences consumers' concepts of an exotic cuisine depends, however, on whether or not the manufacturer is able to present the product as authentic. This ability, in turn, depends on the extent to which the product manager succeeds in choosing culinary elements that still retain a promise of something exotic or unique – that is, elements whose meanings are not yet eroded by the mechanisms of routinization.

The struggle to get the dishes right is, though, only half of a story, of which advertising constitutes the other half. While product development staff were busy with trials for new Bon Appétit products, an advertising agency at the other end of town worked hard to develop ideas for a TV commercial. As product manager, Henrik was in charge of both processes, and, as both responsibilities demanded a strong engagement on his part, his working days involved abrupt shifts of perspective, and required the ability to attend closely to different projects simult-aneously. Most of the time, these processes went on independently of each other, but, as we shall see, there were also times when the problems on the product development side had direct relevance for the marketing activities.

Constructing a Testimonial: Fame and the Ordinary

About six months after the product launch, plans began for the first Bon Appétit TV commercial. Henrik had limited experience with TV commercials, and, as in the case of product development, he had to rely on the advice of experts, in this case advertising agencies and professional film producers. At the same time, as in the case of product development, he was the one who had the final word on any decision, and who would ultimately be held responsible for failure or success.

In the Brand Strategy, benefits of Bon Appétit were defined as a set of 'promises' that would be communicated to the consumer. 'Functional promises' included a wide selection of dishes and portion sizes, time saving, convenience and simplicity in the sense that the dishes would not require any skills to prepare. 'Emotional promises' were defined as an experience of a tasty meal, a healthy convenient food, and a meal that would provide more time for other activities. In addition, the product range would be slightly less expensive than main competitors.

In October 1991, shortly after our visit to ANUGA, Henrik received a storyboard for a Bon Appétit commercial from Viking Foods' long-term advertising partner, an agency called Publicity. A storyboard is an illustrated summary and a key preparatory tool in film production, which indicates the basic chronology of a film by means of shorts pieces of text and a series of visual images. Two films were planned at this stage, one with a male and the other with a female spokesperson. This particular storyboard was based on a testimonial featuring Jon Jonsen, a middle-aged sports commentator, especially known for his knowledge of alpine skiing and soccer.[16] Jon Jonsen would be shown eating spaghetti bolognese, one of the most popular Bon Appétit products at the time, and the film would focus on his busy day, and the need for a fast and ready-made dinner. At this time, Publicity was already familiar with the Brand Strategy. No briefing had been produced for this film, however, as most initiatives and agreements had so far been reached informally, over the phone. Henrik had no particular comments to make on this particular storyboard, but sent a letter to Publicity clarifying general issues related to budget, time schedule and media channels (TV and cinemas). He also emphasized the need to elect a celebrity in such a way that 'the target group . . . experiences identification with spokesman, milieu and not the least, lifestyle.' Regarding the film with the female spokesperson, two figures had previously been discussed over the phone, but no agreement had been reached. In the letter, Henrik asked Publicity to 'come up with suggestions for more suitable women in occupations that appeal to our target group.'

Two weeks later, in November 1991, I joined Henrik for a meeting at Publicity. In addition to Henrik and myself, Johan – a Viking Foods marketing manager and Henrik's superior – was also present. From Publicity, there were four people: Tom, the account manager; Edvard, the creative director; Nina, the art director; and Anne, a consultant whose main functions were secretarial. In addition, a film director was expected to arrive.

The meeting started with a video presentation of recent Publicity commercials. Afterwards, while we waited for the film director to appear, the conversation focused on possible characters. It soon became clear to me that a couple of decisions had been made informally over the phone: Jon Jonsen, the sports commentator, was obviously out, and a replacement was needed. Furthermore, Maria Mortensen, a pop singer in her early thirties who had been successful in a Eurovision song contest, had been suggested as a spokeswoman for the second film. The most important and immediate issue facing the group, therefore, was to select a male celebrity for the first film. At this point, a process of verbal 'name dropping' started, during which Tom wrote a list of celebrity names on the board as they came up. Each name released spontaneous comments, mostly directly related to the target group. Soon, a simple sociograph was sketched on the board, featuring the two main dimensions, modern–traditional along the vertical axis and materialist–idealist along the horizontal. Tom located the target group by drawing an amoeba-like figure on the left side of the vertical axis, and with a movement downwards indicated that the target group was more traditional than had originally been thought.

Throughout the discussion, it became clear that the main criterion for selecting a character was his or her appeal to the target group, a feature that was partly grounded on his or her assumed ability to evoke feelings of identification within the target group. For instance, a singer-songwriter who was considered to be a nice guy was seen to be unsuitable because there was a suspicion that he might appeal more to the 'right' (idealist) than to the 'left' (materialist) part of the sociograph. Furthermore, the person should not be too controversial. This was why a famous comedian, whose performances were often quite satirical, was discarded. In addition, the concept of ordinariness must not imply a publicly low profile: a musician, who had played with a very successful band, but still remained in the shadow of the front-figure of that band, was described as a person whom, in spite of his talents, 'nobody really knows,' and was dropped as a result. In other words, a certain level of fame was required. At the same time, there was a consistent trade-off between fame and financial cost. Obviously, there were many celebrities who were more famous than the ones mentioned during the meeting whose charges would exceed the Viking Foods marketing budget.

One name after another had been brought up and then quickly dropped when someone mentioned a national broadcast program director called Kjell Gregers. For the first time, as the following summary of comments indicates, an appropriate candidate was in sight: 'He's known. He's ordinary. Not controversial. He's in *Se & Hør*" [a celebrity magazine] almost every week. He gets a lot of attention. And he goes to all first night performance parties. It seems like he's on the way up. And besides, he just bought a new car. I read in an article that he was crazy about cars.' At this moment, the film director, Martin – a man in his mid-thirties – arrived, together with a younger female secretary. Instantly, Martin became the center of attention. Without any further introduction, he suggested a celebrity whom he considered to be the right male character for a Bon Appétit testimonial: his choice was Vidar Sande, a well-known racing driver from rural Norway, who was known both for his speed driving talent, and for his rough and outspoken behavior. It seemed as if the film director had made up his mind before entering the meeting, and he spent most of his presentation defending this choice. As he explained:

A lot of people like him. He may be a 'bully' and a reckless driver, but he's a good guy. And one can easily understand that he has little time for cooking. Things must happen fast. And he has a charming dialect. He is likely to appeal to the segment we are talking about. There's a lot to play upon, film-wise.

According to the film director, Sande had already agreed to participate. He had asked a price that was considered quite reasonable, and gradually, as Martin presented his arguments, a consensus was reached to contract Vidar Sande. Shortly afterwards, Anne left the room in order to call him and make an appointment. She returned a few minutes later, saying that he would be home in an hour.

The film director spent the rest of the time elaborating his concept. He wanted pictures of Sande returning to his home in the evening, flashbacks from his busy day, the sound of car tires against gravel, and Sande's voice all along. Now and then, he intended to interrupt this sequence by delicious pictures of raw food material. Henrik expressed some worry that the film might introduce too many different sequences, but the director assured him that it would not. Towards the end of the film, the voice and image would be synchronized, and we would see Sande speaking right into the camera. Then there would be so-called pack shots, and a voice-over saying something about Viking Foods.

A week later, Henrik commented on the meeting this way:

Now, after a while, I'm starting to feel comfortable about these plans for using Vidar Sande. I was more sceptical at first about whether he had a kind of . . . nice and attractive appeal. But then, on the other hand, he might just appeal to the target group of slightly 'rough men' that we are thinking of, so then it's OK.

Henrik's last comment indicates the extent to which he differentiated between his own subjective likes and dislikes, and the assumed preferences of his target group. Clearly, his immediate personal reaction was replaced by a more objective judgment. But what did he look for in a spokesperson? Which characteristics of the potential candidates turned out to be decisive? The discussion prior to the arrival of the film director had given some clues. The spokesperson should be famous, and yet ordinary. Obviously, finding such as person was not an easy task, as fame tends to be based on some personal trait or activity that makes the person stand apart as different, un-ordinary. However, as the comments about Kjell Gregers indicated, such criteria are not always incompatible. Television is important in this respect. Due to frequent appearances on television, Gregers, a fairly 'ordinary' person had become publicly known. His fame was *not* based on any particular trait that made him stand apart, but was rather a function of frequent exposure. In this way, nationwide broadcasting provides possibilities for fame for persons who are *not* talented or outstanding in any particular way, and, in a sense, constructs a celebrity out of the person next door. Television thus helps produce celebrities in which the criteria of fame and 'ordinariness' are reconciled.[17]

While television provides an answer to the question of *how* fame and ordinariness may be reconciled, the question *why* still remains. More precisely, we may ask: why did the spokesperson have to be so ordinary? As we have seen, the three male candidates who were seriously considered (the sports commentator, the program director and the racing driver) all possessed a certain 'ordinariness.' Jonsen and Gregers were both middle-aged men whose fame rested entirely upon their ability to successfully handle the role as leading figures in television programmes. Sande was famous for being a successful racing driver, although his popularity seemed to be related to his ordinary appeal. The fame of the spokeswoman, Maria Mortensen, was definitely based on her abilities as a singer; yet she left the impression of a person who was straightforward, 'natural' and unpretentious, thus contributing to a cultural image of an 'ordinary' Norwegian woman. In other words, the process of selecting a celebrity demonstrates the importance of ordinariness as the common denominator that is required.

This search for ordinariness may be analyzed in light of what Marianne Gullestad refers to as the typically Norwegian notion of equality as sameness. She writes: 'Because sameness (being alike) is a central value, it is problematic to demand prestige and recognition. Norwegians are no less interested in recognition than others, but for them an initiative to attain recognition must be inscribed in the ideal of sameness. Modesty is a virtue, and self-assertion is seen as bragging'.[18] Searching for a character who is famous, yet ordinary, may thus be interpreted as a way of ensuring recognition while at the same time under-communicating social difference. As mentioned above, one way of handling this delicate balance between public fame and ordinariness is through the use of a TV celebrity. But what about the situations in which fame stems from the demonstration of talent? When fame must be inscribed in the ideal of sameness, rendering any explicit claims for extraordinary talent somewhat illegitimate, how then is public popularity achieved?

Looking more closely at the racing driver and the female singer, we find that they share one important characteristic; namely, a direct way of expressing themselves which is readily conceptualized in Norwegian as natural (*naturlig*) or honest (*ærlig*). For the male character this is expressed through a rough and unpolished way of speaking (which also includes a rural dialect). For the female character, it is expressed more subtly through a nice and unpretentious image, which makes her similar to any girl next door. Hence, when Maria Mortensen comes off as ordinary and natural, what we see may be a certain avoidance of artificiality in social encounters that serves to substantiate an implicit claim of being herself; that is to say, of being authentic. Expressing naturalness and authenticity through their behavior, both these celebrities present their talents within a context of ordinariness. It seems reasonable to suggest that it was precisely this ability that made them both stand out as more popular than others who were equally talented, and thus also as preferred candidates for a testimonial. This interpretation is in accordance with Gullestad's assertion that the notion of being natural is a central cultural symbol in Norway: 'Artfulness and style are often experienced as unnatural and artificial and therefore as negative oppositions to the natural.'[19]

A few months later, the Bon Appétit commercial with the racing driver eating lasagne appeared on commercial TV channels and as a preview in cinemas in the four largest cities in Norway. However, the second commercial featuring a female spokesperson was still not released. In the meantime, Maria Mortensen had been substituted by a female actress, Greta Granfoss. This change was made very quickly, when the former suddenly informed the film team of a change of schedule, which implied that she would be off to the Canary Islands on vacation. The actress agreed to replace her on short notice, and, after some changes in the narrative, a commercial with Greta Granfoss eating tagliatelle was produced.

However, a few weeks before this commercial was to be released, Henrik told me that it would have to be withheld because of problems on the product development side:

> We're having some problems with the tagliatelle. There's too much water in it, so they have had to temporarily take it out of production. This means that the film with Greta Granfoss, which was going to be released together with the one with Vidar Sande, cannot be released. Hopefully, the problems will be solved and the film will be released by next fall.

Five months later the tagliatelle commercial with the female actress was released along with a repeated exposure of the commercial with the racing driver. This final incident illustrates once more a point of intersection between the spheres of material production and those of communication.

Authenticity and the Consumers' Gaze

The Bon Appétit case illustrates the complex set of interrelations between the material and the symbolic properties of food products. Sometimes these links are merely accidental, such as, for instance, when a sudden material problem related to a specific product forced Henrik to withhold the testimonial with Greta Granfoss for about half a year, thereby causing a far more male-oriented promotion of the product range than was originally intended. At other times, the interrelations are due to a more consistent interplay, such as when certain material advantages of a product such as pasta contribute to the Italian image of the Bon Appétit product range, or when the need to adapt the products to requirements of mass-manufacture contributes to a growth of 'exotic' product varieties at the expense of the more familiar ones.

The relation between the material content of the product and its visual and symbolic properties may also be analyzed in relation to claims of authenticity, a topic which seems to pervade marketing in relation to both product development and advertising. In his attempt to construct a cultural theory of modernity of the Western world, Charles Taylor introduces the concept of 'modern inwardness' as a descriptive feature. Modern inwardness refers to an underlying opposition in our languages of self-understanding between the 'inside' and the 'outside,' in which thoughts and feelings are thought of as somehow resting inside, awaiting the development which will manifest them in the public world.[20] These aspects of Western modernity are relevant to an analysis of food products in the making. To the extent that a product manager succeeds in establishing a brand product, the product's image or 'personality' ought to reflect some 'inner core' of the product. However, if we consider the awareness among product managers with regard to the arbitrariness of the relation between cultural categories and their material representation, the realization of such coherence is somewhat problematic. On the one hand, product managers may literally pick and choose among a wide range of cultural idioms in order to construct a distinct brand. Through this process they both utilize and contribute to an arbitrariness characterizing the relationship between a signifier and its sign in modern marketing. On the other hand, in their efforts to establish brand products, they try to construct products with an image that is coherent and stable over time: an image which reflects some kind of *authentic character* of the product. Through these interrelated processes, product managers evoke a conceptual framework of Western modernity according to which the 'true' core resides on the inside.

The modern conceptualization of 'self' in terms of an inner–outer dichotomy also implies that authenticity, rather than being a question of either/or, refers to matters of degree. If we think of ourselves in terms of an 'inner' essence which is only partly manifested in public, any expression of the self may, by definition, be ranked according to the degree to which the expression actually reveals this allegedly authentic, inner self. In the Norwegian context, this implies – as we have seen through the selection of a celebrity for the Bon Appétit testimonial – a careful balance of fame and ordinariness establishing what is cherished in Norway as a 'natural' style.

Similarly, as consumers, we may conceive products as more or less authentic representations of whatever they claim to portray, be it 'nature,' 'Italy' or typically 'Norwegian cuisine.' Particularly with regard to claims of foreign origin, we may observe that a wide range of products are, in fact, 'Italian'; yet at the same time we may decide that some of them are more 'Italian' than others. Thus, the competition in the market place is partly structured in terms of another contest in which different products are ranked according to their ability to represent authentically what they claim to represent.

Another significant dimension of Western modernity may be referred to as reflexive disengagement.[21] According to Taylor, the Cartesian notion of a disengaged subject articulates one of the most important developments of the modern era, and has brought about: 'The growing ideal of a human agent who is able to remake himself by methodical and disciplined action. What this calls for is the ability to take an instrumental stance to one's given properties, desires, inclinations, tendencies, habits of thought, and feeling so that they can be *worked on* . . . until one meets the desired specifications.'[22]Although Taylor refers to a reflexive disengagement in relation to the self, reflexive disengagement is also an apt description of the product manager's approach to products in the making. Contrary to what many consumers are led to believe, modern food products rarely exist prior to the production of their Brand Strategy. Although advertising may involve narratives that situate products historically and create an image of continuity through the use of traditional recipes or preparation methods, most products are constructed with a future consumer in mind. In other words, the material process of food manufacture is essentially open-ended, and guided by definitions of potential target groups. Thus, when food products appear in the grocery store, their symbolic and social meaning is literally baked into them.[23] Product managers are, of course, fully aware of this. They know that any success-ful brand product is the result of the effort to successfully create an image that appears as authentic: that is, a brand is thoroughly constructed and 'authentic' at the same time. The swiftness by which this apparent contradiction is handled by product managers may be interpreted as an expression of reflexive disengagement – of ways of being in the world that are firmly located within the condition described by Taylor as Western modernity.

However, the anticipation of consumers' gaze provides some restrictions. As we have seen, exotic food from New Guinea, or 'strange' food from more familiar places, such as *Deutsche Knödeln*, were *not* appropriated in the routinization of the exotic, in spite of their authentic and exotic potential. I suggest that this is because product managers knew that the 'authentic' is only valuable in so far as it is made comparable within a common format, and this common format is defined by the gaze of Norwegian consumers. Thus, when Henrik constructed the Bon Appétit product range, he acted in accordance with an immediate and general knowledge of Norwegian consumers. At the same time, he demonstrated that the quest for authenticity had its limits. It was precisely this awareness, and the disengaged instrumentality with which he selected certain properties, and discarded others, that enabled him to construct and market products that 'met the desired specifications.'

Being There; Between Models and Reality

The production of advertising is rarely a smooth process. While textbooks on marketing and advertising offer a range of rational models on how to proceed, the experience of marketing on a day-to-day basis leaves an impression of a process that is much more pragmatic and contingent upon a variety of exogenous factors. In this chapter we have seen how both construction and interpretation of the material dimension of Bon Appétit offered serious challenges to symbolic representation and caused a significant delay affecting the entire profile of the advertising campaign. This is hardly an exceptional case. During my eight months of fieldwork in Viking Foods I followed cases with far more loops, reversals and 'dead ends' than this one. However, I would not even have been aware of these 'deviations' if my informants had not been so eager to draw my attention to them. I found it interesting, and slightly peculiar, when, during one of our very first meetings, a marketing director told me that I would probably find the process of decision-making in Viking Foods far more contingent than I had originally thought. Similar points were frequently made by product managers, often apol-ogetically, as if they knew they were not always doing things 'right,' and expected me to discover this. Entering the field with little knowledge of marketing, I was clearly much less predisposed to judge their activities critically than my informants assumed. At the same, I learned that marketing is structured through a dialectic between practice and knowledge, or between the need to act pragmatically in relation to day-to-day decisions, and the need to justify such decisions in relation to a body of marketing knowledge which includes models and guidelines for action.

My interest as an anthropologist in this field is not the fact that ideal models do not correspond to everyday realities. Discontinuities between 'maps' and 'territories' are commonplace in ethnographic research and a trivial dimension of social life. However, the exact configurations of such discontinuities, and the ways in which people reflect upon them, differ markedly from one field to another. Thus, the anxiety expressed by my informants, and their frequent comparisons with an idealized model for action (usually drawn from marketing textbooks or seminar material) revealed a field of social practice that is highly self-conscious, reflexive and struggling to come to terms with a state of professional uncertainty.[24] This finding could be a characteristic expression of a marketing department in a part of the world which, in relation to marketing and advertising, is after all in a marginal location. But it could also be a more general trait of the marketing and advertising professions. Anyhow, it is a finding that sharply contrasts with the image of marketing and advertising which is usually portrayed of – and by – the professions themselves in relation to the general public.

Ethnographic research is particularly well equipped to grasp such cultural idiosyncrasies. The fact of being there, and of meticulously tailing informants in and out of meetings, elevators, boardrooms and trade exhibitions, allows us to trace the shifting contexts in which people operate. Through the peculiar combination of the gaze of a distant observer and the emphatic mode of a partner or companion, the anthropologist acquires a sensitivity to the significance of such cultural discontinuities. In this way, the ethnographic approach to marketing and advertising enables us to compare these practices with other practices elsewhere, providing for the profession what is often the most valuable contribution: a view from the outside.

Notes

1. According to a recent survey, the average weight of Norwegians has increased from the early 1960s to the late 1990s by 3,7 kg. for women and 9,1 kg. for men. However, this does not appear to be caused by an increased food intake, but rather by a decrease in levels of physical activity. Statens Råd for Ernoering og Fysisk Aktivitet.
2. For a more complete analysis, see Lien (1997).
3. For an analysis of market metaphors and performative consequences, see Lien (1997, 2000).
4. Geertz (1984: 275).
5. Viking Foods is a fictitious name, as are all other names of persons and products in this chapter.
6. For private manufacturers, these protective measures represented a mixed blessing. Effectively curbing foreign competition, such regulations, on the one hand, forced private manufacturers to rely largely on domestic farmer's cooperatives for supplies of meat and dairy products. In other words, they could not benefit from lower prices on the world market. On the other hand, they largely served to prevent foreign manufacturers from entering the domestic market, allowing players such as Viking Foods to enjoy a leading position in a somewhat captive market.
7. *Deutsche Knödeln* are a kind of dumpling, typical of central European cuisine.
8. Target group analysis, May 1990.
9. Fish au gratin (*fiskegrateng*) is a very common everyday dinner in Norway, while Salmon Hollandaise is a more elaborate meal associated with festive occasions.

10. They had, however, been subject to so-called 'in-home' taste trials. This implies that the products had been tried out at home by a small and non-representative sample of consumers.

11. A content analysis of Norwegian food adverts during the same period revealed that out of all product attributes referred to in the adverts, the correlation between terms referring to foreign origin and the term convenient was the strongest of all bivariate correlations (Lien 1995).

12. '*Spisevaneundersøkelsen*' (The food habits survey), the Market and Media Institute (MMI) 1991/1992.

13. See, for instance, Van den Berghe (1984), Levenstein (1985), and Appadurai (1988).

14. For a more thorough discussion elaborating the case of frozen pizza , see Lien (2000).

15. The term 'imagined cuisines' is inspired by Benedict Anderson's (1983) concept of nations as 'imagined communities.'

16. The purpose of a testimonial is to ensure a steady alliance between the product and the target group. Ensuring this alliance, the spokesperson may be seen as a temporary metaphor, substituting both the product (through testimonial: 'I like it, so it must be good') and its future consumer (through sameness: 'I like it, so you must like it too').

17. These events took place about eight years before so-called 'reality TV' was introduced in Norway. With the emergence of 'reality TV' the production of celebrities out of ordinary persons is even more pronounced .

18. Gullestad (1992: 192).

19. Gullestad (1992: 206).

20. Taylor (1992: 93–4). Taylor argues for what he calls a 'cultural theory of modernity,' i.e. a theory which takes into account the culturally specific traits that shaped modernity in certain regions at certain times. His account addresses Western modernity, and is based on the history of ideas as it evolved in Europe in the eighteenth and nineteenth centuries.

21. See, for instance, Taylor (1992) or Giddens (1991).

22. Taylor (1992: 99).

23. According to Hennion and Méadel (1989: 208) the production of advertising implies that: 'When the object appears at the end of the process, it already contains its market just as it has its technical components. It is just as aware of its own future consumer as of its manufacture.'

24. For a more thorough analysis, see Lien (1997).

References

Anderson, Benedict 1983 *Imagined Communities*, London: Verso.

Appadurai, Arjun 1988 'How to make a national cuisine: Cookbooks in contemporary India,' *Comparative Studies in Society and History*, 30 (1): 3–24.

Berghe, Pierre L. Van den, 1984 'Ethnic cuisine: culture in nature,' *Ethnic and Racial Studies*, 7 (3): 387–97.

Cochry, Frank 1998 'Another discipline for the market economy: Marketing as a performative knowledge and know-how for capitalism,' in Michel Callon (ed.) *Laws of the Market*, Oxford: Blackwell.

Geertz, Clifford 1984 'Distinguished lecture: Anti anti-relativism,' *American Anthropologist*, 86: 263–78.

Giddens, Anthony 1991 *Modernity and Self-Identity*, Cambridge: Polity Press.

Gullestad, Marianne 1992 *The Art of Social Relations*, Oslo: Scandinavian University Press.

Hennion, Antoine and Cécile Méadel 1989 'The artisans of desire: The mediation of advertising between product and consumer,' *Sociological Theory*, 7 (2): 191–209.

Levenstein, Harvey 1985 'The American response to Italian food, 1880–1930,' *Food and Foodways*, 1 (1): 1–24.

Lien, Marianne 1995 'Fuel for the body – nourishment for dreams: Contradictory roles of food in contemporary Norwegian food advertising,' *Journal of Consumer Policy*, 18 (2): 1–30.

—— 1997 *Marketing and Modernity*, Oxford: Berg.

—— 2000 'Imagined cuisines: "Nation" and "market" as organising structures in Norwegian food marketing,' in P. Jackson et. al. (eds) *Commercial Cultures; Economies, Practices, Spaces*, pp. 153–75, Oxford: Berg.

Statens Råd for Ernoering og Fysisk Aktivitet (Norwegian Council for Nutrition and Physical Activity) 2002 *Vekt-Helse* (Weight and Health), report no. 1/2000, Oslo.

Taylor, Charles 1992 'Inwardness and the culture of modernity,' in A. Honneth (ed.) *Philosophical Interventions in the Unfinished Project of Enlightenment*, Cambridge, MA: MIT Press.

-8-

Psychology vs Anthropology: Where is Culture in Marketplace Ethnography?
Patricia L. Sunderland and Rita M. Denny

'Ethnography, which involves observation techniques, in-depth interviewing, and using tape or video to record people in their natural settings, is gaining ground in market research, supplying detailed information on customers that other qualitative research techniques don't provide, experts say.'

Michele Worth Fellman, *Marketing Research*

'These days, with the media world grown as fragmented as the American demographic map, the sales fantasy *du jour* is anthropology.'

Thomas Frank, *Harper's Magazine*

As anthropologists who make their living conducting consumer research for corporate clients, we have benefited from ethnography 'gaining ground' and anthropology's status as 'sales fantasy *du jour.*' We work for advertising agencies or manufacturers ('clients') conducting research that leads them to relevant and resonant ways to market their products or services, or to develop new ones. In the past few years we have conducted research on cars and refrigerators, Internet sites and Internet appliances, luxury and more mundane package goods including beer and frozen dinners, healthcare and financial services. Across this range of assignments we have seen attention shift from the focus group room to the living room. We have had requests to carry out research in people's homes, to interview them and to watch them cook, to go with them in their minivans, to observe them in stores, to shop with them for shoes. Clients do call us and say, 'we need ethnography' and 'we want an anthropologist.' The specific request and the general call for ethnography and anthropologists would lead one to expect that the request is for a cultural understanding of brands, products or services in everyday life. (At least it does us. Isn't that what we do as anthropologists?) Sometimes we are charged with providing a distinctly cultural understanding. Too frequently, however, the questions the client or advertiser would like to address are not anthropological – which is to say, cultural. Rather they are distinctly psychological.

This paper is concerned with, if not preoccupied by, the increasing popularity of ethnography in the marketplace in combination with the absence of what we might call anthropological thinking. Clients situate ethnographic inquiry as on-site or in situ investigative technique. Often, however, the goals or objectives of the research do not include understanding or analyzing the lived culture of people and brands, the meanings consumers invest in brands or products or, even, the shared values imputed to brands or product categories. Rather, for advertisers and marketers ethnographic inquiry is too often embraced as a means to obtain a deeper psychological understanding of a target audience. In a study of pickup trucks conducted in 2000, for example, we were charged with interviewing both brand and competitive brand owners. The study seemed ethnographic at its core: it involved multiple cities and demanded in-home interviews, driving demonstrations and week-plus-long video diaries of owners' and their vehicles' lives. The difficulty for us lay in the questions the client wanted answered: how are Chevrolet, Dodge and Ford pickup drivers different as people? How do pickup owners differ from other drivers? Are they socially conservative? We attempted to reframe the questions as: what does it 'say' in our world to drive one of these brands? We argued, for instance, that a particular brand can convey 'youthful risk-taker' whether the owner necessarily has this psychological profile or not. An owner might want to forge a connection with his kids, for example, or want a youthful, risk-taking vehicle for one occasion or event, i.e. context, and not for another. We suggested that understanding the cultural meanings – not the psychological meanings – of the vehicles was both the key temporal question facing the brand in question and a more appropriate use of ethnography. The client, however, remained tied to the importance of understanding how owners of different brands of pickups were different as people. We argued that sometimes Chevy drivers had recently been Dodge drivers and are, therefore, not different people. At some point mutual annoyance reigned and we simply talked past each other.

The preoccupation with psychological traits is not limited to projects on brand owners but extends to whole product categories. In mid-2000, prior to the technology bubble bust, we were assigned to study people who were 'into' the latest in technology – those who seemed to be on the route we would all eventually take. The ultimate client was a telecommunications firm. We were hired by the affiliated advertising agency and agreed to work in close conjunction with planners there as well as with a consultant (a psychologist) who had worked with them and the client for several years.

To be selected as participants for this study, respondents had to first undergo a screening process which assured not only their ownership/use of a certain array of technological devices but also their designation as 'vanguard' as determined by their responses to a 29-item psychographic, Yankelovich survey instrument. (For instance, they had to agree or disagree with statements such as 'I like to imagine myself doing something I know I wouldn't dare do' and 'I think my IQ is higher than average.') They were then required to submit self-produced video presentations of themselves and the role of technology in their lives. Fewer than half of the people who submitted videotapes were selected. The use of the psychographic screener was neither our idea nor one we had any input on though we did, in principle, have a say in who was selected based on the videotapes. We, along with agency planners and their consultant, viewed the tapes and argued our cases for who should be selected. We then spent a half day or more with each selected respondent, conducting interviews, observing the spaces of their everyday lives and garnering an understanding of the in situ incorporation of technology from our respondents' points of view.

Our chagrin in this study was not centered on the respondent selection process, however tortuous it might have seemed. Rather our chagrin centered on the analysis. More so than in any project we have conducted, the respondents in this study did indeed share a psychological profile – one that was easily discernable and undeniable. It was also highly suspect. First, all respondents had to respond similarly to the initial (psychographic) screening questions. Second, they had been hand-picked based on their videotapes. Assumptions about what kind of person these technology leaders should be had clearly been at work in the selection process. (Witness, for example, the fact that women were truly underrepresented and 'hard to find.') For us, though, overriding the suspect genesis of respondents' psychological profile was the fact that this similarity seemed much less interesting and important (in general and for advertising) than some of the cultural phenomena, in particular the cultural shifts that seemed so readily apparent when we explored their technology-laden worlds.

A striking aspect of the homes and offices of these technology leaders was the (visual) elimination of books – traditionally potent symbols in our society of intellect, reason and knowledge. Desks proudly displayed Internet-ready computer screens, telephones, PDAs and synchronizing cradles, back-up disks and drives. Nearby shelves showed reference CDs, software, and software manuals. Books were relegated to entertainment locations or marginalized altogether. We found books behind the closed doors of entertainment armoires, on family room shelves alongside televisions, in forgotten entranceways and outside propping up an air conditioner. Analytically, we reasoned, computers and related peripherals had replaced books as the icons and symbols of knowledge as well as organization. What mattered culturally in the technology-oriented world was the demonstration of access to and management of up-to-date, changing information and here the computer occupied the central position.[1]

What also emerged from this research was the way in which technological devices did not eliminate, but rather reinforced, pre-existing cultural boundaries. We found that many of the tech-savvy people were using their technological devices and services to mark and separate business realms from personal realms, to keep work and play separate, to bound and define 'free time.' We noted the existence of separate business and personal e-mail accounts and telephones, and the transition to free time that occurred by turning off a cell phone or by closing a laptop. For example, when sailing on a boat, the 'fun' only starts when the laptop is closed. Our finding contradicted journalistic commentary on the 'merging' of work and play in a 24/7, technologically equipped world.[2] Instead, technology was being harnessed to ensure the functional and symbolic separation of cultural spheres of private and public, work and play, human and machine, even if that could now be done practically and cognitively via 'windows.'[3]

These cultural issues comprised only a very small portion of the report to the ultimate client. A much larger portion of the report was centered on respondents' psychological similarities and other issues that had to do with 'the self.' Pre-presentation conversations with the advertising agency planners and consultant assured us that this needed to be the case.

In both of these examples, ethnography, despite its heuristic link to anthropology as a discipline, was translated by agency and client as a method for more in-depth psychological analysis. Ethnography, even when conducted by anthropologists, was interpreted as a means for a more fine-tuned psychographic profile of a target audience. This psychographic perspective assumes, at heart, that a set of personality traits guides consumer motivation, decisions and behavior and ignores the patterns of behavior that might result from cultural values and trends. In the case of the high-tech vanguard, how the vanguard was using technology to manage salient cultural domains such as work and play or devaluing books went unnoticed. For pickup owners, the shared values and meanings of pickups in today's world were secondary. In a time-sensitive, quickly moving society, which approach is more productive for advertising?

The Reign of Psychological Perspectives

How is it that anthropology – or cultural analysis – remains invisible while ethnography draws the limelight? In the United States psychological perspectives and analyses are part and parcel of a shared cultural worldview. To use a psychological framework, or to see things through a psychological lens, constitutes common sense (or a 'default' way of looking at things – to use a more technology inspired metaphor). As such it can be difficult *not* to think in these terms.

In the aftermath of 11 September 2001, the questions framing national discussion in the US were: how threatened do we feel? How much security do we need? Are we in greater need of home? Family? More likely to cocoon? Is our optimism misplaced? The questions that framed news analyses, that were heard on NPR or discussed among work colleagues were born of a psychological way of comprehending our world. A more anthropological or cultural question would be: how have these events reconfigured what it means to be American?

Native theories on childrearing – whether in lore or press – show a similar predilection for the psychological. There is worry over children's self-esteem and cognitive development, and a stress on children's need for developmentally appropriate cognitive tasks and one-to-one emotionally appropriate attention from adults. Without the former, we fear that an ideal network of synaptic connections may not develop in the brain and, without the latter, we fear that psychological problems are likely.

We describe each other most easily and intuitively in psychological terms: introverts, extraverts, narcissists, achievers and so on. We look to psychology for underlying causes in professional success or failure – was a particular attitude self-defeating or winning? Concepts of welfare-dependency push poverty into a psychological discourse. While culture as an idea remains invisible, 'the mind' is an entity firmly ensconced in our cultural epistemology. In the United States, intelligence is a quantifiable entity; people can talk about 'high' and 'low' IQs and might even know the number they scored when tested. Unconscious processes, including their power, are popularly accepted. It is no small wonder that consumption is also thought about in these same terms. To see our cars as mollifying a mid-life crisis or fulfilling a life of quiet desperation is an easy fit.

In 1969, the president of the American Psychological Association, George Miller, encouraged psychologists to 'give psychology away.' Miller believed that what psychology had most to offer humanity was not the provision of services but rather a changed conception of humans. His appeal fell on fertile ground, as psychoanalytic perspectives had had an influence on Americans' ways of looking at the world and themselves long before 1969. Psychologically-oriented techniques had already become a part of the procedures of schools, workplaces, churches, the military and more.[4] In both analytic and popular circles, each new decade just seems to usher in the latest spin of psychology's sway. We have seen things move from psychoanalysis to Maslowian pyramids to the postmodern self – to name a select few trends that have prevailed in both popular and analytic circles. Recently we noted a speed dial option to 'psychologist' in the rooms of an upscale San Diego hotel.[5] Just in case of sudden need, one supposes.

Ethnography is More than a Method

What is troubling is that now that ethnography has been integrated into the toolkit of methodological approaches for use in the marketing world, the cultural analytic framework that traditionally accompanied it in anthropology has tended to be left by the wayside, leaving the focus on the psyche. Ethnography in marketing worlds is a method, not a form of analysis. Slotted into the realm of 'qualitative' methodology that lives in opposition to 'quantitative' methodology, ethnography is depicted as an 'improvement' over the focus group, its qualitative predecessor. In this view ethnography is simply a way to collect or gather data. Implicit in this understanding is the notion of 'raw' data: pieces or patches or parcels of information which can be retrieved and later subjected to analysis. Theory is acknowledged as central to the process only during the analytic, 'cooking' stage. This notion of raw data is integral to traditions of scientific, quantitative research, in which psychology has been a major player.

By contrast, the anthropological stance *vis-à-vis* data is that data are *always* cooked. This cooking process takes place at every stage of the research process. Researcher stance, theoretical perspectives, technologies and techniques of recording all affect what is found. We find the answers to the questions that we ask, explicitly and implicitly. Data are produced, not gathered. In the field of anthropology there is a long history of discussion on these issues. These ideas are evident in the methodological statements of Malinowski,[6] an acknowledged founder of the in-situ ideals of ethnographic fieldwork, which date back to the early 1900s. They can also be found in the more recent discussions of reflexivity, the writing of ethnography, and the problematics of Malinowski's in-situ ideal in a contemporary world of both considerable human movement and non-local, remote communication and interaction.[7]

Coupled with notions of the rawness of data is the sense of the transparency of meaning. As researchers we experience these beliefs when clients join us in the field and then are surprised at what we 'took away.' We encourage clients to accompany us during fieldwork or to look at videotaped recordings of these encounters. We want clients to engage in the lived worlds of their customers and products. But we do not believe that we are necessarily all thinking about, or attending to, the same things in that environment. Based on our anthropological training and approach, we are generally listening and looking for the 'invisible' cultural meanings and categories that organize people's perceptions and actions. While we watch someone clean a floor we might be thinking: what is a floor? What is clean? What is a cleaner? We are trying to discern the assumptions the person must have in order to clean the floor in this particular manner. We might ask that person or ourselves: what does clean mean? What is different about a clean floor versus a clean chair? So what is the difference between a floor and a chair? We use the term invisible for these cultural meanings because they can be so familiar or so tacit that neither the performers nor the observers can immediately discern their existence. We are trying to make the very familiar, the very tacit, and the very new (for instance new ideas of what constitutes a clean floor) obvious to ourselves and our clients.

Ethnographic methodology was developed by anthropologists for situations where the researcher was unfamiliar with the social or cultural worlds of the participants, and an important goal of that research was to explicate and translate these worlds for outsiders. One needed to ask things such as, 'What are chairs and their social uses?' because chairs and what was accomplished with them were often not what the researcher – or anyone in the researcher's society – would have expected. We continue in this tradition in our research and continue to believe that the analysis of cultural issues remains a strong suit of this methodology. Other methodologies have been honed for psychological analyses, for instance projective techniques; the intense, emotion-focused depth interview; or hypnosis. Quantitative fixed response survey techniques remain well suited for uncovering distributions across populations, censuses, voting, and the like. Focus groups have their place in brand and category inquiries, concept testing, and even – we would argue – as a forum for uncovering cultural, not only psychological, meanings. But in advertising circles, qualitative research of which focus groups and now ethnography are a part has been permeated with a psychological framework for understanding consumer behavior. This is a framework that assumes individual motivation and make-up are the key to consumption practices. We would suggest that the use of a psychological framework is itself a cultural issue, conditioned by American cultural predilections to think in those terms. Though, this decoupling of cultural theory from the ethnographic method is not only true of US practices. In a 2001 ESOMAR – Europe's largest professional market research organization – conference, ethnographic studies were highlighted even as they grounded their analyses in psychological theory. In a study of Russian cooking, for example, researchers discussed women's cooking activities in relation to a Maslowian hierarchy (a 'culinary pyramid') and self-actualization.[8]

As anthropologists, we find social and cultural life worth studying in its own right. As consumer researchers we also find it crucial. In recent years, more than one American toothpaste brand has repositioned itself as a 'whole mouth' solution, in response to a contemporary sociocultural shift away from a focus on cavities. Due to fluoridation as well as advances in dentistry, cavity prevention is less of a concern than gum disease. Consumers tell us, as dentists told them, that if they want to keep their teeth they need to take care of their gums. That is why they brush – and are concerned with – much more than just their teeth. Good smelling breath, another socially emphasized reason to brush, also necessitates brushing the tongue and the roof of the mouth, or so many consumers believe these days. Would a campaign launched on the basis of psychological profiles of users really be a better one?

It's not Simple and Easy

We do not mean to imply that the distinction between psychological and cultural frameworks is a simple or easy one. Nor is it one that should mutually exclude. The separation of what is cultural and what is psychological is not clear-cut but, we would strongly argue, how we as a society articulate the make-up of our minds, our selves and our emotions is culturally influenced. Research conducted over the last two decades on the cultural construction of emotion, the self and personhood has clearly illustrated this to be the case.[9] In the American cultural context, for example, what it means to be an individual is socially and culturally constructed in such a way that we think of ourselves as independent of others and strive to be more so when we find this not to be the case. The notion of a self that is completely independent of others would not apply to a definition of ideal personhood in India, Japan or Ethiopia, for example.

As anthropologists, we also know that American anthropology itself follows a decidedly psychological tradition in comparison to analytic schools emanating from other countries. One need think only of American (cultural) anthropology's 'culture and personality' schools versus British (social) anthropology's structural functionalism. With some transparency, American anthropology's interest in psychological matters is itself part and parcel of our national, cultural leanings.

Of late, with sound analytic rationale, American anthropologists have also seen the need to focus more on individual actors than on the extra-individual cultural realm. These attempts to focus on individual cultural actors have been means to incorporate theories of human agency and power in sociocultural life, as well as to acknowledge that cultures are not static entities, situated and sequestered in one place or time. To show the dynamism of cultural processes across place and time and to show the ways in which differently positioned human action and reaction have an effect, there has been a renewed focus on exactly who does and says what, when, where, and how.[10]

The analytic focus on the individual by anthropology still assumes a structure of shared meanings that give coherence to our everyday lives. Culture, as a set of meanings, metaphors, ideas and practices, is made visible through individual action; but the meanings are inherently social and extra-individual.[11] As anthropologists in the US, we are left with the need to acknowledge the cultural importance and place of native (and analytic) theories of action grounded in psychology, and to go beyond them. As anthropologists in the commercial world, we are further left with the task of making culture visible.

Drugs and The Self

One of the most successful studies we have undertaken succeeded because we were able to unwind and make visible the strands of both psychology and culture. This study, on drugs in the lives of mainstream 'Tweens' (children aged 9–13), had issues of the self at its core.[12] The purpose of the research was to develop a drug prevention campaign strategy targeting this age group. We conducted the study with Michael Donovan, a fellow anthropologist and colleague. A central tenet of our findings was that drugs are thoroughly implicated in American Tweens' development of autonomous, bounded, private selves.

This tenet is both psychological and cultural. On the one hand, we found that drugs are deeply implicated in the process of self-construction: forbidden, secret and dangerous, yet an expected part of the growing up experience. We observed that Tweens are a work in progress and that their boundaries between self and other are still somewhat open and permeable; Tweens have 'thin skins.' Drugs are a major player in their development of autonomy and privacy *vis-à-vis* adults. Drug behavior is a means for Tweens to define the boundaries of the private, secret worlds – akin to fashion or music tastes, and like snowboarding or other extreme (non-adult) forms of behavior.

On the other hand, we noted that concepts of the person and the self are socially constructed. The cultivation of an 'interior life' is a pervasive *cultural* expectation in the United States, often first expressed in terms of tastes and 'extreme' kinds of activities. In our society the twin anchors and signposts of the self are autonomy and privacy and the nascent self is both a psychological phenomenon and a cultural construction. Given this meshing of drug behavior with the psychological and cultural process of gaining maturity, for adults to say 'just say no' is to say 'don't grow up.'

Beyond the role of drugs in the development of the self is the culture of drugs in which the Tweens participated. This arena provided advertisers with a clear venue for messaging. Marijuana, alcohol, and cigarettes were the normative drugs for Tweens. Speaking anthropologically, we called this the unmarked cultural category. These drugs were accepted and acknowledged as quotidian examples of ubiquitous drugs. Tweens expected to try these drugs; adults assumed Tweens would try these drugs. Other drugs were seen as different – special cases for special kinds of people. They conceptually resided in non-normative categories, the marked categories: Scary (hallucinogens), Death (heroin), Addiction (cocaine), and Stupidity (inhalants). These 'exceptional' drugs (or marked categories) were nuanced in ways we have glossed with their titles. Inhalants, for example, were for idiots, unusual rock bands or one's self when being really stupid. While the normative category (marijuana, alcohol and tobacco) might elicit a shrug of the shoulders and a 'just is' comportment from Tweens (even as they talked about these as drugs they did not want to have around in their lives), the non-normative categories were marked as special, behaviorally and linguistically. Talk of heroin, we noted, was generally accompanied by a visible shudder.

Beyond the psychological self and into the cultural frame of everyday living, we found the language of drugs to be an important component of children's lives. The language of drugs was part of the social currency and showed what you did and did not know. The language itself, the talk, marked Tweens and their friends *vis-à-vis* other groups, other individual Tweens, parents, and adults in general. Mastering the language *is* part of the experience. Tweens garnered drug language via an outside, official track such as school programs, science teachers and anti-drug advertising, and elaborated and mastered that language via an inside track of movies, music and friends. Stories, stories and more stories about drugs were part of the milieu. Kids told stories to each other about who was doing what and when. Adults told apocryphal stories about drug users and use. Specific vocabularies marked the social categories of speakers. For example, ads and adults might call marijuana 'pot,' whereas Tweens used the indexical 'stuff.' Language mastery suggested membership in the 'drug using group.' Thus, for a Tween to discuss drugs with parents entailed a risk. As a seventh grader told us, 'If I asked a question they'd freak. They'd assume I'd be doing it.' Another Tween reasoned that if he started talking to his mother about drugs, she would then start searching his backpack. What Tweens would often like is to know about drugs though not to take them. For instance, they might want to be included in the group but not to engage in the behavior, whether with alcohol, cigarettes, or marijuana.

Finally, we made the case that a drug metaphor permeates the fabric of American lives. Existing in an unmarked, normative guise – and thus hard to see – the metaphor of drugs is an organizing metaphor of our cultural lives. This unmarked cultural metaphor became apparent to us while we were trying to make sense of Tweens' stories of snorting sugar, Pixie Stix and Altoids, as well as tales of inhaling WiteOut, Magic Markers, rug cleaner or just about anything with 'a strong smell.' In all of these practices, be it with sugar or solvents, the expectation was that one could, possibly, get high.

From the time these Tweens were very young they had heard messages about being 'hyped up' on sugar. (So, as one Tween pointed out, since 'they' say you get high from sugar, maybe the girl she sees snorting Pixie Stix in the school yard is getting high.) Tweens knew of Ritalin as the drug of their classmates, of Prozac as the drug of their parents (or friends' parents) and the uses of Viagra. They told us about their own experiences with antibiotics and pain relievers and could contribute to a reasonable discussion of the relative efficacy and tastes of Advil versus Tylenol. Substances such as alcohol and tobacco, while illegal for them to use, were nonetheless openly part of their everyday worlds: available in neighborhood stores, often consumed within the home, part of adult life. As noted above, stories, stories, and more stories about drugs were part of their lives. Drugs were relentlessly discussed, officially and unofficially, by young and by old.

These Tweens conceptualized many ideas, things and activities in terms of drugs. Foods such as caffeine, chocolate, sugar, and soft drinks were routinely thought of as drug-like. Other foods were also discussed in this light. For example, they spoke of being 'addicted' to chips, to food and the action of eating in general, not only when pathologized in terms of 'eating addictions.' Favored activities, whether video games, shopping, sex or love, were described as addictions. Behavior, thought, and affect, even when not literally drug induced, were frequently spoken of with terms such as hyped, spaced, and tripping. The Tweens drew on this cultural context when they redefined virtually everything as a drug. Given this metaphor, it made sense to smoke incense, to believe that 'anything with a strong smell' could be sniffed and make you high, to maintain that a certain girl could be a drug for one of your friends, or to chop up and snort an Altoid.

In the recommendations we provided the agency, we suggested that it not exempt cigarettes and alcohol from messaging around marijuana. These all live in the same cultural category for Tweens. We also suggested that there was a need to address the ubiquitous status of drugs in our cultural world and that, since Tweens individuate by creating distance from a perceived status quo, an advertising campaign might challenge the pervasive status of drugs in the US. We advised the agency to provoke Tweens to challenge the model of drug experience that the culture at large supports, in order to get to a more 'real self.' With these last recommendations, we also came full circle; we brought the insight into the means by which the self is constructed in American society together with our insights into the permeation of the unmarked, cultural metaphor of drugs.

Language and Culture

As is perhaps obvious for anthropology insiders, our analytic approach is rooted in linguistic anthropology. We accept that language and experience are intimately intertwined, that language is a social resource and that language is itself a culturally defined and specified practice. Our perspectives have been particularly informed by the traditions of the Prague School structuralists, ethnomethodology, and the socialization of language.[13]

We use insights grounded in this intellectual arena in our work for clients. We pay great attention to meaning context, looking for situations where a given meaning prevails and where it does not. As we illustrated in the above Tweens and drugs example, we obtain hints about what is culturally salient and what is culturally unusual by noticing what is marked and unmarked. Paying attention to what is marked and unmarked also gives us – as in the technology study – the means to both witness and map dynamic changes in what is normative about private and public, work and play and other cultural categories that so invisibly organize our daily lives and experience.

Our notion of culture is, in good anthropological tradition, adequately fuzzy. For most of our everyday purposes, we use a notion of culture derived from theorists such as Geertz and Bourdieu, as articulated by Schieffelin, and tempered by the ideas of anthropologists such as Appadurai, Abu-Lughod and Ortner.[14] In her 1990 ethnographic study of language socialization among Kaluli children, Schieffelin provided a succinct outline of her sense of what culture means that has heuristically held up well. The five principles she puts forward there are worth quoting in their entirety:

1. Language and culture comprise bodies of knowledge, structures of under-standing, conceptions of the world, and collective representations that are extrinsic to any individual.
2. These contain more information than any individual could know or learn.
3. There is variation among individual members in terms of their knowledge. This variation is crucial to the social dynamic between individuals, but it is also socially structured, and as such is extrinsic to individuals.
4. It is important to distinguish between the symbolically constructed contexts in which individuals live and the knowledge, attitudes, interpretations, and under-standings they must have to operate appropriately in their place within the culture. These are not the same thing. Thus,
5. One does not 'acquire culture'; one acquires a set of practices that enable one to live in a culture.[15]

We applaud the criticisms of culture theorists who have maintained that notions of culture are flawed when they make it seem that an abstract concept like culture has the ability to act, when a vision of static places and homogeneous actors is produced, or when people and real, mutable, places are forgotten altogether.[16] But we are not ready to eschew all notions of culture. In good anthropological fashion, we use the concept pragmatically. It serves us well. As Ortner writes:

> Without denying the profound and far-reaching importance of this critique, I would suggest that the issue is not so much one of . . . banishing the concept of culture . . . Rather the issue is, once again, one of reconfiguring this enormously productive concept for a changing world . . . What I am trying to say is that the fate of 'culture' will depend on its uses. (1999: 8, 11)

In the End

Mazzarella (this volume) notes the quandary of the anthropologist in the com-mercial world – aiding and abetting, on the one hand, aloof and analytic, on the other. He queries how the intellectual tradition of anthropology can come to grips in a productive, illuminating and theoretical way with advertising as a cultural practice. And, given the enormity of advertising's impact on life beyond merely the business it is designed to affect, how can anthropology and advertising be mutually engaged in a dialogue and critique?

We would pose a different (and presupposing) question: how does an anthropological and distinctly cultural worldview find a presence and a meaning in advertising practices? We have suggested that a psychological framework – one that is understood in our society to be independent from the culture that gives it resonance – permeates ethnographic research in the commercial workplace for reasons both historical and cultural. The idea of culture as a framework for comprehending the world is backgrounded, much as it is in the everyday life we observe, in the analytic models of our clients or in our conversations with respondents about their construction of things, themselves, events and consumption.

We have suggested in this chapter that anthropology has a practical place for advertisers. A cultural analysis illuminates the shifting, ongoing engagement of meanings between consumers and producers, mediated by advertising – whether in reference to pickup trucks, new technologies or drugs in Tween lives. Terrio (2000), in her ethnography of French luxury chocolate, notes that individual chocolatiers as well as state-level authorities exploited the cultural meanings of chocolate in their marketing efforts. Store windows and sponsored ceremonies invoked the French cultural authenticity of fine chocolate with roots in local history and craft tradition; purveyors knew to emphasize the culturally valued tradition of gifting of chocolate for important ritual occasions as well as the highly valued 'familial' nature of their businesses. Moreover, there were active efforts on the part of craft leaders and 'cultural tastemakers' to influence consumption by altering cultural-level meanings, for instance by encouraging the value of fine, French chocolate consumption not only for ceremonial occasions, but also as part of the daily, healthful French diet. As Terrio (2000: 41) explains, 'They sought to increase consumption by altering the culturally constituted uses and symbolic meanings of chocolate in France. Consumers were urged to eat more refined French chocolates not just on the ritualized ceremonial occasions traditionally associated with them but regularly, even daily.'

Cultural meanings are, perhaps, more accessible to members of French society. In France there is a considerable tradition of intellectual and emotional attention to cultural matters. Taste, etiquette, entertainment, fashion, consumption, and what it means to be French have a history of being appreciated in both high and anthropological culture terms. Sociologist Pierre Bourdieu's *Distinction*, is a case in point.[17] For anthropology to be successful in US arenas, an awareness of culture as a theoretical and native theory must be brought to the fore. It is only in becoming part of a collective consciousness that anthropology can hope to become part of an ongoing conversation about who we are in our work and in our lives. In our own work this means making culture visible in advertising's ethnographic practice and, in so doing, making it available to a scrutinizing lens for our society at large.

Notes

1. See Sunderland and Denny (in prep.).
2. Compare Wellner (2000).
3. In Sunderland and Denny (in prep.) we argue that Windows has become our metaphor for windows of action.
4. Sunderland's 1985 thesis covers some of these issues.
5. Observed in late 2001.
6. See Malinowski's introduction to *Argonauts of the Western Pacific*.
7. See Myerhoff and Ruby (1982), Marcus and Cushman (1982), Marcus and Fischer (1986), Clifford and Marcus (1986), Geertz (1988), Gupta and Ferguson (1997a, b). Note also Miller's (this volume) remarks that in anthropology methodology 'is part of the research findings.'
8. See Vladimirova and Petrin (2001). Malefyt (this volume) provides an example of yet another use of the Maslowian model. These psychological analytic models are the ones drawn upon, even when the real concern is not so much centered on understanding the consumer, but rather on strengthening relationships and appearances of expertise.
9. For a range of examples, from both psychologists and anthropologists, see Shweder and Levine (1984), Lutz (1988), Kondo (1990), Turkle (1984, 1997), and Fader (2000).
10. See Abu-Lughod (1991), Kondo (1990), and Appadurai (1996).
11. Wenger's (1998) *Communities of Practice* provides a very useful introduction to the inherently social nature of meaning and individual activity. Note also Muniz and O'Guinn's (2001) work on brand communities.
12. This work was conducted for The Geppetto Group and Ogilvy & Mather Worldwide. The findings were presented in person to the then head of the O.N.D.C.P, General McCaffrey.
13. The thinking and work of Michael Silverstein, Bambi Schieffelin, and Erving Goffman have been of primary influence.
14. Bourdieu (1977, 1984), Schieffelin (1990), Appadurai (1996), Abu- Lughod (1991), Ortner (1999) and Geertz (1973, 1983).
15. Quoted from Schieffelin (1990: 15).
16. Gupta and Ferguson (1997c), Appadurai (1996), Abu-Lughod (1991). See also Eagleton (2000).
17. Müller (2002) discusses the public reception of Bourdieu in light of his death and his politics.

References

Abu-Lughod, Lila 1991 'Writing against culture,' in R. Fox (ed.) *Recapturing Anthropology: Working in the Present*, pp. 137–62, Santa Fe, NM: School of American Research Press.

Appadurai, Arjun 1996 *Modernity at Large: Cultural Dimensions of Globalization*, Minneapolis: University of Minnesota Press.

Bourdieu, Pierre 1977 *Outline of a Theory of Practice*, Cambridge: Cambridge University Press.

—— 1984 *Distinction: A Social Critique of the Judgement of Taste*, Cambridge, MA: Harvard University Press.

Clifford, James and George E. Marcus (eds) 1986 *Writing Culture: The Poetics and Politics of Ethnography*, Berkeley: University of California Press.

Eagleton, Terry 2000 *The Idea of Culture*, Oxford: Blackwell.

Fader, Ayala 2000 'Gender, morality, and language: Socialization practices in a Hasidic community,' PhD dissertation, New York University.

Fellman, Michele Worth 1999 'Breaking tradition: "Untraditional" market research techniques from the social sciences are gaining ground,' *Marketing Research*, Fall, pp. 21–4.

Frank, Thomas 1999 'Brand you: Better selling through anthropology,' *Harper's Magazine*, July, pp. 74–9.

Geertz, Clifford 1973 *The Interpretation of Cultures*, New York: Basic Books.

—— 1983 *Local Knowledge: Further Essays in Interpretive Anthropology*, New York: Basic Books.

—— 1988 *Works and Lives: The Anthropologist as Author*, Stanford: Stanford University Press.

Gupta, Akhil and James Ferguson 1997a *Anthropological Locations: Boundaries and Grounds of a Field Science*, Berkeley: University of California Press.

—— 1997b *Culture, Power, Place: Explorations in Critical Anthropology*, Durham: Duke University Press.

—— 1997c 'Beyond "culture": Space, identity, and the politics of difference,' in A. Gupta and J. Ferguson (eds) *Culture, Power, Place: Explorations in Critical Anthropology*, pp. 33–51, Durham: Duke University Press.

Kondo, Dorinne 1990 *Crafting Selves: Power, Gender, and Discourses of Identity in a Japanese Workplace*, Chicago: University of Chicago Press.

Lutz, Catherine 1988 *Unnatural Emotions: Everyday Sentiments on a Micronesian Atoll and Their Challenge to Western Theory*, Chicago: University of Chicago Press.

Malinowski, Bronislaw 1984 [1922] *Argonauts of the Western Pacific*, Prospect Heights, IL: Waveland Press.

Marcus, George E. and Dick Cushman 1982 'Ethnographies as texts,' *Annual Review of Anthropology*, 11: 25–69.

Marcus, George E. and Michael M. Fischer 1986 *Anthropology as Cultural Critique: An Experimental Moment in the Human Sciences*, Chicago: University of Chicago Press.

Miller, George A. 1969 'Psychology as a means of promoting human welfare,' *American Psychlogist*, 24: 1063–75.

Müller, Anne F. 2002 'Sociology as a combat sport,' *Anthropology Today*, 18 (2): 5–9.

Muniz, Albert M. Jr and Thomas C. O'Guinn 2001 'Brand community,' *Journal of Consumer Research*, 27: 412–32.

Myerhoff, Barbara and Jay Ruby 1982 'Introduction,' in J. Ruby (ed.) *A Crack in the Mirror: Reflexive Perspectives in Anthropology*, pp. 1–35, Philadelphia: University of Pennsylvania Press.

Ortner, Sherry B. 1999 'Introduction,' in S. Ortner (ed.) *The Fate of Culture: Geertz and Beyond*, pp. 1–13, Berkeley: University of California Press.

Schieffelin, Bambi B. 1990 *The Give and Take of Everyday Life: Language Socialization of Kaluli Children*, Cambridge: Cambridge University Press.

Shweder, Richard A. and Robert A. Levine (eds) 1984 *Culture Theory: Essays on Mind, Self, and Emotion*, Cambridge: Cambridge University Press.

Sunderland, Patricia L. 1985 'The Psychologization of Everyday Life,' Master's thesis, University of Vermont.

—— and Rita M. Denny (in prep.) 'The rhetoric of computing metaphors in everyday life.'

Terrio, Swan 2000 *Crafting the Culture and History of French Chocolate*, Berkeley: University of California Press.

Turkle, Sherry 1984 *The Second Self: Computers and the Human Spirit*, New York: Simon & Schuster.

—— 1997 *Life on the Screen: Identity in the Age of the Internet*, New York: Simon & Schuster.

Vladimirova, Ekaterina and Kyrill Petrin 2001 'Russia: "pyramid" on the table,' *The Business Value of Emotional Intelligence*, pp. 289–96, Amsterdam: ESOMAR.

Wellner, Alison Stein 2000 'The end of leisure?,' *American Demographics*, July, pp. 51–6.

Wenger, Etienne 1998 *Communities of Practice: Learning, Meaning, and Identity*, Cambridge: Cambridge University Press.

Afterword: Looking Forward, Looking Back
Marietta L. Baba

The third generation of American and European anthropologists in business and industry has spoken, and it is with a voice unlike any other before it. They tell of a landscape that few have witnessed, and they peer through a lens that is both strange and familiar. These are anthropologists who practice inside the world of advertising, a branch of our institutional diaspora that could not have been imagined fifty years ago. How anthropologists got inside the advertising industry, and what they are doing there is worthy of commentary.

The first generation of anthropologists in business made their appearance more than seven decades ago, in the American manufacturing companies of the Midwest and North-east. They worked squarely in the colonial tradition, trying to understand the indigenous people (industrial workers) in hopes of tranquilizing resistance to management's push for higher productivity. Their mandate came first from the Great Depression and then from the Second World War. Once these 'good wars' were over, however, anthropologists deserted their niche in business, lured by other opportunities abroad. Some may have felt embarrassment at having abetted the corporate analogue of colonialism. For better or worse, this first generation produced no immediate heirs. Business was abandoned to the psychologists and economists.

Not until the last quarter of the twentieth century did a second generation of business anthropologists struggle to be born. The fall of American manufacturing at the hands of foreign competitors triggered a social and economic process that propelled a handful of anthropologists back into companies. This came at a time when many in the discipline believed this kind of work was unethical. Like an endangered species, anthropologists balanced precariously inside businesses during the 1980s – not accepted by the business mainstream, often turned to only as a last resort, hounded inside anthropology – it is no wonder that their numbers never exceeded more than a few score (100 is the estimate). Though small in number, this generation radiated out to create new niches for itself. Unlike the first generation that stayed primarily inside the corporation, this new line ventured outside, into the marketplace, to trace down the material and symbolic flows that connected the corporation to the larger society. The true pioneers of this generation were those visionary anthropologists who recognized the cultural epicenter pulsing inside American consumption, and risked their careers to go there. Their practice of ethnography and related techniques in the marketing domain was made possible by a crisis of confidence that shook the foundations of mainline marketing methodology. Critical theory was beginning to diffuse the aura of scientific validity that surrounded the standard quantitative and statistical techniques, and ethnography was in many ways an answer to the criticism. With global competition remaking the markets of the world, and American industry fighting for survival, new approaches that brought fresh insights were welcomed in some corners of the private sector. Business anthropology thus developed two (small) branches, one for management and the other for marketing. Crossover between practitioners was not uncommon, because, after all, these domains of business are connected.

No one predicted what would happen in the late 1980s and early 1990s. The world as we knew it morphed into the unknown when the Soviet Union collapsed. Suddenly, the world was awash with new and emerging markets, with standards of living rising spectacularly in some places, while improvements were promised in others. Lucrative rewards awaited those that got to these markets first. Planned economies were in disgrace, and everyone was a marketer, even the Chinese communists. How disrespectable could it be now to be an anthropologist in business? The stigma was fading, and the field was ready for explosive growth.

The big change can be traced to anthropologists at Xerox who showed how ethnography could yield major insights into product and service design and innovation. Although Xerox itself was never able to fully exploit this brilliant discovery, and ultimately lost the creative group of anthropologists who opened this incredible new source of wealth, other manufacturing and consulting firms the world over took note, and a new field was created – design ethnography – the queen of anthropological research strategies married to the thing that is consumed. Ethnography became the handmaiden of product development. Watching people use products in the field turned out to be a perpetual fountain of new ideas for product innovation and improvement. Significantly, this field blurs the distinction between the anthropologies of management and marketing. Design ethnography in its most holistic form invites us to understand the intricate connections between the corporate entity on the one hand, and the products and services it designs, makes, sells, and services on the other. The reason is that the corporate organization can facilitate product development, or hugely hamper it. Ethnography also uncovers this truth.

This is how anthropology lost one of its two foremost iconic symbols – ethnography. Once it became clear that ethnography could be a powerful capitalist tool in the new knowledge economy, the anthropologist's era of hegemony over this methodological strategy came to an end. Earlier, our other icon – culture – also had been lost to business. That happened in the 1980s, when the anthropological mainstream declined to translate esoteric cultural theories for the business world, leaving the management professors and consultants free rein to do the job their way. Yet that loss was not so dangerous, because in most cases the corporate use of the culture idea is not very potent. Two reasons account for this; one, the idea is poorly grasped, and two, it is used defensively as an excuse for why things aren't working as planned. But when ethnography escaped our grasp, a serious danger crept in. Yes, the corporate appropriation of ethnography ensures a major niche expansion for anthropology in business, and in fact that is how the third generation of business anthropologists came into being and why there are so many more of us now than ever before. But it also means that we no longer control how or why ethnography is practiced. And that is dangerous, because businesses can use ethnography offensively, as a weapon or tool to appropriate knowledge from consumers and employees, and then turn that knowledge to exploit the very people whose lives created the knowledge to begin with. A simple example is the ethnography of poor children in a ghetto that aims to pump up their purchases of designer clothing. The success of the knowledge gained in this exercise tightens the grip of the capitalist machine on these children, and enforces their labor in low-wage ghetto jobs or, worse yet, nudges them toward crime. No such scenarios were depicted in this volume, but the example is, in fact, a very plausible application of ethnography in marketing and advertising, and it is difficult to see what we can do to avert it.

We live in a global marketplace that is supersaturated with digital media going 24/7, and nothing is sacred or secret. Companies literally cannot count on any asset to sustain their competitive advantage these days except for one – knowledge, and the innovation it delivers. Human knowledge, and the social process that creates it, is the most significant source of new wealth on earth today. Three quarters of the value of all manufactured goods now derives from knowledge. Knowledge is an inexhaustible resource and its frontier is truly endless. Business has discovered that ethnography is the technology best suited to extracting knowledge from human beings, and, like a newborn infant, this reality cannot be stuffed back into its anthropological womb.

Now, in the midst of clear and present danger, we return to the third generation of business anthropologists working in advertising. The anthropological boom in advertising is related to business' discovery that ethnography extracts knowledge. Advertisers require knowledge – both of the consumer and of the client – otherwise they cannot win in the marketplace. Also, like product design, advertising is a creative practice, and so is ethnography. They fit well together. Who better to field when creative knowledge is needed than a 'real' ethnographer (i.e., an anthropologist)? And for its part, anthropology has learned that advertising is the engine of the capitalist machine that 'makes its object' – the construction of consumer communities whose hunger for things that have been designed to produce longing fuels a never-ending quest for the next purchase and the next addition to the bottom line.

Afterword

The third generation speaks with a voice that is distinctive because it stands in a relation to the capitalist machine that is different from the stance of the two generations past. These anthropologists are not naïve handmaidens to the machine, either in the intellectual or technical sense. Nor are they searching desperately for legitimacy inside a brave new world. Rather, these voices are full of self-consciousness, as well as self-confidence. They know who they are, where they are, and why they are there. They practice inside business, but they do not hide their identity as anthropologists, nor do they forget that identity. Instead, they perform a feat of double practice in which they ply their craft while simultaneously observing themselves doing it. This is a very difficult form of art, but one that provides all of us with a never-before-available vantage point from which to gaze upon the inner workings of capitalism's advertising engine. By straddling two worlds, they give us something of great value. But the dangers and discomforts of this difficult performance are not lost on us. The third generation knows that it does not do double practice with impunity. There are costs to an anthropological consciousness and identity in business, one of which is conscience. Conscience joins the anthropologists in advertising to the rest of us in a pressing obligation to our discipline and its future generations. All anthropologists situated in business one way or another must confront the risks inherent in an ethnographic practice that now 'belongs' inside the machine. We must, all of us, engage with the field in a way that enables us to reassert the legitimate exercise of vigilance over ethnographic practice in business. If this is not done, then nothing we gain from a view inside the machine will be worth the price. As members of the third generation contemplate their next move, I respectfully request that they consider tackling the question of anthropological ethics in advertising practice, and invite the rest of us to join the conversation. While the answers are unlikely to be simple or clear, if they come at all, just asking the question will change the nature of the craft, and move our practice toward a habitus that is more just, humane, and sustainable.

List of Contributors

Marietta L. Baba is Professor of Anthropology and Dean of Social Science at Michigan State University. Her research interests focus on the interaction of strategic change and organizational culture. She is the author of *Beyond Dilbert: The Cultural Construction of Work Organizations in America* (Peacock, 2001), *Theories of Practice in Anthropology: A Critical Reassessment* (AAA, 2000), *Trust, Distrust and Information Technology in American Work Organizations* (Human Organization, 1999). Dr Baba can be reached at mbaba@msu.edu.

Rita Denny, PhD, is a founding partner of Practica Group, LLC, an anthropological consulting firm. She holds an anthropology degree from the University of Chicago. Her interests include linguistic, semiotic and symbolic traditions. Recent publications include 'Consuming values: The culture of clients, researchers and consumers' (ESOMAR, 1999), 'Communicating with clients: Issues of intelligibility' (in B. Byrne and S. Squires (eds) *Anthropologists in the Product Development Industry*, Greenwood, 2001), and 'Speaking to customers: The anthropology of communications' (in John F. Sherry Jr, (ed.) *Contemporary Marketing and Consumer Behavior*, Sage, 1995). She can be contacted at rdenny@practicagroup.com.

Steven Kemper, Professor of Anthropology at Bates College, is the author of *The Presence of the Past: Chronicles, Politics, and Culture in Sinhala Life* (Cornell, 1991) and *Buying and Believing: Sri Lankan Advertising and Consumers in a Transnational World* (University of Chicago Press, 2001). His research interests range from monasticism and astrology to transnational forces such as advertising and higher education. He can be reached at (207) 786-6083.

Marianne Elisabeth Lien is Associate Professor of Social Anthropology at the University of Oslo, Norway. She has previously worked as a researcher at the National Institute for Consumer Research in Norway, where she conducted research on nutritional policies, advertising, attitudes to meat, mediations between consumers and suppliers in the marketplace and food production. Her current research interests include topics related to globalization, transnational flows, and salmon farming. She has published *Marketing and Modernity* (Berg, 1997), and has contributed to several anthologies on markets, consumption and culture. She can be reached at m.e.lien@sai.uio.no.

Timothy deWaal Malefyt, PhD, is Director of Cultural Discoveries at BBDO Advertising in New York City. He holds a PhD in anthropology from Brown University. A former professional ballet dancer, his interests include performance. tourism and popular culture. His publications include, 'Gendering the authentic in Spanish flamenco,' in *The Passion of Music and Dance*, (Berg, 1998); 'Inside and outside Spanish flamenco: Gender constructions in Andalusian concepts of flamenco tradition,' (1998) *Anthropological Quarterly*. He may be contacted at timothy.malefyt@bbdo.com or timothy_malefyt@hotmail.com.

William Mazzarella is Assistant Professor in the Department of Anthropology at the University of Chicago. His book, *Shoveling Smoke: Advertising and Globalization in Contemporary India* will be published in 2003 by Duke University Press. He is currently researching censorship and the cultural politics of obscenity in post-liberalization India. He can be reached at University of Chicago, Department of Anthropology, 1126 E 59th St, Chicago, IL 60637, tel: (773) 834-4873, or mazzarel@uchicago.edu.

Daniel Miller is Professor of Material Culture at the Department of Anthropology at University College London. Recent books include *A Theory of Shopping* (Cornell/Polity), *The Internet: An Ethnographic Approach* (Berg, with D. Slater), *Car Cultures* (Berg), and the *Dialectics of Shopping* (University of Chicago Press). Currently he is co-writing a book about the sari in India and conducting fieldwork in sites ranging from government audit to finance capitalism for a study of value and political economy. He may be contacted at d.miller@ucl.ac.uk.

Brian Moeran is Professor of Culture and Communication at the Copenhagen Business School. He trained as an anthropologist at the School of Oriental and African Studies, University of London. His main research interests are in advertising, media, fragrance, and Japan. He is the author of *A Japanese Advertising Agency* (1996) and editor of *Asian Media Productions* (2001, both Curzon/ University of Hawaii Press). He may be contacted at bdm.ikl@cbs.dk.

Barbara Olsen is Associate Professor of Marketing at the State University of New York, Old Westbury. She attained a PhD in Anthropology and is currently teaching in the areas of advertising, consumer behavior and international marketing. She supplements these academic endeavors by consulting and providing pro bono artistic and creative assistance to various causes while continuing research on consumer ethnography. She can be reached at (516) 876-3331, olsenb @oldwestbury.edu.

John F. Sherry, Jr is Professor of Marketing at the Kellogg School, Northwestern University. His research interests include the sociocultural and symbolic dimensions of consumption, and the cultural ecology of marketing. Sherry's work appears in a score of journals (including the *Journal of Consumer Research,* the *Journal of Retailing,* the *Journal of Consumer Psychology*, and the *International Journal of Research in Marketing*). He has edited *Contemporary Marketing and Consumer Behavior: An Anthropological Sourcebook,* as well as *Servicescapes: The Concept of Place in Contemporary Markets;* he is co-editor of *Advances in Consumer Research, Vol. 19.* You may reach him at jfsherry@kellogg.northwestern.edu, or (847) 491 2714.

Patricia Sunderland, PhD, is a founding partner of Practica Group, LLC. She holds a degree in psychology from the University of Vermont and in anthropology from New York University. Her research interests include ethnographic methodology and its representation in video consumer research. She has authored 'Fieldwork and the Phone,' (1999) *Anthropological Quarterly.* Together with Rita Denny she authored 'Performers and partners: Consumer video documentaries in ethnographic research' (ESOMAR, 2002). She can be contacted at psunderland@ practicagroup.com.

Index

Index

Index

ethnicity 36, 38, 46, 76, 87, 173
  see also food, ethnic
ethnographer xi, 18, 22, 35–38, 50, 59, 94, 128, 205
  corporate 14, 22
  folk 12, 24, 35, 51
ethnographic 40, 50, 62
  account 36
  authority 35
  data 116
  encounter 21, 22, 23
  knowledge 16, 50–1
  method 10, 21, 166, 192, 193
  observer 58
  practice 28, 192, 193, 206
  research 13, 21, 182, 199
  site 119
  skill 42
  text 36
  writing 61
ethnography xii, 1, 13, 17, 19, 21, 24, 27, 30, 51, 56, 75, 76, 78, 86, 144, 158, 159, 187, 188, 190–3, 199, 204
  advertising 50, 144
  and fieldwork 6–12, 17, 191
  and management 23
  and marketing 23, 24, 187, 188, 190, 191, 193
  experience of 7–8, 76
exotic 28, 36, 92, 105, 135, 173, 174, 180, 181
  routinization of the 174

family 166, 190
fashion 9, 53, 76, 100, 101, 117, 120, 195, 199
  symbolism 119
  tribe 119
fees *see* payment
feminism 117, 119, 128
field 12, 14, 15, 60, 92, 93–5, 182, 204, 206
fieldwork 1, 12, 14, 16, 17, 25, 27, 28, 29, 55–70, 92, 95, 116, 119, 121, 166, 192
  and ethnography 6–12
  as experience 7–8
  management of 21–4
  multi-sited 17, 31, 75
fieldworker 11
film 4, 175, 177
  director 175, 176, 177

finance 87
focus group 23, 24, 120, 192, 193
food 3, 11, 27–8, 165, 179, 196
  Bon Appétit 167–72, 174–9, 182
  convenience 165–83
  ethnic 171
  market 11, 167, 173
foreign 40, 41, 49, 92, 170–2
  brand 56, 64, 65
  culture 48
  product 41, 45
foreignness 41

GATT 167
Geertz, Clifford 166, 197
gender 27, 38, 113, 114, 130–2, 134
  and advertising 19, 76, 132
  and fieldwork 8
  identity 129
  politics 119
  role 119
  see also women
Germany 26, 92, 94, 96, 97, 98, 104, 106, 109, 168
gift 19, 39, 122
global 9, 28, 40, 59, 107, 205
  advertising 40, 44, 105, 107–8, 109
  and local 3, 24–5, 40, 41, 42, 43, 44, 49, 50, 65–6, 87–9, 107–9
  brand 25, 61, 94, 108
  production 9
  reach 2, 45
  style 26, 107
globalization xii, 25, 26, 29, 56, 60, 61, 62, 86, 88–9, 108
  of ideas 29, 57
government 39, 40, 41, 48, 56, 59, 61, 67, 88
  policy 52
  regulation 167, 183
Gucci 3

hegemony 28, 45, 63, 104, 204
hierarchy *see* cultural hierarchy; needs, hierarchy of
history 63, 87, 113, 117, 133, 199
  of ideas 184
  see also retail history
Hollywood 8

Index

Malaysia 48, 49, 52
Malinowski, Bronislaw 6, 192
manager 102, 139, 145, 148
  -ial practice 107
market 16, 35, 38, 40, 42, 43, 45, 47, 49, 53,
    62, 63, 65, 77, 78, 80, 86, 92, 103, 104,
    107–9, 132, 150, 166, 183
  analysis 15, 19, 94, 102, 110
  domestic 42
  emerging 204
  expansion 67
  philosophy 131
  place 14, 119, 121, 132, 180, 203, 205
  research xii, 4, 12, 28, 42, 62, 80, 85, 165,
    170, 172, 187, 193
  segment 3, 38, 64, 168
  share 43, 128, 165
  see also consumer market
marketer xii, 1, 8, 9, 10, 11, 12, 20, 23, 24, 113,
    130, 142–4, 146, 147, 150, 152, 159, 188
  and anthropologists 1
marketing xii, 2, 3, 6, 7, 9, 10, 11, 16, 21, 23,
    24, 27, 41, 61, 65, 66, 95, 100, 105,
    113–34, 142, 143, 155, 156, 158, 168,
    174, 180, 182, 204, 205
  budget 176
  department 165, 168, 170, 172, 182
  discipline of 64, 115, 130, 147, 170
  discourse 156
  expertise 66
  guerrilla 155
  integrated 4
  knowledge 182
  manager 79, 80, 175, 182
  mix 115
  need 5
  objective 22, 154
  phenomenon 126
  plan 5, 123, 155
  practice 1
  problem 4, 5, 11, 12, 26–7, 113, 119
  professional 1, 21, 151, 155, 166
  rationale 113
  relationship 122
  research see market research
  strategy 5, 12, 66, 91, 93–5, 97, 165, 170
  theory 28
  trend 117

tool 10
  see also ideology, marketing;
marketization 63
Marxism 75, 76
Maslow, Abraham 23, 24, 147, 148, 191,
    193
mass production 166, 173, 179
media 2, 8, 14, 17, 27, 31, 37, 39, 48, 52, 88,
    91, 98, 104–5, 113, 115, 155, 187, 205
  buying 4, 5, 95
  placement 139
  planning 3, 5, 97, 101, 114, 175
  spending 155
meeting 79, 80, 81, 97–8, 114, 119, 139, 141,
    144–6, 151, 154–6, 182
merchandizing 3, 4, 84, 95, 125, 126–7, 132,
    134
metaphor 144, 154, 159, 183
  of drugs 196, 197
  of war 27, 31, 114, 154–7
method see methodology
methodology xii, 6, 8, 10, 12, 13, 21–2, 31,
    119, 192, 193, 204
  anthropological 7–8, 10, 23, 75–7, 200
  marketing 1, 11, 192, 193, 204
model 43, 45–6, 83, 119, 123–5, 127, 143, 146,
    148, 149, 151–7, 159
  agency 4, 143, 144, 146–8
  Asian 49, 53
  consumer 146–8, 152, 153
  see also theoretical model
modernity 44, 169, 180, 181, 184
motivations 9, 12, 147, 152, 190, 193
multinational 61, 108

narrative 13, 181
  ethnography 26–7, 113–34
nation 16, 17, 40, 63
  state 40, 50, 51, 66
nationalism 52, 87, 108
need 9, 64, 105, 126, 146–9, 150, 152, 153,
    157
  hierarchy of 23, 24, 27, 147, 148, 193
Nestlé 84, 85
network 39, 111
  television 4
newspaper 2, 31n, 37, 47, 52, 60, 115, 123
Norway 1, 11, 27, 110, 165–83